Guadalupe and Her Faithful

Lived Religions
Series Editors: *David D. Hall* and *Robert A. Orsi*

Guadalupe and Her Faithful

Latino Catholics in San Antonio,
from Colonial Origins to the Present

Timothy Matovina

The Johns Hopkins University Press
Baltimore

The Johns Hopkins University Press
2715 North Charles Street
Baltimore, Maryland 21218-4363
www.press.jhu.edu

Library of Congress Cataloging-in-Publication Data

Matovina, Timothy M., 1955–
   Guadalupe and her faithful : Latino Catholics in San Antonio,
from colonial origins to the present / Timothy Matovina.
      p.   cm. — (Lived religions)
   Includes bibliographical references and index.
   ISBN 0-8018-7959-0 (hardcover : alk. paper) —
   ISBN 0-8018-8229-X (pbk. : alk. paper)
      1. Guadalupe, Our Lady of—Cult—Texas—San Antonio—
History.   2. Hispanic American Catholics—Religious life—Texas—
San Antonio—History.   3. San Fernando Cathedral (San Antonio,
Tex.)—History.   4. San Antonio (Tex.)— Religious life and customs.
I. Title.   II. Series.
   BT660.G8M35 2005
   282′.764351′0896872—dc22   200505142

A catalog record for this book is available from the British Library.

For Elida and Carlos

Se quedó (she stayed).

—GUADALUPAN DEVOTEE

Contents

Preface

I first came to know of Our Lady of Guadalupe during a course I took in 1982 at the Mexican American Cultural Center in San Antonio, Texas. Though previously I had heard of Guadalupe, a class presentation by Sister Rosa María Icaza, C.C.V.I., awakened me to the significance of the Guadalupan image, story, and tradition and to the intense fervor Guadalupe inflames among millions of devotees. Inspired by the lecture, I visited the Guadalupe basilica in Mexico City later that year. I was overwhelmed by the immense crowds of pilgrims and tourists and by the juxtaposition of the vendors selling their wares and the pious crawling through the plaza en route to the sanctuary of their celestial mother, the priests presiding at Mass on the main altar and the multitudes in constant motion toward the Guadalupe image in the devotional area behind it, the countless flickering candles and the fervent gaze of those praying before this feminine icon of the sacred.

I have participated annually in the December 12 Guadalupe feast ever since. The genesis of this book is my fascination, as an Irish-Croatian American Catholic, with the Guadalupan devotion I have witnessed in Mexico City as well as in the various places I have lived and worshiped over the past two decades, from California to Washington, D.C., from Indiana to Texas. My hope is that this volume will illuminate the beauty, strength, and multiple meanings of Guadalupan devotion, as well as respectfully reveal some of the ways this devotion has failed to fully reflect its practitioners' proud affirmations of Guadalupe's liberating, unifying, and life-giving potential.

The study primarily focuses on San Fernando Cathedral in San Antonio, Texas, a congregation that for nearly three centuries has sustained its Guadalupan devotion through times of progress and political upheaval, war and peace, ecclesial change and social change. I was a parishioner at San Fernando from 1992 to 1995, during which time I completed a doctoral dissertation on religion and ethnicity among nineteenth-century San Fernando congregants and collaborated with cathedral rector Virgilio Elizondo on a congregational study of the parish. My friendship with Father Elizondo had led me to worship at San Fernando during previous visits to San Antonio, and I had marveled from a distance at the cathedral's international television ministry, particularly the weekly Sunday Mass and the annual broadcast of the *serenata*—the serenade to Our Lady of Guadalupe on the eve of her feast. In the course of the congregational study I interviewed hundreds of parishioners and cathedral visitors. Father Elizondo and I also conducted eleven focus groups that included parishioners, other San Antonio residents, and scholars we invited to join the congregation in worship and then engage in conversation about their experience and observations. To this day I return frequently to visit and worship at San Fernando. During 2003, when I made two key research trips, I attended the first Guadalupe feast-day celebration in the newly renovated cathedral and conducted interviews crucial to the final editing of this volume.

In the first and final chapters of the book, which treat Guadalupan devotion at San Fernando from World War II to the early twenty-first century, I credit parishioners and other interviewees by name for direct citations and other information they provided, except in cases in which I merely describe my informants because they did not tell me their names or preferred that their names not be revealed. I conducted interviews in English, Spanish, or a combination of both languages according to the preferences of each interviewee; in order to reflect more clearly interviewees' ideas and sentiments, a number of Spanish and bilingual citations are given in their original form with parenthetical English translations as needed.

My sincere thanks to Father Elizondo; his successor and current San Fernando rector, Father David García; parochial vicar Jake Empereur, S.J.; and the numerous parishioners who encouraged me in this project and generously shared their wealth of knowledge and recollections about San Fernando. I am especially grateful to Gene and Sylvia Rodríguez for hosting an evaluation session on a working draft of the manuscript and to participants in that session, all of whom have assisted and guided me in this project for over a decade: Mary Esther and Joe Bernal, Janie Dillard, and Esther and Joe Rodríguez. I have incorporated many of their ideas, corrections, and critical observations though, of course, I am responsible for the final text. Other parish leaders interviewed for this study are too many to enumerate, but I would also like to thank Charles Acree, Al Aguilar, Enrique and Leticia Barrera, Ramona Bell, Emma Casarez, Roberta and Roberto Castro, Carmen Cedillo, Rosie Chacón, Felix Díaz Jr., Patti Elizondo, Richard and Zulema Galindo, David and Leyvia García, Janie García, Albert Garza, Sally Gómez-Kelly, Victor Landa, Mario and Guadalupe

Mandujano, Joann Montez, Tina Cantú Navarro, Mary Navarro Farr, Frank Paredes Jr., Doroteo "Pete" Pedroza, Felipa Peña, Alfredo Ramírez, Josefina Rodríguez, Graciela Sánchez, Lionel and Kathy Sosa, and Homer Villarreal. Ruben Alfaro, whose photography has documented much of San Fernando's recent history, provided various striking illustrations, which I'm sure many readers will appreciate as much as I do.

Though I cannot begin to list the names of all the friends and colleagues who have helped shape this volume, I am deeply grateful to all of them. At the University of Notre Dame I presented portions of the work to the liturgical studies area of the Department of Theology, the Cushwa Center for the Study of American Catholicism, the interdisciplinary Catholic Studies group, and the Erasmus Institute. Special thanks to those who invited my participation in these respective groups and led them in offering critical commentary on select portions of the manuscript: Michael Driscoll, Scott Appleby, John McGreevy, Anne Martínez, and Jim Turner. Students in the doctoral seminar I helped lead at Notre Dame during spring 2004 critiqued a draft of nearly the full manuscript: Kim Belcher, Natalia Imperatori Lee, Micaela Larkin, Heliodoro Lucatero, Rudy Reyes, Anthony Suárez, and Neto Valiente. I also want to thank my good friend and colleague Jerry Poyo for our extended conversations about this volume at nearly every stage of its development.

Various other colleagues offered helpful comments on the research and manuscript; particularly Juan Alvarez Cuauhtemoc; Adán Benavides Jr.; Miryam Bujanda; Rudy Busto; Gilbert R. Cadena; Kevin Caspersen; John Cavadini; Kathleen Cummings; Karen Mary Davalos; Allan Figueroa Deck, S.J.; Jesús F. de la Teja; Mary Doak; Orlando O. Espín; Eduardo Fernández, S.J.; Alejandro García-Rivera; Roberto S. Goizueta; Michelle González; Brad Gregory; Daniel Groody, C.S.C.; Paula Kane; Martha Ann Kirk, C.C.V.I.; Tom Kselman; Juanita Luna Lawhn; Luis D. León; Nancy Pineda Madrid; Lara Medina; Gary Riebe-Estrella, S.V.D.; Steven Rodríguez; Bob Sullivan; Chris Tirres; Jaime Vidal; Maria Watson Pfeiffer; and Bob Wright, O.M.I.

Furthermore, I benefited greatly from responses to parts of this work presented at the 2002 Henry Luce III Fellows in Theology Conference and at the annual meetings of the American Academy of Religion, North American Academy of Liturgy, Academy of Catholic Hispanic Theologians of the United States (ACHTUS), College Theology Society, Comisión para el Estudio de la Historia de la Iglesia en Latinoamerica (CEHILA), American Historical Association, National Association for Chicana and Chicano Studies, American Catholic Historical Association, American Society of Church History, Texas State Historical Association, and Texas Catholic Historical Society.

A Henry Luce III Fellow in Theology sabbatical grant gave me the time to finish an initial draft of the manuscript. I am thankful to the Henry Luce Foundation for funding the grant program, especially John W. Cook and Michael F. Gilligan; and to the Association of Theological Schools in the United States and Canada, which administers this sabbatical award, especially Daniel O. Aleshire. Summer study stipends from the Louisville Institute, the National Endowment for the Humanities, and Loyola Marymount University enabled me to make substantial progress on the manuscript at crucial points in its development. Some significant research employed in this volume stems from the San Fernando congregational study, which the Lilly Endowment generously funded and endowment officers Olga Villa Parra, Jim Wind, and Craig Dykstra supported with their expertise and encouragement.

I am particularly grateful to Bob Orsi for his collegiality, guidance, and friendship, and to both him and David Hall for their advice and support as general editors of the series in which this volume appears. Henry Tom and his colleagues at the John Hopkins University Press also provided outstanding editorial oversight. Tara Whipp, at the time a graduate student in the Department of Theology at the University of Notre Dame, ably assisted in preparing the book's notes and bibliography. Paula Brach, a colleague at Notre Dame's Cushwa Center for the Study of American Catholicism, effectively conducted numerous research tasks.

I am also indebted to various archivists and librarians whose expertise guided my research. These include Brother Edward Loch, S.M., Catholic Archives at San Antonio, Chancery Office, Archdiocese of San Antonio; Father John Raab, C.M.F., past director of the Archives of Claretian Missionaries, Western Province, U.S.A., Claretian Center, Los Angeles; Kinga Perzynska, past director of the Catholic Archives of Texas, Austin; Tom Shelton, University of Texas Institute of Texan Cultures, San Antonio. I thank those charged with the care of collections at the San Antonio Public Library; the Center for American History, University of Texas, Austin; the Nettie Lee Benson Latin American Collection, University of Texas, Austin; the library at San Antonio College; the Daughters of the Republic of Texas Library, San Antonio; the Witte Museum, San Antonio; the University of Notre Dame Archives, South Bend, Indiana; the Archives of the Mexican American Cultural Center, San Antonio; Special Collections, Our Lady of the Lake University, San Antonio; the Incarnate Word Archives,

Incarnate Word Generalate, San Antonio; the Vincentian Archives, St. Mary's of the Barrens, Perryville, Missouri; the Library of Congress; the National Archives, Washington, D.C.; the Houston Public Library; the Ethnic and Gender Studies Library, University of California, Santa Barbara; and the Bancroft Library, University of California, Berkeley.

An earlier version of chapter 2 appeared as "New Frontiers of Guadalupanismo," *Journal of Hispanic/Latino Theology* 5 (August 1997): 20–36. Chapter 4 was published in an earlier form as "Companion in Exile: Guadalupan Devotion at San Fernando Cathedral, San Antonio, Texas, 1900–1940," in *Horizons of the Sacred: Mexican Traditions in U.S. Catholicism*, Timothy Matovina and Gary Riebe-Estrella, eds. (Ithaca, NY: Cornell University Press, 2002), 17–40.

Finally, for their patience, support, example of faith, and unwavering love, *muchísimas gracias* to my wife, Elida, and our son, Carlos, to whom this book is dedicated.

Guadalupe and Her Faithful

An Evolving Tradition

In his 1556 sermon on the feast of the Nativity of the Virgin Mary, Fray Francisco de Bustamante sharply criticized Mexico City archbishop Alonso de Montúfar's promotion of Guadalupan devotion. Bustamante reportedly avowed that "one of the most pernicious things that anyone could sustain against the proper Christianity of the natives was the devotion to Our Lady of Guadalupe." He called on the viceroy and other royal officials present in the congregation to "remedy this great evil" and "punish the inventors [of the devotion], giving each of them 200 lashes." He went on to accuse the archbishop of being "very deceived" in his enthusiastic support of the devotion, especially because many Indigenous neophytes believed Guadalupe was a goddess and that her image itself worked miracles, and a number of them wavered in or abandoned their Christian faith when their pleas for miracles went unanswered. Archbishop Montúfar immediately ordered an investigation of Bustamante's oration. Though the nine witnesses selected for the inquiry were deferential toward the archbishop, no punitive action was ultimately taken against Bustamante; a note in the official documentation for the inquiry declared without explanation that the proceedings were "suspended" and "dead."[1]

The conflict between the two clerics reflected sixteenth-century ecclesiastical politics in New Spain, as it pitted the Franciscan Bustamante against the Dominican Montúfar. More precisely, it illuminated conflicting views on the Guadalupe cult, particularly the early Franciscan missioners' reticence about and even hostility toward the devotion. The Franciscan view was most famously expressed in the observations of Fray Bernardino de Sahagún, the great chronicler of ancient Mexico. Sahagún decried Guadalupan veneration because it disguised the "idolatry" of Indigenous devotees, whose people had in pre-Columbian times "had a temple dedicated to the mother of the gods, whom they called Tonantzin." The temple was on the hill of Tepeyac, the same site as the Guadalupe chapel, and thus devotees continued to worship Tonantzin in the image of Guadalupe.[2]

When nineteenth-century historians first encountered the testimonies from the 1556 inquiry (first published in 1888), they were immediately embroiled in the debates about Guadalupe's origins, which by then had dominated Guadalupan studies for more than two centuries. Because none of the witnesses who testified had mentioned the Indigenous neophyte Juan Diego's experience of the Guadalupe apparitions, and several recounted Bustamante's claim that an Indigenous artist had painted the Guadalupe image, the anonymous editors of the first published edition of the depositions argued that traditional beliefs about the miraculous origins of the Guadalupe cult and image were false. Two years later, in 1890, Fortino Hipólito Vera, a leading figure in the collegiate chapter at Tepeyac and a future bishop of Cuernavaca, defended the apparition tradition in a rival publication of the 1556 depositions. Among other arguments, Vera contended that Bustamante and his fellow Franciscans were iconoclasts and that the comparison of Guadalupe to miraculous-origin European images of Mary revealed a presumption that Guadalupe's derivation was also miraculous.[3]

Not surprisingly, Vera's publication also included an Indigenous Nahuatl reprint of the *Nican mopohua* (a title derived from the document's first words, "Here is recounted") and Spanish and Latin translations of the document. For Vera and other proponents of the Guadalupe tradition before and since, the *Nican mopohua* is the foundational text recording the 1531 Guadalupe apparitions to Juan Diego. It narrates how Guadalupe sent Juan Diego to request that Juan de Zumárraga, the first bishop of Mexico, build a temple at Tepeyac in her honor. At first the bishop doubted the celestial origins of this request, but he came to believe when Juan Diego presented him exquisite flowers that were out of season and the image of Guadalupe miraculously appeared on the humble *indio's tilma* (cloak).

No one doubts that a chapel dedicated to Guadalupe was active at Tepeyac as early as the mid-sixteenth century, as is clear from the 1556 inquiry into Bustamante's sermon. The disagreement is over which came first, the chapel or the belief in the apparitions. In other words, did reports of Juan Diego's miraculous encounter with Guadalupe spark the construction of the chapel and the beginnings of Guadalupan devotion, or is the apparition narrative a later invention that provides a mythical origin for an already existing image and pious tradition? Those who hold the latter position point to evidence such as the lapse of more than a century between 1531, when the apparitions reportedly occurred, and the earliest publication of apparition accounts. They also note the lack of documentation about the apparitions among the works of prominent sixteenth-century Catholic leaders in New Spain, including the complete absence of such references in the known writings of Zumárraga. Conversely, those who hold the former position argue that the Spaniards' disdain for the allegedly inferior native peoples accounts for the lengthy delay before an official inquiry recorded Indigenous oral testimony about Guadalupe and Juan Diego. They also contend that there is written documentation for the apparitions that dates back to before the *Nican mopohua*'s publication, such as a recently discovered codex depicting Juan Diego's encounter with Guadalupe that Jesuit Xavier Escalada argues is Juan Diego's 1548 death certificate. Thus the heart of the debate is disagreement about the validity of oral testimony, the viability of historical arguments from silence, and especially the authenticity, authorship, proper dating, and significance of critical primary sources, particularly the *Nican mopohua* itself.[4]

Despite ongoing controversies, millions of devotees have no doubt about the authenticity of the apparition narrative and the miraculous origins of the Guadalupe image. Long acclaimed as the national symbol of Mexico and officially recognized within Roman Catholicism as the mother and patroness of the Americas, Guadalupe continues to appear in the daily lives of her faithful: on home altars, t-shirts, tattoos, murals, medals, refrigerator magnets, and wall hangings; in parish churches and in countless conversations and daily prayers. Her basilica in Mexico City is the most visited pilgrimage site in the Western Hemisphere. She is the most conspicuous sacred icon of Mexican-descent residents in the United States. The inordinate attention given to historical origins in Guadalupan studies—an issue repeatedly addressed but never resolved—overshadows an equally vital question that is rarely addressed: Given the plentiful miraculous images of Christ, Mary, and the saints that dotted the sacred landscape of colonial Mexico, how did the Guadalupe cult rise above all others and grow from a merely local devotion into a regional, national, and then international phenomenon?

Numerous devotees concur with the *Nican mopohua* that news of Guadalupe's miraculous presence on Juan Diego's tilma immediately attracted people from "everywhere," who came "to see and marvel at her precious image." Extant scholarship on the historical evolution of Guadalupan devotion, particularly the influential work of William B. Taylor, demonstrates a more measured growth. These studies document the gradual spread of Guadalupe paintings, medals, sermons, *cofradías* (confraternities, or pious societies), and feast-day celebrations, as well as the incremental increase in the choice of Guadalupe as a name for places, children, shrines, and churches. The devotion was initially concentrated in Mexico City and its environs, and then expanded toward the north. By 1731 settlers had established a parish at the town of San Fernando de Béxar (present-day San Antonio, Texas); it was the first parish congregation in what is now the United States to honor Guadalupe as a primary patroness. By the time of Mexican independence in 1821 the devotion had spread throughout the viceroyalty. Several factors contributed to Guadalupe's growing acclaim, most notably her devotees' multitudinous testimonies about her compassion and miraculous aid, the foundational influence of the earliest theological writings on Guadalupe, the urban networks that linked other municipalities to the trend-setting center of Mexico City, Guadalupe's multivocal appeal to diverse castes and races, and her role in the rise of Mexican national consciousness.[5]

From Local to National Patroness

The 1556 depositions in the Bustamante-Montúfar controversy are the earliest uncontested primary sources that illuminate the contours and extent of Guadalupan devotion at Tepeyac. One crown official favorably compared Guadalupan devotion to that of Nuestra Señora de Atocha in Madrid and Nuestra Señora de Prado in Valladolid, stating that he had been to the Guadalupe chapel "many times," had heard of the miracles that occurred there, and had observed how visits to this sacred site had replaced more frivolous and "illicit pleasures" among the residents of Mexico City. A lawyer related that he had seen both Spaniards and native people enter the chapel "with great devotion, many of them [proceeding] on their knees from the door to the altar where the blessed image of Our Lady of Guadalupe is located." He also noted that the stream of women and men, healthy and infirm, who went from Mexico City to pray, attend Mass, and hear sermons at the shrine was so continuous it induced young children to "agitate" their elders "to take them there." The final witness testified that he had been to the chapel more than twenty times and that his young daughter had been cured of a bad cough after he prayed with her there. Though no natives were called upon to offer depositions in the official inquiry because Bustamante preached his controversial sermon to the viceroy and other dignitaries in the chapel of a Franciscan cloister, this final witness also commented that at the command of the Franciscans some natives had grown lukewarm in their devotion to Guadalupe. He added, however, that Bustamante's sermon "had not stopped the devotion, but rather it had increased even more" in the weeks following his oration.[6]

Over the following century Mexico City archbishops, the viceroy and other public officials, and devotees from the general populace helped propagate the Guadalupe cult through their patronage of increasingly elaborate celebrations and facilities at Tepeyac. Most notable among the buildings was the first Guadalupe basilica, which was dedicated in 1622 and, like the original chapel, was financed through the donations of the devout. Some viceroys made the three-mile trek from Mexico City's main plaza to visit the Guadalupe chapel as often as once a week, providing an example of piety for other residents. Also facilitating the spread of Guadalupan devotion was the 1572 arrival in New Spain of the Jesuits, whose attitude toward "pagan" sources and practices as potentially integrative with Christianity provided an alternative to the more exclusivist approach prevalent among the early Franciscans. In 1573 Pope Gregory XIII provided further impetus for Guadalupan devotion by granting a plenary indulgence to those who visited and prayed at the Guadalupe chapel; three years later Jesuit superior general Everard Mercurian assisted the archbishop of Mexico City, Pedro Moya de Contreras, in securing the pope's ten-year extension of this indulgence to encourage the faith and devotion of a growing population, especially numerous natives "recently converted to faith in Christ."[7]

Tepeyac's location at a principal crossroads also abetted Guadalupe's growing popularity. Situated on the outskirts of New Spain's capital of Mexico City, it was the point from which travelers could take one road northward to the interior and its silver mines, or another road to the east and Veracruz, the primary port for transatlantic travel. From the 1560s onward archbishops, viceroys, and other prominent Mexico City residents met arriving Spanish dignitaries at Tepeyac and ceremoniously ushered them into the city. The practice of visiting the Guadalupe image and chapel was widespread among local travelers as well, as Englishman Miles Philips observed when he went by Tepeyac in 1573: "Whensoever any Spaniards passe by this church, [they] . . . come into the church, and kneele before the image, and pray to our Lady to defend them from all evil."[8]

As with many sacred sites and images, the primary reason Guadalupe's fame initially spread among residents of Mexico City and the surrounding area was devotees' testimonies of miracles and trust in her aid. The Spanish Catholic imagination tended to view God as stern and distant, which intensified appeals to Guadalupe and other Marian figures as compassionate mothers and intercessors. Philips observed that devotees who bathed in the cold-water springs near the Guadalupe chapel, attended feast-day celebrations there, or prayed before the image said that "our Lady of Guadalupe doeth worke a number of miracles." Other sixteenth-century sources also attest to claims of miraculous cures, such as a 1575 letter of Viceroy Martín Enríquez to Spanish king Felipe II, which stated that the chapel and growing Guadalupan devotion at Tepeyac evolved from the claim of a herdsman that he "had recovered his health" when he visited the Guadalupe image in an original hermitage on the site.[9]

The trust of devotees in Guadalupe's help and intercession is also revealed in sixteenth-century wills, such as that of Francisco Verdugo Quetzalmamalitzin, a Nahuatl lord from the town of Teotihuacan, a short distance from Mexico City. Verdugo Quetzalmamalitzin left four pesos so the priest assigned to the Guadalupe chapel would offer masses on his behalf after his death; his will also stated: "To our lady the Blessed Virgin Mary, queen of heaven, I ask that she be my advocate before her precious son, the redeemer of the world." Samuel Stradanus, a Flemish artist and New Spain resident who ran a lithography business, made an engraving (c. 1615) that depicts the Guadalupe image surrounded by eight scenes of the more renowned miracles Spanish devotees attributed to her, apparently drawn from ex-votos (objects representing a prayer request or memorial) enshrined by supplicants at the Guadalupe chapel. The miracles in the eight scenes and six others are also described in the *Nican motecpana* (Here is an ordered account), which begins with three miracles Guadalupe reportedly granted to Indigenous devotees. These accounts range from stories of petitioners being saved from a misfired arrow, a horse accident, a falling lamp, or an unspecified epidemic, to tales of healings of headaches, dropsy, and severe swelling of the feet and neck.[10]

Increasing claims of healings and other miraculous interventions on behalf of individual supplicants led devotees to petition Guadalupe to intercede for communal needs, most conspicuously during the devastating Mexico City flood of 1629. Archbishop Francisco Manso y Zúñiga mandated that the Guadalupe image be moved from the basilica to the cathedral in the center of the city (the only time the Guadalupe image has ever been publicly processed from Tepeyac). It remained at the cathedral until 1634, when the flood subsided. Many devotees credited Guadalupe with tempering the effects of the floodwaters after the initial torrents of 1629 and with bringing final relief from the inundation. Accompanied by the viceroy and the archbishop, they returned the Guadalupe image back to Tepeyac in a victorious procession, amidst music, fireworks, and colorful decorations. Despite her rising acclaim, however, Guadalupe was not yet the predominant celestial patroness, even in the local area of Mexico City, as is evident from the more frequent communal appeals during times of drought, epidemic, and threat of foreign attack to Nuestra Señora de los Remedios (Our Lady of Remedies), the Spanish Virgin whose image reportedly accompanied and assisted Hernán Cortés and his men in the conquest of Mexico. The inconsistent flow of financial contributions to the Guadalupe basilica further indicates that her rise to prominence was still in its initial stages.[11]

Theological and pastoral treatises on Guadalupe have helped expand, refashion, and codify Guadalupan devotion for centuries, but none more extensively than the works of two Mexico City diocesan priests: Miguel Sánchez's *Imagen de la Virgen María* (1648) and Luis Laso de la Vega's *Huei tlamahuiçoltica* (By a great miracle, 1649). Sánchez was a pastor and theologian who specialized in early Christian writings; the primary focus of his book was to examine Guadalupe and the evangelization of Mexico vis-à-vis the wider Christian tradition, particularly the writings of Augustine and the image of the "woman clothed with the sun" in Revelation 12. His erudite and somewhat convoluted volume has five major sections that successively treat Guadalupe's providential role in the conquest of Mexico, the Guadalupe apparition narrative (the first published account of the apparitions), a theological reflection on the Guadalupe image, a summary of postapparition developments in the Guadalupe site and tradition, and a narration and analysis of seven miracles attributed to Guadalupe.[12]

Laso de la Vega, who was appointed vicar of the Guadalupe basilica in 1647, penned a glowing commendation included in Sánchez's volume and published his own book just a few months later. Though the precise relation between the two works remains a debated topic, the contents of the *Huei tlamahuiçoltica* reveal their close correlation. It is a composite text and encompasses an author's preface; the *Nican mopohua* apparition narrative; a brief description of the Guadalupe image; the *Nican motecpana* miracle accounts; a short biographical sketch of Juan Diego; the *Nican tlantica* (Here ends [the story]), which summarizes the history of Mary's influence in New Spain and exhorts the faithful to Guadalupan devotion; and a concluding Guadalupan prayer. But the *Nican mopohua*'s extensive use of poetic devices, diminutive forms, and the Indigenous narrative style of accentuating dialogue, along with the absence throughout the *Huei tlamahuiçoltica* of the theological elaboration and the numerous scriptural and patristic references found in *Imagen de la Virgen María*, reveal Laso de la Vega's aim to provide a pastoral manual to promote Guadalupan devotion and Christian faith among Nahuatl-speaking residents.[13]

Though Sánchez and Laso de la Vega situated Guadalupe within the context of Marian apparitions generally, one way that they promoted Guadalupe's evolving devotional primacy was to symbolically indicate her preeminence over her chief rival among Marian images in Mexico City, Nuestra Señora de los Remedios. Both authors recount the healing of an Indigenous convert named Juan (de Tovar), who, according to tradition, found the Remedios image after one of Cortés's men hid it among maguey plants as the troops retreated following an early loss to Indigenous forces. Significantly, Juan's grave illness was not healed in response to prayers offered before the Remedios image, for which he was the caretaker. Rather, he had his loved ones carry him a distance of more than two leagues to the Guadalupe sanctuary, where Guadalupe effected his cure and sent him back to build a chapel for Remedios. In his usual fashion of engaging biblical typologies to explain contemporary events, Sánchez contended that Guadalupe and Remedios parallel the biblical figures of Naomi and Ruth. Like Naomi, the native of Bethlehem, Guadalupe was a native of Mexico; like Ruth, Remedios was a foreigner who migrated to provide her love and assistance in a new land. Though both he and Laso de la Vega carefully noted that all Marian images are manifestations of the same mother of God, Sánchez planted the seeds of Mexican nationalism by arguing for Mexico's divine election on the basis of the singular honor of Guadalupe being "a native of this land." These seeds came to fruition a century and a half later in the struggle for Mexican independence, when for a time Guadalupe and Remedios served as the banners of insurgent groups and their crown-loyalist opponents, respectively.[14]

Imagen de la Virgen María and *Huei tlamahuiçoltica* had a relatively small circulation, the former because it was primarily intended for the clergy and other learned readers of Mexico City and the latter because it was written in Nahuatl. Neither work was reprinted in its entirety before the twentieth century, but Sánchez's volume had a pronounced effect on the propagation and meaning of Guadalupan devotion during his own lifetime. Jesuit Mateo de la Cruz eliminated much of the expansive biblical imagery and theological erudition of *Imagen de la Virgen María* in a popular 1660 abbreviation of the text entitled *Relación de la milagrosa aparición de la santa imagen de la Virgen de Guadalupe de México.*[15] The more widespread appeal of de la Cruz's condensed volume was complemented by Sánchez's influence on prominent Mexico City clergy and his fellow criollos, the designation in the Spanish caste system for persons of Spanish blood born in the New World.

Approximately one hundred published Guadalupe sermons from 1661 to 1802 are extant. Collectively they elaborate various themes that echo Sánchez's criollo, patristic-based analysis of Guadalupe, such as God's providential guidance in Mexican history, Guadalupe's appearance as a foundational event for the church in Mexico, and the blessings and miracles that await those who appeal to Guadalupe and contemplate her countenance in the sacred tilma. A number of sermons even repeat directly Sánchez's biblical typologies, such as his association of Moses, Mount Sinai, and the Ark of the Covenant with Juan Diego, Tepeyac, and the Guadalupe image. As David Brading has observed, "Nowhere was [Sánchez's] influence more obvious than in the application of Augustinian typology to the interpretation of the Mexican Virgin."[16] Moreover, following Sánchez and Laso de la Vega, theologians who have considered Guadalupe have not tended to focus on traditional questions about Mary, such as her title of *Theotokos* (Mother of God), her virginity, and the Immaculate Conception. Rather, the Guadalupe image, the account of the apparitions, and the historical context are means to explore the collision of Old and New World civilizations and the ongoing implications of this clash for Christianity in the Americas and beyond.[17]

As Sánchez, Laso de la Vega, and de la Cruz, along with their readers, promoted the Guadalupe cult and argued for its solid foundation in scripture, theology, the apparitions to Juan Diego, and the miraculous origins of the tilma, Guadalupe's faithful propagated her devotion in other ways. Most conspicuously, Guadalupan devotion spread through the construction of the first church edifices dedicated to her beyond the vicinity of Tepeyac, beginning in 1654 with the efforts of leaders in San Luis Potosí (about 250 miles north of Mexico City) to secure a "real portrait" of Guadalupe and "build a house for she who housed

our God and Lord . . . the true effigy of the queen of angels." Even new generations of Franciscans, whose predecessors had expressed the strongest reserva-
tions about the devotion, founded establishments under Guadalupe's patronage
such as a mission for propagating Christianity among the natives in what is now
Ciudad Juárez (across the river from El Paso, Texas) in 1659 and later a missionary training center at Zacatecas, where friars prepared for apostolic work
among the Indigenous peoples of New Spain's northern frontier.[18]

Seeking to further augment the rising tide of Guadalupan devotion, the Mexico City cathedral chapter began pursuing a goal that would take nearly a century to realize: securing a papal declaration of 12 December, the traditional date
of Guadalupe's final appearance to Juan Diego, as the Feast of Guadalupe. Their
first attempt to achieve this goal involved a 1666 inquiry intended to document
that an oral tradition for the Guadalupe apparitions to Juan Diego had been extant since the inception of the devotion at Tepeyac. Twenty elderly witnesses
gave depositions for the inquiry, including seven Indigenous residents of Cuau-
titlán, who testified through an interpreter that Juan Diego was a "native" of
their town and was so renowned for his holiness and love of Guadalupe that numerous natives "asked him to intercede with the Most Holy Virgin" for their
needs. Subsequently a growing number of books on Guadalupe disseminated
more widely the wonders of her "miraculous origin" and "admirable apparition"
in Mexico, most notably Luis Becerra Tanco's *Felicidad de México* (1675) and
Francisco de Florencia's *La Estrella del Norte de México* (1688). All of these developments helped multiply the pilgrimages, celebrations, and prayer offerings
at Tepeyac, as did the viceroy's 1675–1676 construction of a grand highway that
linked the Guadalupe basilica with the main plaza in Mexico City and was lined
with fifteen chapels dedicated to the fifteen mysteries of the rosary. The 1709
completion of a formidable new Guadalupe basilica at Tepeyac both reflected
and enhanced Guadalupe's rising prominence.[19]

The catalytic event for the official declaration of Guadalupe as patroness of
New Spain was the disastrous *matlazahuatl* (typhus or typhoid fever) epidemic
of 1736–1737, which claimed more than forty thousand lives in Mexico City
alone. As the death count began to soar, Mexico City residents followed the
long-standing Spanish Catholic practice of successively appealing to celestial intercessors with processions through the streets, novenas (nine days of prayer services), and other supplications until one of their heavenly patrons provided relief. According to a contemporary account, devotees first implored Our Lady of
Loreto, then Nuestra Señora de los Remedios, and eventually various other

saints and Marian images. Juan Antonio de Vizarrón y Eguiarreta, archbishop of Mexico City, refused the city council's request to have the Guadalupe image brought to the cathedral as had been done during the flood of the previous century, advising instead that they organize a novena at the Tepeyac sanctuary Guadalupe had chosen for herself. When the epidemic continued to rage after this novena, the city council petitioned the archbishop to join with them in naming Guadalupe the patroness of the city and promoting her designation as the patroness of New Spain. On 24 May 1737, a massive citywide procession celebrated the ecclesiastical and civic officials' solemn oath that they would declare Guadalupe their municipal patroness and honor her annually on 12 December.[20]

Finally the epidemic ended, and the city's residents attributed its abatement to Guadalupe's intercession. This, in combination with Mexico City's centrality as a capital and a trend-setting city for other municipalities and the immediate efforts of Mexico City officials to extend Guadalupe's patronage throughout New Spain, soon led city councils and cathedral chapters in other cities and towns to declare Guadalupe their patroness. This burgeoning initiative reached its ultimate goal in 1754 when Pope Benedict XIV declared Guadalupe the patroness of New Spain and named 12 December her feast day. Thereafter the geographic range and density of Guadalupan devotion increased even further, a process frequently facilitated by priests sent to rural parishes after receiving their seminary training in Mexico City, the epicenter of the devotion. A sign and cause of the widening devotion was petitioners' supplication for Guadalupe's help for an ever-growing variety of needs. They increasingly solicited her protection not just from illness, floods, and epidemics but from other maladies as well, such as drought, failed crops, fire, earthquakes, and enemy attacks.[21]

Yet another factor in the proliferation of Guadalupan devotion was its appeal to a variety of interests and social classes because of its polyvalence, an element of the devotion illuminated in its ambiguous meaning among native peoples. Some scholars have overstated the case with claims that Guadalupe's "early cult was overwhelmingly Indian" and that she was "unifying Indians in a single religious movement." It is true that Indigenous participation was discernible from the outset, as demonstrated by primary documentation, such as wills, the Bustamante sermon inquiry, and the *Nican motecpana*. Some natives remained close to the devotion because they resided at Tepeyac; according to the chaplain of the Guadalupe chapel, in 1570 the adults in this small settlement numbered 250. Given the association of Tepeyac with pre-Columbian worship, the Nahuatl tendency to absorb rather than resist the gods of their rivals, and the catastrophic effects of the conquest and European diseases on Indigenous communities—five decades after the conquest the native population of central Mexico was less than one third what it had been before the Spaniards arrived—it is not difficult to imagine that Guadalupe was a paradoxical figure for Indigenous devotees. She was a powerful mother and intercessor, a brown-skinned woman like them who provided continuity with an ancient Nahuatl image and pilgrimage site and came to symbolize the Indigenous peoples' dignity and right to self-determination.[22]

But Guadalupe was also a force whom Spaniards engaged to enhance native peoples' acceptance of colonial rule and missionary efforts. In a telling passage, the *Nican motecpana* notes that Mary of Guadalupe "cherished, aided, and defended the local people" in the wake of the Spaniards' arrival, but it also presents her as a protagonist in the Spanish efforts to extinguish Indigenous ways, since because of her compassion the natives "despised and abhorred the idolatry in which they had been wandering about in confusion on the earth, in the night and darkness in which the demon had made them live." Even during the struggle for Mexican independence from Spain in the early nineteenth century, when numerous Indigenous combatants fought with Father Miguel Hidalgo and other insurgents under the banner of Guadalupe, the ambiguity of Guadalupan devotion was evident in the actions of natives like the Zacapoaxtlas, who named Guadalupe their patroness in their defense of the royalist cause and credited her with their victories over Hidalgo's forces. The war and its aftermath marked the culmination of Guadalupe's rise to national prominence. During the course of the war the geographic mobility of both Indigenous and non-Indigenous populations brought residents from isolated areas into more sustained contact with Guadalupan devotion, while the eventual winning of independence and the public homage offered Guadalupe by Mexico's first leaders sealed her status as the national emblem. To this day activists, writers, preachers, and devotees note the ambiguities of Guadalupe, particularly the incongruity between celebratory claims about her power to uplift and unite diverse races and classes and the ongoing plight of devotees like Mexico's Indigenous peoples.[23]

Guadalupe at San Fernando

The spread of Guadalupe's patronage in the wake of Mexico City officials' 1737 declaration making her their municipal patroness extended as far north as present-day San Antonio, Texas, where in 1738 local residents invoked Guadalupe as a primary patroness when they laid the cornerstone for their first parish church. Further developments in New Spain and later Mexico continued to influence the devotees of San Fernando parish, as it came to be called, such as Guadalupe's role in the struggle for Mexican independence, the famous Guadalupe coronation of 1895, the ideological battles connected with the Mexican Revolution and the Cristero Rebellion during the early twentieth century, the 2002 canonization of Juan Diego, and especially the patterns of transnational migration between Mexico and San Antonio, which have consistently brought San Fernando congregants into contact with new devotees and their varied understandings of Guadalupe.

Some recent works have examined elements of contemporary Guadalupan devotion, including dance, pilgrimage, feast-day celebrations, and the influence of those celebrations on social hierarchies and collective identity in Mexican villages.[24] Latina and Latino theologians have articulated claims regarding Guadalupe's significance as the premier evangelizer of Mexicans and Mexican Americans, the mother of new life for the Americas, a source of empowerment for women, a symbol of hope and liberation, an inculturated expression of the Christian tradition, a paradigm of authentic human freedom and relationships, an embodiment of beauty and a rich resource for theological aesthetics, and a vital means to foster dialogue between Nahuatl and Judeo-Christian Wisdom theologies.[25] Contemporary novelists, essayists, poets, and artists have sought to unveil and develop Guadalupe's meaning and potential for groups like undocumented Mexicans in the United States, Chicana and Chicano[26] activists, and farm workers. They have frequently offered a critical analysis of Guadalupe, particularly her power in the lives of women—the power both to transform women's lives and to sanction their subordination in church, family, and society.[27]

This volume enhances the growing body of ethnographic, theological, literary, and artistic works on Guadalupe by grounding Guadalupan devotion in its shifting historical contexts, illuminating both its potent force and its potential limitations in the lives and religious imagination of Guadalupe's faithful. Additionally, the book advances the increasing scholarly interest in exploring the faith and religion of Latinos and other groups as a vital component of larger historical narratives, as do the few historical works that have examined Guadalupe's role in shaping the lives and identity formation of Mexicans, Mexican Americans, and Chicanos.[28] The volume also augments previous studies of U.S. Catholicism. For example, my own individual and collaborative work has compared the nineteenth-century Mexican experience of incorporation into the United States with that of European Catholic immigrants, provided a documentary overview of U.S.

Latina and Latino Catholics, and explored ways in which scholarship on Latinos necessitates a "remapping" of U.S. Catholic historiography and analysis of contemporary church life.[29]

Though Guadalupe is unquestionably the most revered sacred image among Mexicans and Mexican Americans, no previous study has examined Guadalupan devotion in a single faith community from Spanish colonial times to the present. Nor has any previous book-length work examined Guadalupan devotion from the perspective of what many scholars call "lived religion," the focus of a growing cluster of studies on rituals, devotions, and pious practices. The lived religion perspective takes seriously the interconnections between faith expressions and the social structures, cultural horizons, bodily existence, everyday lives, and local circumstances of their practitioners.[30] San Fernando's nearly three centuries as a predominantly Latino congregation, its persistence in Guadalupan devotion since the parish's inception, and its status as a Latino cathedral community with broad influence on the faith and devotion of other congregations make it an apt choice for such a study.

The evolution of Guadalupan devotion at San Fernando is particularly linked to San Antonio's long history as a borderlands settlement, a contested zone of contact between national sovereignties and diverse peoples in which, as Luis León demonstrates, "religious belief and practice are continuously redefined by devotees . . . as a creative and often effective means to manage the crises of everyday life."[31] Established as part of the Spanish crown's efforts to claim Texas, to Christianize and Hispanicize Native Americans, and to shield New Spain's northern territories from French Louisiana, San Antonio was adjacent to emergent Anglo American[32] colonies in Texas after Mexico achieved independence in 1821. When Texas won independence from Mexico in 1836 and was annexed by the United States nine years later, San Antonio became part of the borderlands region between Mexico and Texas, a transnational crossroads where Mexican nationals, Texans of Mexican descent, Anglo Americans, African Americans, and other peoples have interacted ever since; today San Antonio is a U.S. city that many ethnic Mexicans still proudly claim as "the northernmost city in Mexico." The frequent clashes of peoples in San Antonio's history include about a dozen military battles fought in and around the city, more than in any other place in the United States. Violence and peacemaking efforts, ethnic conflict and cohesion, political struggles and economic disparities, and ongoing migration and demographic shifts constitute just some of the changing power dynamics that have shaped and been shaped by devotion to Guadalupe at San Fernando, often accentuating Guadalupan devotion as a means to express, mold, and reinforce worshipers' collective identity in this predominantly working-class, ethnic Mexican congregation.

San Fernando's location and appearance have also consistently shaped the congregation's Guadalupan devotion, revealing the integral links among physical space, material culture, religious traditions, and, particularly in the San Fernando case, ethnic identity and legitimation.[33] As the premier parish church in a Spanish Catholic settlement, San Fernando has always stood at the heart of San Antonio's two original plazas, a place usually reserved for the county courthouse or another governmental "temple of justice" in towns that Anglo Americans founded in Texas and elsewhere.[34] San Fernando congregants have often evoked this physical centrality as a visible reminder of San Antonio's Hispanic origins, a validation of their dignity, and a warrant for just and equitable treatment. The church building's original Spanish colonial architecture, a nineteenth-century French neo-Gothic addition, and periodic alterations of spatial arrangements and Guadalupan and other sacred imagery within its interior have influenced and expressed communal identity, particularly the importance of Mexican traditions like Guadalupe in the life and faith of the congregation. Processions and festivities for the Feast of Guadalupe and other feast days have often spilled out into San Antonio's streets and the plazas on each side of the parish church. When farm fields surrounded the town center, participants in the events offered intercession for good harvests; later the feast days evoked painful memories, and participants prayed amidst the physical reminders of battles and other violent conflicts; and in various eras of the parish's history participants symbolically expressed ethnic pride and solidarity in a pluralistic and contested urban environment. Conversely, the relegation of Guadalupe celebrations to the church edifice for several decades after the U.S. Civil War paralleled ethnic Mexicans' diminished influence in a settlement their ancestors had founded.

Most San Fernando parishioners and devotees have consciously engaged Guadalupe as a powerful celestial mother. Her litany of achievements at San Fernando, many deemed miracles by her devotees, is endless: she has provided rain and abundant harvests, driven back the floodwaters of the San Antonio River, safeguarded immigrants, protected soldiers at war, restored broken relationships, enabled students to succeed in school, provided help with employment, and healed all manner of infirmity and distress. Down through the centuries many San Fernando devotees have called her the Virgin Mary and have understood the Catholic belief that she is not God but an intercessor before God; in practice, however, many turn to her as a mother who herself wields divine power.[35] Prayers of petition and thanksgiving flow to her in a continuous cycle. In the hearts of her faithful followers, Guadalupe never fails. Turning to her is an infallible step in gaining influence in the midst of a difficult or even hopeless situation. What of the cancer patient who fails to recover, the son who shows no sign of turning from wrongful ways, the poverty that is endemic? If doubts ever creep into the hearts and minds of Guadalupe's devotees, they are loath to mention them. Their trust and confidence in her maternal care are so absolute that the mere notion that she failed to listen, respond, or bring about some greater good from tragedy seems a conceptual impossibility.

The Guadalupan devotion of San Fernando parishioners illustrates that religious practices not only express and enliven faith in celestial protection but also shape and illuminate divergent understandings of faith and communal power dynamics that at times have brought laity, clergy, and women religious into conflict. However, contrary to depictions of Catholic clergy in the Southwest as either absent or perpetually in conflict with Hispanic laity, in San Fernando priests have often joined with laity to forge parish traditions like Guadalupan devotion through processes of compromise and conciliation; this is consistent with the findings of scholars like Bob Wright.[36] Though priests typically have the final authority in liturgical matters such as the adornment of the church worship space, San Fernando congregants have influenced the clergy's choices by their level of participation in fundraising campaigns, as well as by choosing their own sacred images to donate. Sometimes these offerings reflect the greater wealth and influence of individual congregants, but in at least two instances parishioners initiated and led successful grassroots efforts to purchase and present likenesses of Our Lady of Guadalupe.

Recognizing Guadalupe's power among congregants, European clergy and religious at San Fernando, who predominated for nearly 140 years after the political separation of Texas from Mexico, tended to engage Guadalupan devotion as a form of Marian piety that fortifies Catholic allegiance and deters the influence of Protestant proselytizers. They also proclaimed a vital link between worthy reception of the sacraments and proper Guadalupan devotion. Exiled Mexican clergy who assisted at San Fernando in the early twentieth century, as well as the Mexican and Mexican American pastors, women religious, permanent deacons, and lay leaders of more recent decades, have also challenged congregants to heed Guadalupe's message and calling. They too interpret that calling in various ways: they exhort congregants to render true devotion, transmit the

Catholic faith to the young, foster harmony in ethnic relations and the wider society, and raise up the lowly "Juan Diegos" of today. They especially connect
Guadalupe with devotees' ethnic identity and their dignity as the chosen sons
and daughters of *la Morenita* (the brown-skinned woman). Diverse understandings of Guadalupe reflect not only the fluidity and multivocality of the devotion
but also the personal charisma, authority, and interactions of clergy, elite parish
members, and organized lay constituencies who shape devotional expressions
and their meanings.

Parish Guadalupe celebrations have reinforced, and at times reconfigured, relationships of power and differences in social status among San Fernando congregants. Though scholars and practitioners of "popular," or lived, religion have
rightly contested analyses that depict everyday religious practices as overwhelmingly superstitious, fatalistic, and oppressive, Robert Orsi correctly avers
that the more recent emphasis on devotees' creative agency in engaging faith traditions like that of Guadalupe frequently obscures the "issues of power, domination, discipline, and authority in religious contexts."[37] At San Fernando, class
distinctions among congregants have often been symbolically reinforced when
the elite occupy places of prominence at Guadalupe celebrations, but Guadalupe's intense association with collective identity can easily hide the sacralization
of social hierarchies in these feast-day rituals and festivities. As Roberto Goizueta explains, Latinos like San Fernando congregants tend to derive their sense
of identity more from "the community [that] forms and shapes" them than from
their lives as "autonomous individuals."[38] Thus participants have a strong urge
to assume their "place" in ritual and in other communal activities—their sense
of identity and belonging depend on it—particularly for an occasion like the
Guadalupe feast, which is central to group pride and solidarity. Parish leaders
and congregants who have protested such social hierarchies frequently proclaim
that authentic devotion to Guadalupe requires egalitarianism in communal and
social relations, but seldom have they decried specific injustices and demanded
concrete action for change within their own faith community.

The differentiation of gender roles in the parish's Guadalupan devotion evi-
dences a similar tendency. Contrary to the stereotypical view that few Latino
males display religious devotion publicly, in predominantly ethnic Mexican
communities like San Fernando a number of men have participated in pious societies that promote Guadalupan devotion and have exercised leadership in
parish Guadalupe celebrations. Both boys and girls are named for Guadalupe,
illuminating the presumption that, like females, males fall under Guadalupe's

maternal care and owe her filial respect and devotion. Some San Fernando lay-men have sung tributes to Guadalupe or written newspaper editorials about her, revealing that Guadalupan devotion provides men with a culturally acceptable means to express sentiment, affection, and faith and its meaning in their lives. In general, however, men have tended to support women's leadership of public prayer by taking on other tasks themselves: organizing games and other festivi-ties, coordinating fundraisers, directing processions, and firing gun and cannon salutes. Historically, for many men, occupying a prominent place in Guadalupe celebrations—whether as planners and organizers or as participants in worship and festivities—has affirmed or even enhanced their status as political or com-munity leaders.

Guadalupe celebrations have often enabled women to exercise greater lead-ership and authority than they have been able to in other areas of public life, il-lustrating what Ana María Díaz-Stevens calls the "matriarchal core" of Latin American Catholicism. Women's autonomous authority in religious devotion at San Fernando has enabled them to oppose presumptions of male privilege, forge bonds of sisterhood for mutual support, and contest, reinterpret, and reimagine Guadalupe's meaning for their lives in the home and in community activism, pol-itics, and civic affairs. Yet, as Catherine Bell has noted, such "temporary inver-sions or suspensions of the usual order of social relations dramatically acknowl-edge that order as normative." Though women have exercised substantial leadership in San Fernando's Guadalupe celebrations throughout the parish's long history, their leadership roles often entail extending domestic duties and models of feminine purity into the public arena of communal worship, thus sanc-tifying male-female distinctions shaped by gender-specific stereotypes. Gender distinctions and expectations of feminine purity have been bodily encoded in Guadalupan devotion, such as when young girls dressed in white were set apart as bearers of the Guadalupe image, or when participants in processions divided into gender groups, with a further separation between married and single women. Articulating the implicit meaning of these symbolic and corporeal rep-resentations, some San Fernando clergy and devotees have invoked Guadalupe as providing divine sanction for women's domesticity and the exaggerated asso-ciation of virginity with feminine virtue.[39]

Guadalupan devotion at San Fernando has also been ambiguous with respect to the power relations among ethnic Mexican congregants, other San Antonio residents, and the social structures of the wider society. As Christopher Tirres has observed, "At its best, the symbol of Guadalupe . . . is an expression of the

life of a people, a collective articulation of the people's distinctiveness and orig-
inality." But he also asserts that this aesthetic representation of group pride, solidarity, and cultural resistance can obscure the need for deeper social transformation or, at its worst, become an escape into the world of the symbolic when
the harshness of reality becomes too overwhelming.[40]

Guadalupe celebrations at San Fernando have often ritually counteracted the
hostility and disdain that ethnic Mexicans have endured in San Antonio, dramatically positing an alternative worldview that reinforces their sense of dignity
and personhood and enables them to combat prejudicial views and the expectation that they become "Americanized." Guadalupe has also been an empower-
ing mother who has inspired numerous devotees in their struggles for social
change and improvement in San Antonio's civic and political life. But San Fernando's Guadalupe celebrations have also reflected congregants' divisions on social questions ranging from the issue of full and equal citizenship for African
Americans during Reconstruction to devotees' divergent perspectives today on
how Guadalupe calls them to participate in U.S. society. Only rarely has the San
Fernando congregation established formal links among their parish, its Guadalupan devotion, and social-action causes, movements, and groups in San Antonio. Ethnic Mexican residents estranged from the Catholic Church have even
criticized Guadalupe celebrations as mere diversions that appease the poor and
downtrodden and thus thwart efforts for substantive social reform. Present-day
congregational leaders attest that parishioners have scarcely begun to proclaim
and act on the full liberating message of Guadalupe, particularly that she is the
mother of all who calls her followers to break down walls of division in a stratified world. San Fernando devotees have also consistently associated Guadalupe
with their own patriotic loyalties, uncritically presuming that although her maternal love extends to all people, she offers special protection for their own side
in war.

Thus the history of San Fernando reveals a range of possibilities for individual and collective empowerment that religious traditions like Guadalupan devotion can mediate, gloss over, or restrict. On one end of the spectrum, Guadalupe has regularly offered her devotees a source of healing, hope, consolation,
and renewed self-worth. In their Guadalupan devotion San Fernando congregants have enacted a liberating countervision to the discrimination and other
harsh realities they face in daily life. They have also forged an arena of mutuality in which clergy, religious, and laity have influenced one another and the contours of communal piety. But the devotion does not usually induce self-critique

about inequalities and double standards within the faith community itself; nor does it provoke critical analysis and action to transform the social structures that perpetuate the affliction and second-class citizenship of many ethnic Mexicans.

From a psychological perspective, none of this is surprising, since for most people personal and ethnic affirmation is more attractive than honest self-examination, and the tensions and reciprocal relations within a familiar communal setting are more easily embraced than the risk of confronting a hegemonic social order. In this regard Guadalupan devotion at San Fernando reveals that religious practices tend to soothe rather than agitate; to change individuals and worship communities rather than the wider social groups and contexts they inhabit; and to provide a respite from daily hardships rather than a collective strategy for overcoming them. At the same time, ritual and devotion can strengthen practitioners and hone their capacity to both persevere and act for change in their faith community and the wider society. The Guadalupan devotion of San Fernando congregants has frequently embodied the popular expression, "Prayer doesn't change things; prayer changes people, and people change things." Or, as Durkheim articulated it, "The believer who has communicated with his god is not merely a man who sees new truths of which the unbeliever is ignorant; he is a man who is *stronger*. He feels within him more force, either to endure the trials of existence, or to conquer them."[41]

The dynamic interplay among power relations, material culture, physical space, and social functions, practices, and meanings in the sacred orbit of Guadalupan devotion at San Fernando has yet another element of complexity, namely, devotees' theological analyses and affirmations of their faith and its expressions—an element of ritual and devotion addressed only implicitly or not at all in many studies of lived religion. Amid the often harsh realities that have influenced their daily lives—attacks by Native Americans, changes of national government, poverty, racism, exile, family conflicts, social hierarchies, and struggles for their own dignity and advancement, to name but a few—Guadalupan devotees at San Fernando have consistently assessed their faith and their lives against the backdrop of the wider Catholic tradition. Consciously and unconsciously parish leaders and congregants have understood, affirmed, and contested the congregation's Guadalupan devotion with appeals to that wider tradition: its saints; iconic representations of celestial beings; liturgical and pious practices; teachings on morality, justice, and human dignity; and biblical events and themes such as the Babylonian exile, Christ's lowly birth in a stable, divine providence, and covenant. They have, as Orlando Espín has so succinctly put it, engaged tradition as "an interpretation of the past, made in and for the present and in anticipation of an imagined future."[42] The vast array of Catholic images, rituals, and beliefs has enriched even as it has limited and defined the religious imagination of San Fernando congregants and, more importantly, strengthened their assurance that the symbolic world of their devotion illuminates a truth larger than the visible realities of their daily lives. Though the breadth and ongoing development of the Catholic tradition enabled congregants to disagree on that tradition's priorities and meaning, parishioners' common conviction that an ancient and divinely revealed tradition guided Guadalupan devotion at San Fernando significantly influenced the contours and evolution of the devotion.

EVERY ATTEMPT at scholarly analysis is filtered through the lens of the interpreter's biases and social location. I am a theologian with a background in history and ritual studies, a North American Catholic of Irish-Croatian heritage, a former parishioner of San Fernando, and a participant in Guadalupan devotion who never ceases to be amazed at its intensity and meaning in people's lives. My research, teaching, and involvement with Latino faith communities have been ongoing for more than two decades. Equally important is my interpretive stance. In this volume I foreground in my analysis the insights, convictions, sentiments, and ritual actions of San Fernando's Guadalupan devotees. I have endeavored to highlight devotees' diverse understandings, prayer expressions, and ritual enactments and to avoid preconceived interpretations—whether from Catholic dogma and official teaching or from scholarly theories of religion. To be sure, my religious experience and commitments and my academic training have consciously and unconsciously shaped the analysis in this volume, but I have attempted to resist reductionism along both confessional and theoretical lines and to focus my attention primarily on what Guadalupan devotion has meant in the lives of San Fernando congregants. Indeed, even my critiques of Guadalupan devotion are grounded first and foremost not in my personal views or in predetermined criteria of judgment, but in San Fernando leaders' claims about Guadalupe's capacity to heal, unify, empower, incite faith, and forge a community of mutual respect and equality. The goal of this volume, then, in the words of Brad Gregory, is to offer insofar as is possible a depiction of the subjects under study "in which they would have recognized themselves."[43] Although this is not the only interpretive stance that could be adopted for examining Guadalupan devotion, it is particularly appropriate for my primary purposes: to increase appreciation and critical understanding of this fascinating faith expression and to help animate its ongoing celebration and development.

The organizational structure for this book reflects the evolution of Guadalupan devotion at San Fernando. Chapter 1 introduces the reader to the topic through a description of the 2003 Guadalupe feast, the first such celebration at San Fernando after the church was temporarily closed for a major renovation. The remaining chapters are arranged both chronologically and thematically; that is, they are divided into time periods that reflect major shifts in the life of the San Fernando congregation and its Guadalupan devotion. Critical exposition and analysis of written and oral sources provide a basis for presenting pertinent elements of the changing historical context in which Guadalupan devotion took place, examining Guadalupan devotional practices within the wider constellation of the congregation's sacred traditions, and interpreting those practices in light of the context in which they were enacted. Each of these chapters ends with some comparative analysis of Guadalupan devotion at San Fernando and in other locales, particularly the towns and cities of what is now the Southwest United States, collectively revealing the vital and varied roles Guadalupan devotion has played in the lives of Mexican-descent residents from the colonial era to the present. Photographs and other illustrations reveal the evolution of the San Fernando church building, its physical surroundings, its interior space, and elements of the congregants' daily lives and their ritual and devotional practices.

Though Guadalupan devotion is presented throughout the book as complex and multilayered, each of these four chapters highlights a primary theme for the devotion in the given era. Not all devotees expressed these meanings with the same fervor, of course, and some congregants even implicitly contested them. But they are arguably the most significant meanings that link San Fernando Guadalupan devotion to the shifting contours in successive time periods of parish, municipal, and regional history. Chapter 2 explores how Guadalupe became San Fernando's primary patroness in the century following the establishment of this rural settlement on the northern edge of New Spain, later the Republic of Mexico, illuminating the theology of divine providence that underlay the communal practice of naming patron saints. The following chapter reveals how Guadalupan devotion at San Fernando was a significant public expression of group pride and identity in the tumultuous six decades following the political separation of Texas from Mexico; it also explores the possibilities and limitations of collective devotion as a means of symbolic resistance to dominant-culture expectations. Chapter 4 explores the reanimation, the growing nationalistic fervor, and especially the exilic overtones in Guadalupan devotion as successive waves of Mexican émigrés dramatically increased San Antonio's and San Fernando's Mexican-descent population during the first four decades of the twentieth century. The final chapter spans the period from World War II to the dawn of the twenty-first century and examines the appropriation of Guadalupe as a symbol of hope and a call to action among new generations of ethnic Mexican devotees adapting to life in the United States. An epilogue assesses the future of Guadalupan devotion at San Fernando and in other faith communities.

In her study of Guadalupe in the lives of Mexican American women, Jeanette Rodriguez reports that when she asked an Indigenous woman in Mexico what makes Guadalupe different from other apparitions of Mary, the woman simply responded "se quedó" (she stayed).[44] This volume's point of departure is Guadalupe's abiding presence in the lives of numerous devotees like the San Fernando parishioners, as well as the historical circumstances, social arenas, and webs of relationships that have formed the shifting context for her devotees' enduring faithfulness to her. The history of the Guadalupe-devotee bond at San Fernando enhances understanding of Guadalupan devotion as it has evolved from the earliest encounters with Guadalupe at Tepeyac to the most recent feast-day celebrations and prayers offered in the numerous faith communities where she is venerated.

CHAPTER I

"Nuestra Madre Querida"

The crowd in front of San Fernando Cathedral applauded as the singer on the stage at the edge of the plaza urged people to dance and dedicated his next song to "nuestra madre querida Guadalupe, quien siempre nos cuida" (our dear mother Guadalupe, who always cares for us). It was a clear December evening in downtown San Antonio, and the lights on the front of the church magnificently illuminated the façade, which had recently been cleaned and repointed as part of a cathedral restoration project. Already there were far more people than the cathedral could hold, though it was still four hours before the church celebration of the traditional Guadalupe *serenata* (serenade), in which devotees pay their celestial mother musical homage on the eve of her feast day, just as an admirer might serenade a beloved woman on her birthday or Mother's Day. Some of the faithful huddled at the church doors, their offerings of fresh or artificial roses in hand, hoping to get a seat when the doors opened. Many others formed a semicircle at a respectful distance from a Guadalupe statue perched on a pedestal in front of the cathedral. Intermittently individuals or small groups of devotees approached the Guadalupe image, gazed at her countenance, and silently offered prayers. Some left flowers, while others had their picture taken

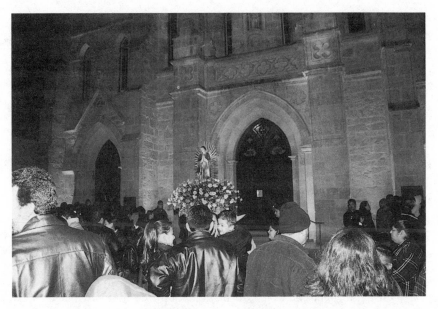

Crowd gathers around a Guadalupe statue in front of San Fernando Cathedral before the 2003 *serenata* celebration. Courtesy Ruben Alfaro.

as they stood before her. Most ended their moments of devotion in the Mexican manner of forming a small cross with their right thumb and index finger, making the sign of the cross, and then kissing the small cross they had formed with their hand.[1]

Festivity abounded all around the plaza. Although a few of the songs were traditional Guadalupe hymns and all the singers publicly acclaimed Guadalupe and dedicated their performance to her, the main fare was the upbeat rhythms of popular music such as cumbia and salsa. Some onlookers waved Mexican flags or dressed in the Mexican colors of green, white, and red; a number of them bore the ever-present flower offerings for their beloved mother and patroness. Food booths with flautas, fajitas, tamales, buñuelas, champurrado, hamburgers, tacos de carnitas, tripas, funnel cakes, gorditas, and menudo added a mix of tantalizing aromas to the ambiance. Vendors also sold flowers and religious goods such as candles, holy cards, and Guadalupe images. Some people gathered around the stage to hear the music and watch the revelers dancing. Others milled about the plaza, browsing at the food booths, finding a space to sit or stand apart and eat, greeting friends and acquaintances, and passing by the Guadalupe image. The event drew partakers like an African American couple holding hands and a white man who asked a vendor what the occasion was, but most of the crowd were of Mexican descent—children and the elderly, families and groups of young people. Spanish was the primary language heard around the plaza, though many spoke English or a combination of the two languages. Even children too young to speak took part: a little boy looked on in wonder from his father's shoulders, and a girl in a stroller energetically jumped up and down and clapped her hands with the beat of the music.

The sights, sounds, and smells resembled those of a fiesta in a small Mexican town or a San Fernando Guadalupe celebration from a bygone era, but there were also physical reminders that the time and place was a twenty-first century U.S. metropolis. Looming over the plaza were the Bexar County Courthouse and the Frost Bank building. Municipal buses and other traffic rolled by steadily. Service trucks for the Univisión television network and the local radio station Estéreo Latino were parked conspicuously in front of the cathedral as technicians prepared to broadcast the serenata later that evening. On both sides of the plaza were large screens on which the majority of the devotees would later view the serenata as it took place within the church. A copper-skinned young man in blue jeans, a flannel shirt, and a cowboy hat was one of several participants who conversed on a cell phone; he described the event in exuberant terms after holding up the phone so the person on the other end could hear the music and the noise of the shuffling crowd.

Felipa Peña spent the evening at her usual post as volunteer at the cathedral gift shop, where she is renowned not only for her decades of managerial service but also for her constant presence and hospitality, her mastery of the art of conversation, and the wealth of information she offers about the cathedral and its community. As I entered she greeted me warmly and proudly pointed out the enlarged space for the gift shop in the newly constructed Cathedral Centre. I had met her a decade earlier as I began interviewing parishioners, a number of whom suggested I speak with her because she "has been at San Fernando desde un principio" (from the very beginning). When I first visited Felipa and mentioned this, she flashed her trademark wry smile and playfully admitted that she may have missed a few years of the parish's nearly three centuries of history.[2] Statements about Felipa's continual presence reflect the sense of ownership among many San Fernando congregants. By thus acknowledging venerable members of the community, parishioners implicitly stake a claim for the continuity with ancestors and religious traditions that makes San Fernando such a privileged site for their expressions of faith and sense of identity. Similarly, Felipa's comment on the 2003 serenata placed that year's Guadalupe celebration in a longer time frame: "Como siempre [as always]. It reminds me of the outdoor masses we used to have. It's going to be beautiful."

Another parish leader, Leyvia García, was still beaming about her experience of playing the part of Guadalupe in a reenactment of the apparitions at one of San Fernando's Sunday masses the previous weekend. When cathedral rector Father David García (no relation to Leyvia) first asked her to take on this role, she felt she was too unworthy for such an honor because she is such a "bromista" (practical joker). But now she recounted: "All I can remember is my contact with the eyes of Juan Diego and it was like God was giving me a sign. . . . Then [after Mass] the people are weeping and they want to touch you. . . . In the moment of such fame and popularity, what you actually feel is more humble." She explained that she was now more aware of how important Guadalupe is and expressed a strong desire to be "more faithful" in her life as a Catholic. As the time was approaching for *las posadas* (literally the "dwellings" or "shelters"), which reenact the pilgrimage of Mary and Joseph to Bethlehem, she had decided to have her two young children play these parts in a home posada celebration so that they might "feel what I felt and receive the same message I received. I want them to not focus so much on material things but on their religion."

Inside the cathedral, parish leaders and television technicians bustled about making preparations for the serenata and the live broadcast, and a handful of devotees were already seated and waiting. As her husband Félix nodded in agreement, María Teresa Sáenz explained that they had arrived at 3:30 that afternoon so they could be in place before the cathedral was closed for these final preparations. María Teresa's mother had watched the serenata for years on television at her home in Falfurrias, Texas, a town about 170 miles south of San Antonio. When her mother died the previous summer, María Teresa vowed that she would journey to the serenata and pray for her. As she sat waiting for the celebration to begin, her conviction deepened that "the most important part of La Virgen is passing on the faith to our children and grandchildren." Rita and Eduardo Blanco sat directly in front of the Sáenz couple. Rita attested that "Guadalupe has helped me keep the faith. . . . The doctor told me there is no way I should have been alive after this last accident, but here I am." Rita had come "en peregrinación" (on pilgrimage) from her home in Omaha for her fourth consecutive serenata; this was the first time she had convinced her husband to accompany her. She began making her annual pilgrimage after the death of her own mother, who also had participated in the San Fernando serenata via television.

As they prayed and waited for the serenata to begin, Rita and María Teresa met each other and came to realize that each had come to their heavenly mother's feast-day celebration in remembrance of her earthly mother. They both perceived this as a providential occurrence, and by the time I approached them, they were deeply engaged in conversation about their children and grandchildren and about faith, miracles, and the dignity of motherhood. Echoing numerous devotees' contention that Guadalupe unites her children, particularly those who share with her the bond of motherhood, María Teresa confidently averred that "la Virgen nos trajo juntas" (the Virgin brought us together).

The church doors were opened at around 8:30 p.m. and the building was immediately filled to capacity. By 10:00, still an hour before the serenata would start, the live music outside was replaced with a tape recording of softer, more meditative songs. The crowd had swelled to thousands of people, most of whom stood silently facing the Guadalupe statue outside the cathedral. When I asked a Mexican American police officer assigned to crowd control how everything was going so far, he replied, "Very orderly. Guadalupe brings out the best in everyone." Inside, the altar had been removed from its usual central location, and a Guadalupe image surrounded by flowers adorned one side of the sanctuary, leaving ample open space for singers and dancers to offer her their tributes. These performers, other invited dignitaries, and parish leaders like the members of the Guadalupanas devotional society occupied about a quarter of the available seating space toward the front of the church; devotees who had stood in line to get a place filled the remaining seats.

Twenty minutes before the serenata began, Father García greeted the participants. Those outside the cathedral saw his greeting on television screens set up on the plaza. He especially thanked the people outside for their patience and explained that after the serenata the doors would be opened so all could enter and personally express their "love and respect to our mother, the Virgin of Guadalupe." As camera and sound crews around him adjusted their equipment, he also made an announcement that seemed both a declaration and a plea: "This is not a show, but a prayer, a devotion, an offering to Our Lady of Guadalupe."

At precisely 11:00 p.m. a television producer signaled for the celebration to begin, and a procession of young people in Aztec attire entered, playing Aztec drums, dancing, and waving incense. They danced before the Guadalupe image, waved incense at her with feathers, and reverently placed their incense bowls before her. Television host Jackeline Cacho then successively introduced the performers, who offered Guadalupe artistic tribute; Father García gave occasional commentaries on the event and its significance. Performers included another group of Aztec dancers; the traditional Mexican dancers of the Danzantes de Guadalupe; and Mexican-descent singers from both sides of the border, including popular performers Huracanes del Norte, Angeles Ochoa, and the mariachi group Campanas de América. Applause followed each presentation, and at times participants cried, as when Tejana singing star Patsy Torres offered a stirring rendition of "Madrecita del alma" (Mother of my soul). For the finale, just before midnight, all the performers led the congregation in singing the traditional *mañanitas* (literally "morning songs") to Guadalupe. As they did so, young women from a local middle school, dressed in mariachi outfits and bearing the flags of Mexico, Texas, and the United States, processed into the sanctuary, where, on cue, the performers and the crowd joined them in throwing confetti streamers in the air. Once the televised serenata had officially concluded with this festive salute to Guadalupe, devotees from the plaza streamed into the cathedral and waited in line to present their prayers and offerings before her image. Meanwhile, the Aztec troupes headed outside to dance before the representation of Guadalupe on the plaza, where the celebrating continued until just after 2:00 a.m.

Young people in Aztec attire begin the *serenata* with their offering to Our Lady of Guadalupe. Courtesy Ruben Alfaro.

Singer presents her musical tribute to Guadalupe. Courtesy Ruben Alfaro.

The 2003 Guadalupe serenata reflected the public role of the cathedral as the citywide gathering place envisioned in San Fernando's "City Centre" project. San Antonio archbishop at that time, Patricio Flores, along with Father García and a committee of core collaborators announced their plans for the project in February 2000. The City Centre Capital Campaign brought together business and civic leaders, Catholics and adherents of other faiths, corporate and individual donors, and people from throughout the city and from all walks of life. Commenting on this broad base of support, general chairman for the campaign Edward Whitacre, a business executive and a Presbyterian, claimed that the project was a citywide, interfaith endeavor because San Fernando is "not only for San Antonio's Catholics but for the community at large." Rabbi Samuel M. Stahl, a member of the Interfaith Steering Committee for the campaign, concurred that San Fernando is "the central religious address of the San Antonio community." In only eighteen months campaign organizers, led by Father García, whose energy and vision for the project is widely acclaimed, exceeded their $15 million fundraising goal; about two-thirds of the funding came from non-Catholic sources.[3]

The banquet to celebrate the attainment of this goal was set for 14 September 2001, three days after the attacks on the World Trade Center and the Pentagon. Despite the tragedy, organizers decided to go ahead with the event, which included an interfaith prayer service led by an imam, a rabbi, and Christian ministers of various denominations. Articulating the sentiments of many banqueters, *San Antonio Express* editor Robert Rivard opined that for nearly three centuries

Finale of the *serenata* in the San Fernando sanctuary. The flags of Texas and Mexico are in the background. Courtesy Ruben Alfaro.

San Fernando "has stood as a monument to the unshakable spirit of this community." With the banquet, the prayer service, and the City Centre project, he wrote, "an old, still-living church in the Southwest, in the center of our city, renewed itself as a refuge from despair" in the face of catastrophe.[4]

The capital campaign funds were used to finance a three-phase project: the repair and restoration of the church edifice, construction of the parish's first community center for social and community outreach programs, and a new cathedral center with parish facilities like a museum, a gift shop, a cafeteria, a sacristy, and counseling rooms. During the summer of 2002, the congregation gathered in a temporary worship space for Sunday Mass while workers and artisans stripped layers of plaster from the interior church walls, restored and reconfigured the pinewood church pews, secured the building's foundation, and created new *retablos* (ornamental backdrops) and sacred images to adorn the cathedral, including a retablo to enshrine a 1770 Guadalupe painting purchased for the renovation. By the time of the 2003 Guadalupe feast, both the renovated cathedral and the adjacent cathedral center had been dedicated, and construction on the nearby community center was about to begin. The televised serenata, which reached an estimated eighty million viewers in sixteen countries, exemplified the style of public ritual that García and other parish leaders had envisioned as they undertook the renovation. In García's words, the media outreach enables a single multifaceted event like the serenata to "saturate" the city and places beyond, adapting to modern times elements of an age when the great European cathedrals were "truly the center of the religious, social, cultural and educational life of the city."[5]

San Fernando's location and physical appearance attest that it has played just such a vital role in San Antonio since the settlement's inception. Its prominence on the main plaza in the heart of the downtown area reveals its significance in the lives of San Antonio's founders. The stained-glass windows, ancient baptismal font, century-old pipe organ, and aged stone contribute to the sense that the cathedral is a living testament to the heritage and spirit of the congregation's pioneer ancestors. A sign at the church entrance declares San Fernando as the "first place of worship for Texans," and the cover of the weekly parish bulletin acclaims it as "the oldest cathedral sanctuary in the country."[6] These assertions resonate with parish leaders like the late Richard Galindo, who proudly avowed that "this church was here before there was a United States."[7] Plaques that hang on the interior walls further reveal that San Fernando bears witness to the tragedies and triumphs of the people who established this sacred place and those

Devotee prays before San Fernando's Guadalupe *retablo*. Courtesy Ruben Alfaro.

who continue to claim it as their spiritual home. Memorials to deceased parishioners date from before the U.S. takeover of Texas and recall the community's struggles and sacrifices as they founded and developed San Antonio. Recollections of events like the 1987 visit of Pope John Paul II, along with various episcopal ordinations and installations dating back over a century, reflect San Fernando's development from a town parish on the northern edge of New Spain to the cathedral of a major U.S. metropolis.

Parish organizers for the cathedral renovation commissioned a painting to honor the extensive role of women in the parish and the community; called "Las Tres Marías," it depicts the Easter-morning scene of the women at the empty tomb, whom many ethnic Mexicans have called the three Marys: Mary Magdalene, Mary the mother of James, and Mary Salome.[8] Other sacred images link contemporary devotees to heroes of faith who were the celestial companions of San Antonio's founders, including the community's four original patrons: Our Lady of Guadalupe, Nuestra Señora de la Candelaria (Our Lady of Candlemas), San Antonio, and San Fernando. When devotees leave votive candles, flowers, photographs, notes, letters, braids of hair, hospital bracelets, and *milagritos* (miniature hands, arms, or other limbs) before these icons, their offerings of petition and thanksgiving continue a stream of prayer that is linked to familial, municipal, national, and international concerns dating back to the eighteenth century.

During the decade preceding San Fernando's restoration, more than a dozen U.S. Catholic cathedrals were constructed or renovated. Several of these projects, most notably those in Los Angeles, Milwaukee, and Seattle, met with criticism and protest, and so did the renovation of the historic and venerable San Fernando Cathedral. The most controversial aspect of the renovation was the relocation of the altar farther out among the congregation. Several parishioners commented publicly that they thought the altar had been moved out too far. "This theater-in-the-round looks commercial," opined one parish leader. Others supported the change, saying, "Now we're closer and feel more involved in the Mass. Moving the altar was a great idea." Sylvia Rodríguez reflected the views of many congregants when she commented that parishioners were just being "very respectful and aren't making a big fuss about it. Overall, the entire church looks gorgeous. But I hope the altar will be moved back a bit." The most vocal opponent of the cathedral renovation was Edmundo Vargas, who is not a San Fernando parishioner. Vargas heads Defenders of the Magisterium, an organization of San Antonio lay Catholics "established to help combat the serious crisis of faith within the Catholic Church today." The Defenders led a petition drive to notify Archbishop Flores of their "deep concern and disappointment at the proposed plan to move the altar at San Fernando Cathedral." They contended that the modification was "clearly due to a spirit of novel modernistic trends only serving to permit a greater lack of reverence in Church." In reference to events like the serenata, they further objected that "the problem could worsen even more with the altar to be moved, from time to time, to other locations to allow gatherings, such as symphonic and dancing performances, as well as other non-religious activities."[9]

The most tragic, and bizarre, act of protest in the renovated cathedral occurred a month after the Guadalupe feast. A man who declared himself the "Prince of Peace" and announced that he was intent on "saving souls from idol worship" entered San Fernando and, before onlookers could call police or stop him, toppled seven statues from their pedestals. Four statues were completely ruined, and the damage was estimated at one hundred thousand dollars, though the Guadalupe image and other retablos in the devotional area behind the sanctuary were spared because all the destruction occurred in the nave of the church. Once in police custody, the man reportedly stated that he was God and that his destructive spree was "done in the name of his father." Meanwhile his wife called Father García to apologize and explain that her husband had failed to take his medication for paranoid schizophrenia. Some parish leaders and concerned citizens expressed their sadness and outrage over the incident and also raised the question of whether more security was needed in a place as public and accessible as San Fernando. In a press interview Father García publicly forgave the man and called for prayers that he might be restored to health. He also took the opportunity to explain, "Statues are family members that surround us and give us strength. You don't worship them, you talk to them. It's a very gritty, familial relationship." Like the City Centre project, the response to this tragedy was an interfaith outpouring of financial and moral support from throughout the city.[10]

Few if any participants at the serenata complained about the altar being moved to accommodate the artistic Guadalupe tributes, much less about the cathedral's ample statuary, but immediately following the grand finale, tensions arose that illuminated the serenata's dual status as a public media event and an act of devotion. Once the church doors were opened and devotees who had waited outside for hours made their way into the cathedral, the television producer called for quiet so the performers could be interviewed on camera in front of the Guadalupe image. As the growing crowd pressed to reach the sanctuary and the producer's pleas for silence continued, voices of protest became audible. One woman waiting with a floral offering asked sarcastically, "Is this the fiesta of Univisión or the fiesta of la Virgen de Guadalupe?" Over the next day several congregational leaders commented privately on the contradiction of parishioners and grassroots devotees being kept at a distance from Guadalupe. In the words of one leader, "she's the mother of the poor." Regarding media exposure, the leader insisted, "It's not worth it no matter how good the program is." Father García, who was greeting people outside the cathedral as the commotion occurred, participated in several such conversations and, with his fellow parish leaders, vowed, "We won't let this happen again."

Most participants didn't seem to notice any conflicts or shortcomings related to the event. Devotees like the Sáenz and Blanco couples stayed long after the serenata ended, making further visits to Guadalupe, taking photographs, walking in and out of the cathedral, and chatting in superlative terms about the marvelous experience, which was worth "every mile we traveled" to be present. A Mexican American mother with an eighteen-month-old daughter explained, "Our Lady of Guadalupe helps me to reconnect with my heritage and my relatives still in Mexico." Her Anglo American husband related, "I was raised Protestant and we emphasized more the mind, but at this the whole experience speaks to your heart, your mind, your body. It's about beauty. . . . You get the holy coming at you through all of your senses." Though the couple regularly attends Mass at a suburban parish on San Antonio's north side, they have been participating in the San Fernando Guadalupe celebration since a friend first invited them two years earlier, and they are now committed to coming every year so their daughter will "know Guadalupe and her Mexican background."

As Verónica Alvarado watched the serenata on television at her home in Raleigh, North Carolina, she "was moved to tears" and became determined to "offer all my sufferings, pains, memories, and joys and pray for the conflicts and necessities of all América" by beseeching Guadalupe, who is "our mother, a star, a sun, a hope, love, faith, everything." On the other side of the country, Socorro Durán in San Leandro, California urged her children, grandchildren, and members of the confirmation class and youth group she leads to watch the serenata so they could "conocer mejor a la Virgen y a Jesucristo" (know the Virgin and Jesus Christ better). She attested that young people who have viewed the serenata in the past have been inspired to participate in the apparition drama she organizes at her parish and asserted that "the impact this has with youth is something the church needs more of. . . . When the parishes don't have these traditions, [the youth] lose their faith."

Congregational leaders like Gene Rodríguez (the husband of Sylvia, mentioned above), who was co-chair of the parish steering committee for the City Centre Capital Campaign, are pleased to hear such testimonies. A few months after the cathedral rededication, Gene Rodríguez expressed concern that the regular Sunday attendance at San Fernando had dipped below the pre-restoration level of about five thousand. Apparently some worshipers who frequented other parishes while the cathedral was closed for renovation had not returned for weekly participation, an occurrence Rodríguez attributed in part to disagreement about the renovation but more generally to the need for reestablishing congregants' worship habits after the disruption of the construction period. As a leading member of the parish finance council, Rodríguez also noted the rising maintenance expenses for the renovated church and new buildings, as well as the growing cost of broadcasting events like the serenata due to the diminishing number of public service hours that television networks are willing to donate. As Rodríguez explained San Fernando's major challenge: "We are moving from being a simple parish to managing a large parish complex with a tremendous increase in visitors, activities, and services—all in an historic cathedral building that has its own special needs." Despite the difficulties, he expresses pride in the City Centre project and all it has accomplished, pointing to events like the San Fernando Health Fair, which drew the largest crowd in its thirteen-year history the first time it was held in the new cathedral center, and to the serenata, which is one of the core annual celebrations that make San Fernando "more and more a place of pilgrimage," a spiritual home both for parishioners and for visitors from far and near.[11]

Just three hours after the last participants in the 2003 serenata left the cathedral and the plaza, San Fernando began to fill once again for the early morning mañanitas, a song tribute offered to Guadalupe before daybreak on the day of her December 12 feast. The multitude of flowers around the Guadalupe image were a visible reminder of the serenata, as was the relocation of the Guadalupe statue that had been enshrined on the plaza the previous evening to the center of the devotional area behind the sanctuary. But the return of the altar to its central position, the hushed ambiance, the tidiness of the church after the previous night's dispersal of streamers, the song leadership of a single parish choir, and the prominence of San Fernando Guadalupanas in welcoming worshipers and distributing song sheets and candles revealed immediately that this was not a televised event but a ritual primarily for parishioners and other Guadalupan devotees. The church was comfortably full by the time the celebration began just after 5:30, but without the overflow crowd of the previous evening. A few children were present, but most of the worshipers were adults, many dressed in uniforms or other work clothes so they could report to their jobs after leaving the cathedral.

As congregants lit the candles they would hold throughout the mañanitas, the singing of traditional Guadalupan hymns opened with the popular "Buenos

Días, Paloma Blanca" (Good morning, White Dove), a song that begins and ends with an expression of the sentiment of the mañanitas offering to Guadalupe: "Buenos días, Paloma Blanca, hoy te vengo a saludar. . . . Recibe éstas mañanitas, de un humilde corazón" (Good morning, White Dove, today I come to greet you. . . . Receive these mañanitas, from a humble heart). Songs such as "Las Mañanitas a la Virgen de Guadalupe" and "Las Apariciones Guadalupanas" followed, interspersed with prayers and an occasional poetry recitation. The music was all in Spanish and resembled that in mañanitas celebrations in numerous locales throughout Mexico and in ethnic Mexican communities in the United States, asking Guadalupe's blessing and protection and emphasizing themes such as her motherhood, purity, miraculous apparitions to Juan Diego, and connection to Mexicans and the Mexican nation.[12]

Prayers, on the other hand, were offered alternatively in Spanish and English and, besides echoing some themes from the songs, introduced additional perspectives on Guadalupe and her meaning. One prayer noted the connection between Guadalupe and Advent, the pre-Christmas liturgical season during which her feast falls; she was called the "mother of the Lord of light" during a "season of darkness, as we await the coming feast of the birth of the Son of God." Another prayer extended the musical proclamation of her patronage over Mexico and Mexicans by naming her "Our Lady of America" and the "patroness of those who are poor and oppressed." Linking Guadalupe's maternal care to the task of Christian discipleship, this prayer ended with an invocation: "Teach us all that justice is a condition for a world of solidarity. Help our people to know Jesus." Many of these prayers were recited in alternating parts between a Guadalupana leader and the congregation or between the worshipers seated on the two sides of the church, mirroring the ancient practice of praying the psalms and other sacred texts in the divine office antiphonally.

The bilingual Mass that began at 7:00 flowed from the mañanitas without pause, with the Guadalupanas serving as lectors for the Bible reading and prayer intentions and as distributors of communion. Once again traditional songs reflected long-standing Guadalupan themes like maternal love and Mexican nationalism, but now other elements of the celebration expanded the scope of these themes, especially the homily of Jesuit priest Jake Empereur, a renowned theologian and expert in liturgy who had begun serving as a parochial vicar (assistant pastor) at San Fernando a decade earlier. Empereur opened by placing the theme of the Guadalupe feast within a Marian reflection on the season of Advent, then reminded his hearers that "Guadalupe is in us to deepen our faith and help us seek the progress of the American continent." He concluded his homily with Mary's admonition to obey her son at the wedding feast of Cana (John 2:5), asserting that Mary of Guadalupe calls her devotees to "hacer lo que él les dice" (do whatever he tells you). Reflecting Vatican II's call for active participation in the liturgy, Empereur went on to lead the Eucharistic prayer, the central prayer of the Catholic Mass, in dialogue fashion, with the choir and congregation singing acclamation responses to the words he prayed as presider. The celebration concluded with the traditional song "Adiós, Oh Virgen de Guadalupe," which fittingly ends "Adiós, oh Madre. . . . Aquí te dejo mi corazón. . . . Dame, Señora, tu bendición" (Goodbye, oh Mother. . . . Here I leave you my heart. . . . Give me, Lady, your blessing). Devotees then filed up to offer Guadalupe their prayers and flowers, and with the start of the work day now upon them, most left within a few minutes after the end of the Mass.

The mañanitas celebration accented a different vision for San Fernando than the focus on media outreach, public ritual, and pilgrimage reflected in the serenata. In Father Empereur's words, San Fernando congregants' conspicuous devotion to Mexican Catholic traditions like the Guadalupe feast provides an opportunity to "reimagine how liturgy and popular religion can be integrated," enabling San Fernando to exercise the "spiritual leadership of a cathedral" by providing a viable model for this integration between Catholic sacramental liturgies and the everyday prayer practices of ethnic Mexicans and other believers.[13] Rooted in this conviction, Empereur played a leading role in preparing and celebrating the mañanitas and the Guadalupe feast within the wider context of Advent, the prayer of the Eucharist and divine office, and the Christian call to discipleship, justice, solidarity, and a universality that transcends nationalism. Sally Gómez-Kelley, the San Fernando parish coordinator of ministries, concurred that the renovation and new facilities provide an opportunity "to look at ourselves in terms of the universal church and not just in terms of being the center of the city." She expressed her hope that San Fernando will increasingly become "not just a place to offer hospitality and be validated" in Latino/a identity and traditions, "but also to model good liturgy that takes seriously a sense of mission and helps us fulfill our responsibility to make a more just world." A Puerto Rican who came to know Guadalupe after she moved to Texas, Gómez-Kelley accentuated Guadalupe's capacity to empower her devotees for mission: "I identify with her as a mother who always believes her children can do it."[14]

For the 2003 Guadalupe feast the Guadalupanas exercised many of the same leadership roles they have since the devotional society's inception during the mid-twentieth century, such as offering hospitality, raising funds, decorating the church, organizing processions, making floral offerings, and engaging in other devotional expressions. The group had about fifty members, half of them active, including the first three male inductees in the society's history, whom the group's leaders had recently invited to join. To men who objected that the San Fernando Guadalupanas had always comprised only women, organization president Graciela Sánchez pointed out the historical precedent: "Juan Diego was the first Guadalupana." She also explained that the Guadalupanas thought the men "should be recognized since they are always here to help us for the feast and it's important that they wear the medallion" of the organization.

One of the male members, Felix Díaz Jr., said that because of his previous involvement in the Guadalupe feast and other Guadalupana activities, he felt "honored" and "very special" when the women invited him to formally join the organization. Díaz recalled that he had first heard of Guadalupe from his grandmother, but deepened his relationship when he joined San Fernando in the early 1990s, began to help with the cathedral's televised Sunday Mass and the serenata, and witnessed the faith and Guadalupan testimonies of the Guadalupanas and other San Fernando devotees. All of this led him to "read the accounts of the apparitions and the tilma" and to realize more profoundly that "this is real. . . . She is this Aztec princess, this mother of God, my mother, this lady that somehow said, 'I am all things to all people. I can become who you need me to be so I can bring my son to all people.' She is this person, a mother who loves, who cares about me, who wants me to be okay."

Like that of many Guadalupanas, Graciela Sánchez's experience of Guadalupe began in childhood with the example of a significant woman in her life. Sánchez explains that her mother "was very devoted to la Virgen but she never pushed it on us." Reflecting many devotees' association of Guadalupe with maternal intimacy, which for some is a desire never fully realized with their own mother, Sánchez's most poignant childhood memory of Guadalupe was of a time "when I was eleven or twelve. I had a dream and la Virgen appeared to me. And I wanted to get closer to her but then I woke up." Now that she is an adult, her relationship with Guadalupe is still linked to her relations with other women. In one instance she was upset with another Guadalupana leader who had failed to tell her of a society event until the night before its occurrence, but after praying about the situation she decided that her resistance to "accepting orders from someone else was something I had to change in myself." When she went to the event as requested, she had a deep sense of peace and reconciliation with the

Guadalupana who had upset her. Upon her return home that evening, she detected the scent of roses in her home even though there were no roses there, and she took this wonderful aroma as a miraculous sign of approval from Guadalupe for her harmonious interaction with her sister in the society.

As Guadalupana president, Sánchez introduced or expanded on several organization initiatives, such as hosting an annual retreat to unify society members and prepare them for the Guadalupe feast; inviting Guadalupanas from other parishes to San Fernando events and celebrations; and organizing mañanitas to St. Juan Diego, whom Pope John Paul II canonized in July 2002, before the morning Mass on December 9, the day of his feast. She and other Guadalupanas have also helped to coordinate parish participation in an annual pilgrimage to the Basilica of Guadalupe in Monterrey, Mexico, where San Fernando congregants have presented a dramatic reenactment of Guadalupe's apparitions to Juan Diego. Sánchez emphasized that all of her efforts support the Guadalupanas' evangelizing call: to attract more male and female members to the society and its mission of increasing knowledge and appreciation of Guadalupe and, more importantly, to "make people feel at home and have a beautiful experience [during the Guadalupe feast] so they come back." Other leaders accentuated the internal mission of the Guadalupanas. Past president Joann Montez asserted that "the main function of the Guadalupanas is to empower women, especially Latina women. . . . We support one another. Now we have men [in the organization] and that's good too. But that's who we are, a support group, and not just for women who are Guadalupanas. Look what she did for Juan Diego. Guadalupe came to lift and empower our people. And she's still doing it today."

The vast majority of devotees who stopped at San Fernando to visit Guadalupe on her feast day that year—and indeed most participants in the serenata and the mañanitas—seemed to be aware of neither pastoral leaders' vision for cathedral and parish groups like the Guadalupanas nor the tensions and disagreements surrounding the renovation project. Most viewed the cathedral as a venerable and beautiful church where their cherished faith expressions are honored and approached Guadalupe as a mother, protectress, and miracle worker. One couple with a daughter who appeared to be in her thirties attested that "Our Lady of Guadalupe has done many miracles for us. . . . The most recent is that our daughter has improved greatly from a serious muscular disorder." A middle-aged couple offered thanks that their son was graduating from the University of Texas at San Antonio the next day; the young man's mother had tears in her eyes because "muchos jovenes se desaniman, y con mi hijo siempre pedí a la Virgen

Guadalupanas with their society insignia during the 2003 Guadalupe feast. Courtesy Ruben Alfaro.

para que pudiera cumplir" (many young people become discouraged, and with my son I always asked the Virgin that he could finish).

As a father knelt before the Guadalupe image with his wife and three young daughters, the eldest, who was about eight years old, asked him where the tilma came from. In response he explained that after Guadalupe appeared to Juan Diego no one would believe him until the miracle of the roses verified his testimony. Bringing his teaching about Guadalupe closer to home, he then told the girl that Guadalupe had saved her youngest sister from death after a premature birth, and that that is why the family faithfully comes to thank their celestial mother each year on her feast day. Other devotees came to pray with heavy hearts: a ten-year-old girl and her mother, who had delivered a stillborn daughter a week earlier; three boys who had come with their parents directly from the hospital where their grandmother was dying. Reflecting the sentiments of numerous devotees, one woman testified that "Guadalupe never fails us" and prayed for a series of intentions: "the conversion of the young, peace, that wars end, the health and salvation of my family."

At the 7:00 p.m. Mass, the final celebration of the day, the music, liturgical leadership of the Guadalupanas, and size of the crowd were similar to those of the earlier celebration, though there were more children present this time and a Nahuatl and Spanish reenactment of the Guadalupe apparitions preceded the homily. In this message Father García repeated the theme that Guadalupe calls her devotees to mission. He connected the apparitions drama, the well-known Gospel account of the angel's announcement to Mary (Luke 1:26–38), and the evening's Gospel reading about Mary's visit to her kinswoman Elizabeth (Luke 1:39–45) by observing that the initial response of Juan Diego, Mary, and Elizabeth in their respective stories was "no soy digno" (I am not worthy). Father García told his listeners that they too may feel unworthy of their calling and the things of God, but that God chooses the insignificant and makes of them something great. Like Juan Diego, he said, all of us are called to keep growing and to do great things for God in our everyday lives. Our Lady of Guadalupe gives us the capacity to do this because "there is something of Guadalupe in each one of us. Guadalupe is our mother, and there is something of our mother in each one of us." At the end of the Mass Father García thanked the Guadalupanas and led the congregation in applauding them for their work on the Guadalupe feast.

After the Mass, as yet another line of devotees processed before Guadalupe and offered flowers and candles, Father García huddled with a tired but obviously pleased group of Guadalupanas and other parish leaders. Still concerned about the clash between devotees and television personnel the previous evening, García shifted the focus from the group's praise of the feast-day celebrations to his thoughts on how to improve for next year: "Maybe we can have people come through from the plaza in a continuous stream and make their presentation to la Virgen before the serenata. We've got to do something to receive all those thousands of people on the plaza."

IN MANY WAYS San Fernando and its Guadalupan devotion typify the prayer and communal dynamics of numerous other U.S. congregations. People come to ask celestial succor for their needs, express gratitude for favors received, participate in religious traditions that link them to their childhood memories and ancestors, obtain inspiration for themselves and their children to live their faith more vibrantly, and discover and testify to the miraculous in their lives. Conflict occurs around the physical layout of sacred space, the intermingling of "secular" artistic expressions and religious devotion, and the use of images in prayer and worship. For some celebrations seating arrangements reflect participants' level of parish involvement or their status as visiting dignitaries, while for other gatherings a more egalitarian ethos prevails. Distinctions are evident in the leadership roles of laity and clergy, women and men, though in some ways those distinctions are increasingly blurred. Pastoral leaders' efforts to forge a ministerial vision reveal the frequent challenges and tensions in renovation and building projects for cathedrals and other prominent downtown congregations: to preserve a church or synagogue's historical character while meeting the demands of contemporary worship; to enhance the congregation's mission both as a religious center for the city and the spiritual home of a parish faith community; to allocate sufficient resources to maintain new facilities without neglecting essential ministries and outreach to the poor; and to foster community-wide public rituals, civic events, and social involvement while retaining a strong sense of the sacred.

But in other ways San Fernando is distinct from many U.S. congregations. It is a predominantly ethnic Mexican, working-class parish, but most of the financial support for the City Centre project came from non-Hispanic and non-Catholic sources. Its most conspicuous characteristic is its rootedness in Mexican Catholic traditions like the Guadalupe feast, but it is also renowned as a center of interfaith and citywide worship. San Fernando is a downtown parish so hemmed in by urban growth that it doesn't even have a parking lot, but it still attracts regular worshipers from around the city, pilgrims and visitors from various backgrounds, and numerous devotees who participate via television.

San Fernando is also the first parish in what is now the United States to embrace Guadalupe as a primary patroness. Though other celestial guardians and ritual traditions have also been important in the congregation's history, parish celebrations in honor of Guadalupe have been its most constant and prominent public devotion. San Fernando congregants have sustained their public Guadalupan devotion under the flags of Spain, Mexico, the Republic of Texas, the United States, the Confederate States of America, and then the United States again. For nearly three centuries devotees in this enduring community of faith have celebrated, shaped, and developed their Guadalupan traditions as they responded to ongoing changes in San Antonio and its environs. In the process, devotional practices were altered, added, and abandoned, and the meanings of practitioners' Guadalupan devotion shifted dramatically across successive historical eras and generations. Yet like that of millions of other devotees, San Fernando parishioners' most persistent belief about Guadalupe has been that her maternal presence is a source of strength, hope, and miracles. The history of their testimonies, theological interpretations, and collective rituals and of their enduring veneration of their "madre querida," along with the histories of countless other devotees and faith communities, constitute the sacred landscape that must be traversed if we are to more fully grasp the significance, contemporary meanings, and future prospects of the evolving Guadalupe tradition.

Patroness of *la Frontera,* 1731–1836

The first Spanish subjects to visit the location called Yanaguana by Native Americans were soldiers and Franciscan friars led by Domingo Terán de los Ríos. A military leader, Terán de los Ríos echoed the title of Francisco de Florencia's popular book *La Estrella del Norte de México* (1688) by acclaiming "the powerful Virgin of Guadalupe" as the "North Star and guide" of his expedition. Arriving at Yanaguana on 13 June 1691, they named the place for the renowned Franciscan preacher San Antonio de Padua, whose feast is that day. Since the following day was the feast of Corpus Christi, they did not continue their journey until the fifteenth. On the Corpus Christi feast day, the friars celebrated Mass and the soldiers expressed their devotion by firing gun salutes during the liturgy. According to Fray Damián Massanet and his companions, members of a local Indigenous group called the Payayas also were present during these festive rites. The friars observed that the Payayas had voluntarily placed a tall wooden cross in their settlement, a Christian practice the natives said they imitated because reverence for the cross "was a thing that was very pleasing to him who was God and Lord of all."[1]

Though Terán de los Ríos asserted that the countryside around San Antonio was "the most beautiful in New Spain,"[2] the Spanish crown waited nearly three decades before establishing settlements there as part of its claim to Texas. But by 1731 Spanish subjects had founded a *presidio* (garrison) and civilian settlement, along with five missions dedicated to propagating Christianity among local Indigenous groups. Over the following century a process of political, economic, social, and religious accommodation and integration resulted in the evolution of these originally distinct institutions into a single municipality.

Local inhabitants in this isolated outpost on the northern edge of New Spain (and later Mexico) turned to heavenly guardians like Guadalupe in times of drought, flood, and epidemic. Frequently confronted with these, as well as endemic poverty and the threat of attacks by Native Americans, Guadalupan devotees extended the celebration of her 12 December feast into the Christmas season, a prolonged period of rituals and revelry that served as the annual harvest festival for this heavily agricultural community. The boisterous crowds, the aroma of *caldo* and *cabrito*, the sound of hands patting out *masa* into *tortillas*, the taste of *aguardiente de caña* (rum) and the children's much-loved *piloncillo* (brown sugar cane), the dramatic spectacle of bullfights, and the dances and games on the two plazas surrounding the parish church joined with solemn masses, traditional hymns, and prayers of thanksgiving and supplication to mark another year of the community's survival and to express its hope for future protection and sustenance. These exuberant celebrations, along with Guadalupe's status as an image indigenous to the New World and the concurrence of her feast with a natural break in the community's agricultural cycle, facilitated Guadalupe's gradual emergence as the town's primary celestial patroness. Just as the parish church with its tower and clanging bells shaped the rhythms of daily life in the town and surrounding farm fields, so too the December feast-day celebrations stood at the center of the annual ritual calendar, reflecting and refashioning the local populace's collective identity, social hierarchy, and faith in divine providence.

Founding Settlements and a Parish Church

The area's first settlements under the Spanish crown were established in 1718, when Fray Antonio de San Buenaventura y Olivares founded a mission, and soldiers established a presidio on the west side of the San Antonio River; a few years later the friars moved the mission a short distance to the opposite side of the river. While all settlers were subjects of the Spanish crown, presidio soldiers and their families were a racially mixed group with varied combinations of African,

Engraving of San Antonio, c. 1840. Though the drawing does not accurately depict the church's actual size and shape, the prominence of the San Fernando church tower illuminates the parish's centrality in the predominantly agricultural community. Courtesy University of Texas Institute of Texan Cultures, San Antonio.

Native American, and Spanish blood lines; Fray Olivares described these settlers as "mulatos, lobos, coyotes, and mestizos, people of the lowest order." The friar's comments reflect the Spanish caste system that placed Spaniards at the top of the social hierarchy, Blacks and Native Americans at the bottom, and *castas* (mixtures of these groups) in-between.[3]

Since the Terán de los Ríos expedition had already named the site San Antonio, early settlers placed both the mission and the presidio under the patronage of this saint. Presidio soldiers and their families frequently crossed the San Antonio River for baptisms and other rites at Mission San Antonio de Valero because military chaplains were not always available and the accommodations for worship at the presidio were rudimentary. By 1731 the Franciscans had extended their evangelization efforts among the Native Americans by adding four missions located on the San Antonio River south of the presidio and Mission San Antonio de Valero.[4]

King Felipe V induced Spanish subjects to found a *villa* (town) in the area as well, and a settlement was established in 1731 by Isleños, or immigrants from the Canary Islands, a string of small islands about seventy miles west of Morocco that had come under Spanish control in 1479. The presidio soldiers and their families had previously formed a civilian settlement, naming it Villa de Béxar to honor the Duke of Béxar, whose brother was viceroy of New Spain at the time, but the Spanish crown did not officially recognize a villa in the locale until the Isleños took possession of lands on a site adjacent to the presidio. In gratitude for the opportunities bestowed on them by the crown, the new arrivals called the villa San Fernando de Béxar in honor of Ferdinand VI, future heir to the throne and namesake of San Fernando, a thirteenth-century king noted for his piety and his recapture of territory from the Moors.

Initially the fifty-five Canary Islanders had conflictive relations with the three hundred other settlers who lived in and around the presidio. In order to encourage voluntary immigration to the northern borderlands of New Spain, Felipe V had promised the Isleños nobility status as *hidalgos* (literally "sons of something") and various other privileges. For example, the crown granted them the right to form the first self-governing *cabildo* (town council) in Texas; shortly after their arrival in 1731 six Isleños received life appointments to this governing body. With their political hegemony in municipal affairs, the Isleños quickly gained the upper hand in disputes over land and water rights. The newcomers claimed for themselves the lands just south of the presidio, which soldiers and their families had already irrigated, as well as all available rights to water from the San Antonio River and San Pedro Creek, the area's only two natural water sources. Since earlier settlers had never established individual claims to their communal fields, the Isleños successfully attained legal title and forced their predecessors off the farmlands. In socially stratified Spanish colonial society, the Isleños presumed that their status as hidalgos and "Old World" Spanish subjects justified their political and economic dominance over the racially mixed population that had preceded them in establishing the settlement.[5]

Despite the Canary Islanders' presumption of their superiority and their right to control local affairs, the economic hardships of life in an isolated outpost facilitated Isleño cooperation with other residents in efforts to construct a parish church. A canonical parish was officially established under the pastorship of Father José de la Garza shortly after the Canary Islanders arrived in 1731, but congregants initially attended services at the presidio chapel or across the river at Mission San Antonio de Valero. In 1736, Father de la Garza's successor, Father Juan Recio de León, wrote that many parishioners had to attend Mass at the mission since the presidio chapel was "so miserable because of its inappropriateness (*indecencia*) that not even half of the people can fit." Town council members concurred with Father Recio de León, claiming that the chapel was "unbecoming for the celebration of the august Mystery."[6]

In February 1738 presidio leaders and the town council met in separate sessions to initiate plans for the construction of a parish church. Father Recio de León led the ensuing parish cornerstone-laying ceremony, at which he declared: "In the exercise of my ecclesiastical jurisdiction I pronounce the said building, the parish church of this villa and the royal presidio of San Antonio." The collection taken for the construction project confirmed the curate's statement that the church would be the joint venture of both villa and presidio; while the majority of donors were citizens of the villa, their offering did not equal the total sum given by presidio officers and troops. Significantly, the site for the new parish church was between the plazas of the presidio and the villa, symbolically linking the two settlements and the communities that constituted them.[7]

The patronesses whom presidio and villa leaders selected for the new church further reflected their joint effort in building a house of worship. Father Recio de León announced the chosen patronesses at the cornerstone-laying ceremony, explaining that since the presidio already bore the name of San Antonio and the villa that of San Fernando, the new church would be dedicated to the Virgin Mary "under the invocation of . . . Our Lady of Candlemas and Our Lady of Guadalupe."[8] Our Lady of Candlemas, or Nuestra Señora de la Candelaria, is the patroness of the Canary Islands, where she is acclaimed for the fifteenth-century evangelization of the islands' native population. Guadalupe was embraced as a patroness by criollos, castas, and other residents throughout New Spain, especially after Mexico City authorities called for an official declaration making her the patroness of the viceroyalty when she reportedly dispelled the deadly epidemic of 1737. Extant documentation does not reveal when residents of the villa of San Fernando and the San Antonio presidio received notification of the call for naming Guadalupe the patroness of New Spain, but news of these events reached other northern locales, like Saltillo, before the end of 1737.[9] In all likelihood both the general spread of Guadalupan devotion and the immediate effort to officially place New Spain under Guadalupe's patronage influenced local leaders' deliberations about the patronesses for their parish church. By providing recognition for both Isleño and the predominantly casta presidio residents, the selection of dual patronesses facilitated the two groups' collaboration in the church construction project.

Notwithstanding the collaborative efforts of presidio and villa residents to raise funds for a church, pervasive poverty limited their contributions, which scarcely accounted for five percent of construction costs. Some donors hauled stone or labored at other tasks in lieu of making cash contributions. Insufficient financial resources resulted in a delay of seventeen years before grants from the royal treasury enabled parishioners to finish the project. Gradually the local house of worship came to be known as the parish church of San Fernando, a shift that reflects the Spanish crown's funding of nearly all construction costs. The first bishop to visit the settlement, Francisco de San Buenaventura Martínez de Tejada of Guadalajara, noted in 1759 that the only image of a saint adorning the parish church was a representation of San Fernando above the main altar. Extant records do not indicate when the congregation enshrined other sacred images in their house of worship, though a Guadalupe representation was present by at least the early nineteenth century. As late as 1843, the parish sacristan told a visitor that he was not sure if the church was dedicated to San Fernando, Our Lady of Guadalupe, or San Antonio (he did not mention Nuestra Señora de la Candelaria). Despite the eventual name change to San Fernando, however, the original choice of Guadalupe as a patroness illuminates the Guadalupan devotion of the early parishioners who helped found and build the parish church.[10]

Upon completion of the church in 1755, town council members met on 12 December, the feast day of Guadalupe, and vowed before God that "now and forever we shall celebrate the feast of Blessed Mary of Guadalupe," a vow later reinforced with the arrival of the news that Pope Benedict XIV had declared Guadalupe the patroness of New Spain and that Bishop Martínez de Tejada had elevated her feast to a holy day of obligation—a day of required attendance at Mass—in his diocese. At their December 1755 meeting the town council also pledged to celebrate perpetually the feasts of la Candelaria and San Fernando. In celebrating these feasts, along with that of San Antonio, the patron saint of the presidio, local residents followed the Spanish custom of designating celestial companions deemed to have a particular relationship with a town or village. These companions formed a constellation of intercessors to whom devotees turned for protection and aid.[11]

In addition to the patronal feasts, the community's annual ritual cycle expanded to include celebrations for the Immaculate Conception, Christmas, Holy Week, and Corpus Christi, as well as religious ceremonies and festive gatherings for events such as peace treaties, the announcement of a new Spanish monarch, and the installation of a new town council. The colorful pageantry of the community's public ritual is illustrated by a 1749 peace-treaty ceremony between the Apaches and the Spanish subjects in the local populace. They cele-

San Fernando church, c. 1865–1868. Courtesy University of Texas Institute of Texan Cultures, San Antonio, #76-858.

brated Mass in their partially completed parish church at the outset of peace talks on 17 August. On 19 August soldiers, citizens, priests, and Apaches dug a hole in the center of the plaza in front of the church and placed in it instruments of war: a hatchet, a lance, six arrows, and a live horse! Then the various groups danced together three times around the hole, and when a signal was given, they symbolized the end of hostilities by covering the hole. They concluded their peace-treaty ritual with the Apaches emitting loud whoops and the Spanish subjects shouting "Viva el Rey" (Long live the king) three times.[12]

The successful completion of the parish church and the fervor of its annual celebrations did not signal an end to the settlement's economic hardships. Even in the most prosperous of times life expectancy was only about forty years; medical conditions like appendicitis could cause death within hours. Though San Antonio de Béxar became the provincial capital of Texas in 1772, a subsequent visitor to the area reported that "the town consists of fifty-nine houses of stone and mud and seventy-nine of wood, but all poorly built, without any preconceived plan, so that the whole resembles more a poor village than a villa, capital of so pleasing a province." He also observed that "the church building is spacious and has a vaulted roof, but the whole is so poorly constructed that it promises but a short life." This visitor's dire predictions for the church building proved incorrect, but his candid assessment of local economic conditions illuminates a struggling community more apt to celebrate survival than prosperity in its annual cycle of feasts.[13]

Guadalupe's Rise to Prominence

Although Guadalupe, la Candelaria, San Fernando, and San Antonio were initially honored as the community's primary patrons, by the late eighteenth century the conflated December celebration of the Immaculate Conception, Guadalupe, and Christmas had emerged as the most prominent local feast. The month-long festivities attracted the participation of military leaders, elected officials, clergy, and a general populace that had reached some two thousand residents by the end of the eighteenth century. Large crowds gathered for feast-day activities from all sectors of the racially diverse local population: in addition to criollos and castas, participants included Native Americans, who had been incorporated into the local community as captives, adoptees of local families, or Christian neophytes who entered Spanish colonial society through the mission system. During times of peace even the settlement's Native American enemies were known to partake in the celebrations, as Texas governor Domingo Cabello was amazed to discover in December 1785 when a Comanche husband and wife warmly greeted and embraced him during festivities on the plaza. Devotees interwove religious ceremonies like masses, processions, and rosaries with bullfights, games on the two plazas, and dances held throughout the settlement. With the prayers, sermons, and hymn-singing of Mass; the flavors and aromas of customary foods; the colors of festive clothing and decorations; the warmth of friendly greetings; and the sounds of children running through the plazas and elderly people telling stories—the December celebrations engaged all the senses, creating an ambiance that publicly displayed the central values and social structure of the Béxar populace: their collective identity, agricultural livelihood, social hierarchy, and theology of divine providence. The religious services and festival surrounding the Guadalupe feast became the primary annual event in which Béxar residents shaped and transmitted their fundamental assumptions about faith, life, and their local community.[14]

One reason for the growing prominence of the Guadalupe feast was the emergence of a regional spirit and identity for which the indigenous Guadalupe had

Artist José Cisneros's 1991 drawing depicts the racial diversity among eighteenth-century San Fernando parishioners. Courtesy University of Texas Institute of Texan Cultures, San Antonio, #88-377.

more appeal than Old World sacred figures like la Candelaria. Initial clashes between Isleños and other residents regarding issues like land and water rights gradually dissipated, as did the cultural differences reflected in the decision to place their parish church under the patronage of both la Candelaria and Guadalupe. Over time the common struggle to survive in an isolated outpost caused these two groups to ally with each other, with later arrivals who migrated to the settlement from adjacent regions of northern New Spain, and with Native

Americans incorporated into the local community. As the eighteenth century progressed, cooperative efforts to develop the region's economy, collaborative negotiation and defense in relations with nonmissionized Native American groups, the increasing ethnic mix among electees to the town council, the marked tendency of residents to identify themselves as a single community, the ritual extension of kinship ties through *compadrazgo* (godparentage), and extensive intermarriage reflected the growing integration of the various groups into a relatively homogeneous community. The proximity of the villa and the presidio enhanced the integration of residents from the two settlements; by the end of the eighteenth century presidio lands were incorporated into the town, and the two entities had effectively become the single settlement of Béxar. Undoubtedly the paltry number of Isleños and European-born settlers also influenced the emergence of a regional spirit and identity in the New World, as well as the rising popularity of the Guadalupe feast. Thus, as Gerald Poyo and Gilberto Hinojosa have shown, the Isleños "arrived with their Old World protectress, Nuestra Señora de la Candelaria, but soon accepted New Spain's mestiza Virgen de Guadalupe as their own."[15]

Another reason for the December festivities' growing prominence was their privileged place in a predominantly agricultural community's annual farming cycle. As Jesús de la Teja has observed, the festivities were "timed to coincide with the break between the late maize harvest and the early-year cattle branding and planting preparations," thus enabling the local populace "to celebrate another year of survival as a community." Guadalupe's association with farming at Béxar is consistent with the growing devotion to her as the protectress of agricultural pursuits in eighteenth-century New Spain, a devotion expressed most conspicuously by farmers who offered an annual novena at the Guadalupe basilica in Mexico City during planting season. Father Juan Gregorio de Campos's published sermon from the 1781 novena declared that "the protection of Mary in her image of Guadalupe is proper, special, and specific with regard to the successful cultivation of the land and the plentiful gathering of its fruits." Though geographic isolation separated farmers in far northern settlements like Béxar from the annual pilgrimage to and novena at Mexico City, Guadalupe's widespread association with abundant harvests reinforced the significance and harvest-festival ambiance of December celebrations at Béxar.[16] As community-wide celebrations of the maize harvest and other blessings received during the previous year, the rites of December reflected the penchant for festive public ritual among Catholics in the Spanish empire, as well as their belief that all of life falls under

God's providence. Local residents' sense of divine providence is confirmed by their pleas for celestial assistance during times of communal need, such as the petitionary prayers and processions they offered to "placate the Lord's ire" during a 1786 drought.[17]

The timing of the December rituals at a key moment in the agrarian cycle, as well as their festive spirit and expression of collective petition and thanksgiving to an almighty God, also reflects the traditions that Native American residents brought to the settlement. Most conspicuous among these Indigenous traditions were exuberant communal rituals called *mitotes*, which included singing, dancing, feasting, and the use of hallucinogens like peyote. Coahuiltecans and other native peoples from the Yanaguana area celebrated mitotes on occasions like the summer harvest, hunting and fishing expeditions, the return of the full moon, and victories in battle. Although Native Americans had participated in Catholic rituals at Yanaguana as early as the 1691 Corpus Christi feast, they maintained Indigenous traditions like the mitotes even in the face of Spanish missionaries' attempts to reorient or suppress them. Moreover, the native peoples exerted considerable cultural influence on the newcomers, as contemporary archaeological studies of Béxar's material culture demonstrate. Similarities between mitotes and Catholic ritual traditions could easily have attracted Native American participation in the settlement's December festivities, as well as enabled the natives to incorporate their own interpretations and practices into the annual December celebrations. Though the native peoples of Yanaguana were not closely linked to the Nahuatl-speaking natives of central Mexico, Guadalupe's association with the pre-Columbian goddess Tonantzin; her brown-skinned, Indigenous appearance; and her election of the Nahua neophyte Juan Diego as her chosen messenger made her more similar to local natives than any other sacred figure Catholic newcomers introduced.[18]

Despite the collective participation of Béxar's racially diverse population in public celebrations, rituals for Guadalupan and other feast days also illuminated the social class divisions in the local community. Though even the wealthiest residents had relatively modest economic means in comparison to New Spain's urban elites, as in other locales in the viceroyalty prominent citizens exercised some prerogatives over the general populace during feast-day celebrations. Town council members and other leading male citizens organized religious feasts in conjunction with the parish clergy, and citizens selected to plan a given feast were expected to make monetary contributions. For example, the town council appointed two captains and two assistants to assume financial responsibility for the Guadalupe festivities, and by the 1780s the minimum contribution for each sponsor was twelve pesos. This requirement limited participation on official planning committees to residents who could bear the financial burden. The planners would then occupy positions of prominence during communal celebrations. The prestige of sponsoring feast days is evident in the efforts made to meet the mandatory contribution, as in 1786 when Amador Delgado sold some cattle to cover the costs of serving as a newly selected assistant sponsor of the Guadalupe feast.[19]

Social class was not rigidly stratified along racial lines, however. Although Native Americans and castas tended to occupy the lowest rung on the social ladder, some castas joined the ranks of the more prosperous citizens in the settlement. Alicia Tjarks notes that the most striking demographic feature of Spanish colonial Texas was "a marked racial diversification, combined with and induced by an active biological and cultural miscegenation. As an immediate consequence, these factors encouraged a strong social and ethnic mobility, tending toward a free and heterogeneous society." The rise in status through marriage, development of artisan skills, acquisition of land or wealth, display of courage in battle, or other means was often accompanied by election to a position of civic leadership as a town council member or a sponsor for communal feast days. For example, Antonio Rodríguez Baca, a mestizo (person of mixed European and Native American ancestry) and native son of the settlement, advanced from his position as a soldier at the garrison to become a successful merchant, an employer of a number of workers, and one of the area's major landowners. His selection as one of the sponsors for the 1789 Guadalupe feast came in the midst of his rise to prominence in the community.[20]

The number of women in Béxar approached, then surpassed the number of men in the late eighteenth and early nineteenth centuries. This and Béxar's isolation enhanced the possibility that women would participate and exercise leadership in local affairs. Women were among the settlement's first residents; they headed households, occasionally won legal judgments against men, conducted business transactions, and owned ranches, cattle, farmlands, and town lots. In 1780, for example, María Luisa Guerrero successfully petitioned to secure legal title for property she had occupied for sixteen years "so my mother, children and myself will not be placed at jeopardy." As in the case of the men, some of the women were "free people of color," others were slaveholders, and still others were slaves, some of whom managed to claim their freedom, such as Native American María Gertrudis de la Peña, who successfully petitioned Governor

Domingo Cabello to rule in favor of her plea for "mercy, justice, and goodwill." Yet under Spanish, and later Mexican, rule women were denied the right to vote and to hold public office, they could be forced by law to stay with their husbands, they often suffered far harsher legal penalties than did men for offenses like adultery, they bore the brunt of providing for "illegitimate" children, they at times were victims of rape, and in patriarchal households their subordinate status was reinforced when they ate separately from their husbands after serving the men their meal.[21]

Primary sources do not reveal the role women played in preparing and celebrating religious feasts, a documentary silence that speaks eloquently about the division in gender roles for these events. Men supervised plaza entertainments like bullfights and games because women were legally barred from serving on the town council, and they were not included among the official sponsors of these entertainments. Extant records do not indicate who led ritual activities like processions, recitations of the rosary, singing, and decorating of the parish church and the Guadalupe image, but the first available descriptions of such activities from the early 1840s show that women exercised considerable leadership in the community's public Guadalupan devotion, albeit in circumscribed roles that paralleled their responsibilities of homemaking and transmitting communal traditions and faith to their children. These later descriptions illuminate an established tradition of women's leadership in worship that is consistent with the social and economic contributions women made to the settlement from its inception.[22]

The Mexican Period

During the war for Mexican independence from Spain (1810–1821), insurgent forces fought under the banner of Our Lady of Guadalupe, a juxtaposition of religious and political sentiments that royalists decried as sacrilegious. After the outbreak of the war on 16 September 1810, Texas governor Manuel Salcedo decreed a strict curfew for celebrations at Béxar during the December feasts of the Immaculate Conception, Our Lady of Guadalupe, and Christmas. He also limited the time allotted for public entertainments and mandated that they be confined to one of the two plazas adjoining the San Fernando parish church. The annual event had become so popular that participants came from as far away as the Rancho de Santa Margarita, some 110 miles to the south (at present-day San Patricio, Texas). Apparently the large crowd that the celebration attracted, along with the nationalistic fervor attached to the Guadalupe image, convinced the governor that these regulations were necessary "to preserve this province . . . from the fatal destruction of the revolution [that has engulfed] certain settlements in the viceroyalty."[23]

Governor Salcedo's fears were not unfounded, as local residents revolted a month later, arresting him and forcibly removing him from the settlement. A counterrevolutionary movement enabled Salcedo to reclaim his former post, but a further insurgent effort resulted in his capture and brutal execution in April 1813, an act avenged when royalists recaptured Béxar four months later. Although the loyalties of the local populace were divided as control of their hometown seesawed between Spanish royalists and Mexican insurrectionary forces, many supported the struggle for independence, which one resident deemed "the first occasion in which the Mexicans of San Antonio de Béxar announced their desire to break forever the chains of their ancient colonial slavery." When news of independence reached the settlement in July 1821, no protest or resistance movements erupted; within a matter of days the governor, town officials, clergy, soldiers, and citizenry swore a public oath of allegiance to the newly formed Mexican Republic.[24]

Though Béxar residents had celebrated events like the announcement of a new monarch during the Spanish period, the Mexican government more frequently mandated religious services to mark affairs of the nation, such as the defeat of invading armies, the patron saint days of national leaders, the assembling of the national congress, and the death of prominent political figures. Béxar celebrations for Mexican Independence Day in 1829 illustrate the importance of ritual and devotion in patriotic celebrations. On 15 September, the eve of the anniversary of revolutionary hero Miguel Hidalgo's *grito* (proclamation) for independence in 1810, a procession accompanied by music, church bells, and gun salutes wound its way through the streets. On the morning of the 16th, Mass and the Te Deum (a religious chant of praise for God's wondrous deeds) were offered at the parish, followed in the afternoon by another outdoor procession, a speech on the meaning of Independence Day, and evening dances. The next day the populace dressed for mourning and attended a Mass offered on behalf of those who had given their lives in the cause of independence, as well as all their beloved dead.[25]

The confluence of Catholic ritual with public expressions of Mexican national pride provided further impetus for celebrations in honor of Guadalupe. In 1824, the Mexican Congress decreed that the national holidays would be Mexican Independence Day and Constitution Day and that national religious feasts would be only Holy Thursday, Good Friday, Corpus Christi, and the feast of Our Lady of Guadalupe. This law promoted public celebrations that enhanced patriotic fervor while eliminating national recognition of the feasts of European saints. The observations of foreign visitors to the newborn Mexican Republic reveal that this legal prescription of a national Guadalupe feast was accompanied by widespread acclaim of her as a national patroness; one newcomer described Guadalupe as "the most venerated saint in Mexico, especially since independence," whose image was so popular that it was "found not only in churches but even in establishments alien to the faith."[26]

Though Béxar residents supported Mexican independence and celebrated the Mexican Republic, they opposed various policies of national leaders in Mexico City, reflecting the regional autonomy and identity that had taken root during the colonial era. Béxar leaders pointedly expressed their grievances in an 1832 petition that called for reforms to deal with attacks by Native American, inadequate schools, an ineffective judicial system, and colonization laws that impeded population growth and exacerbated the stagnation of the economy. These complaints reveal that the primary concerns of the Béxar populace were local ones. The expression of group solidarity in residents' ongoing Guadalupan devotion reflected the regional loyalties revealed in the 1832 petition as much as, if not more than, national allegiance. For the devotees of Béxar, Mexican identity thus had a decidedly regional bent; Guadalupe's growing acclaim in Mexico buttressed local pride in a patroness who had accompanied them for a century in their lonely struggles on the periphery of the empire.[27]

The prominence of the Guadalupe feast increased even further at Béxar during the period of the Mexican Republic (1821–1836). Whereas previously December festivities had been dedicated to the feasts of the Immaculate Conception, Guadalupe, and Christmas, after 1810 town council minutes and official correspondence mentioned Guadalupe as the sole honoree of these festivities. The annual December celebrations continued to spill out onto the plaza in front of the parish church, where bullfights, games, and food booths complemented Mass and other religious rituals in a convergence of merriment and solemnity that illuminated the celebrations' ongoing vigor as an expression of faith, collective identity, and the social ranking of Béxar residents. Town council decrees that games and booths be taxed and requests that militia members assist with crowd control illustrate the ongoing popularity of the December festivities. The planning for religious feasts at town council meetings would abruptly cease once Anglo Americans became council members after Texas independence in 1836, but up until the last December before the Texas Revolution, elected officials maintained their long-standing practice of overseeing preparations for the community-wide December celebrations.[28]

The December rituals continued to provide a significant festive pause between harvesting and planting. Despite some diversification in Béxar's economy during the Spanish and Mexican periods as local leaders fostered trade with places like Louisiana, Coahuila, Chihuahua, and New Mexico, an 1830 census indicated that more than 60 percent of employed persons at Béxar were farmers. Secularization of the five area missions, which had begun in 1793, was completed in 1824, placing mission communities that occupied large tracts of farmland under the ecclesiastical jurisdiction of San Fernando parish. While trying economic times hampered farming and kept the local population under two thousand for most of the Mexican period, the decline of the missions augmented the number of rural parishioners affiliated with San Fernando and its ritual traditions.[29] As they had over the previous century, the local populace implored the heavens for solace and relief in times of crisis. A visitor to the town who arrived in the midst of a cholera epidemic in 1833 noted in his diary that he had witnessed two "religious parades" held as a means of offering "religious invocation to God for preservation from the cholera."[30]

Social class divisions among participants also remained evident in Guadalupan and other public celebrations. Sometimes two simultaneous dances were held in connection with a communal celebration, separating the elite from the general populace. The tradition of prestigious male citizens serving as official sponsors for the Guadalupe feast lasted into the 1820s. In 1830, the town council began collecting rents for game and food booths set up on the plaza during the December festivities. Although the practice of renting booths represented a somewhat more egalitarian approach to citizen participation in organizing plaza entertainments, wealthier residents could more easily afford the fees.[31]

Though public celebrations reinforced the community's social hierarchy, they continued to unite Béxar residents and shape a sense of commonality among them. Even Anglo Americans who settled in the town were incorporated into the local community and its public rituals; this is not surprising because Anglo Americans were few in number, reportedly accounting for less than 2 percent of Béxar's population in 1828. For example, John Duff Brown was about eight years old when his family moved to Béxar in 1832. Shortly thereafter, he was baptized a Catholic. Although later in life he would observe religious practices learned from his Presbyterian grandmother, for the three years his family lived in San Antonio he joined his classmates from the local school during religious celebrations and "marched with the pupils in double file to the cathedral [San Fernando parish] singing full-voiced some Catholic hymn." Though the Catholic religion was prescribed for all citizens under Mexican law, the number of Anglo Americans in other settlements who ignored or resisted these legal requirements makes Anglo American participation in religious rituals at Béxar all the more striking.[32]

Patron Saints and Divine Providence

Given Guadalupe's widespread presence and influence in the Americas today, it is tempting to presume that her rise to prominence as the primary patroness of Béxar Catholics was predictable, perhaps even inevitable. In the contemporary United States, dioceses from San Diego to New York have at least one parish named for Guadalupe. But in the Spanish and Mexican periods, Guadalupan devotion in the present-day United States was still evolving. Other settlements in what became the state of Texas concentrated their devotion on sacred images such as those of Jesús Nazareno (the Christ figure standing crowned with thorns), Nuestra Señora de los Dolores (Our Lady of Sorrows), and Nuestra Señora del Refugio (Our Lady of Refuge), all popular devotional figures in Laredo, about 150 miles southwest of Béxar. In Los Angeles, devotion to Nuestra Señora de los Remedios, the Marian image that had long rivaled Guadalupe for prominence in central Mexico, surpassed Guadalupe in popularity well into the nineteenth century.[33]

Whether at Los Angeles, Laredo, Béxar, or elsewhere in New Spain, Catholic colonists followed the Spanish practice of developing "a unique [ritual] calendar built up from the settlement's own sacred history," as William Christian has documented.[34] From the vast array of feast days, saints, and Marian images in the Catholic tradition, devotees especially honored heavenly intercessors deemed to have a particular interest in their community. The Béxar case illustrates typical ways that devotees and their patrons came to be linked, as local residents designated as their celestial benefactors the saint on whose day Spanish subjects first arrived in the area, the namesake of a royal benefactor's son, and the Marian images cherished by the settlers who initiated the local parish church construction project. Far from perceiving the emergence of their patrons as mere historical coincidence, New Spain settlers espoused the Spanish Catholic belief that God's providence provided these blessed protectors to accompany them and assist them in their struggles.

The theology of divine providence associated with the naming of patron saints asserted that celestial beings and God's assistance were not distant but, as Ana María Díaz-Stevens demonstrates in her study of Puerto Rican Catholics, were "constantly manifested in daily occurrences, in the forces of nature, in the seeming ease with which, season after season, the once dormant seeds woke up to warmth and sunlight."[35] Consistent with the Yanaguana natives' sense of a pervasive divine presence, this theology envisioned that all was in the hands of God—rain, drought, harvest, health, torment, good fortune, protection from enemies, communal well-being. Daily sustenance and survival were cause for heartfelt gratitude: when residents of Béxar and the environs woke up in the morning, they literally did not know if they would stay alive till the evening. Given this tenuous existence the sense that one's everyday life was in the hands of forces beyond human control is not surprising. This sense was so prevalent that residents presumed that social divisions and one's state in life reflected a divine plan in which stratified Spanish society mirrored the hierarchical ordering of the heavenly dominion. Like the intermediaries who were so often necessary for dealing successfully with local magistrates and crown officials, patron saints linked their devotees to the power of divine succor. By God's design the earthly world imitated the celestial realm: the world was ordered in such a way that natural occurrences, social rank, and human events all conformed to a higher reason and purpose. The primary vocation of the Catholic was to persevere in faith, harmony, and inner peace despite the joys and pains, hardships and travails of life. To this day many Latino Catholics express this understanding of divine providence with the popular saying, "El hombre pone, y Dios dispone" (man proposes, and God disposes).

Yet these theological convictions did not lead all devotees to blindly embrace a rigidly deterministic view of the world. Slaves, women, and men of lower casta sometimes accepted their status with fatalistic resolve, but in Béxar and other settlements those of marginal social rank also strove to improve their position and even symbolically authenticated their advance by assuming public roles in feast-day celebrations. Deeply held convictions about a divine plan and God's ordering of the universe were tempered by human experiences that led Guadalupan and other devotees to conclude that fortune, chance, perseverance, or sacrifice could alter one's situation in life. Fervent prayer and the performance of ritual duties could also influence life outcomes, but faith was not a simplistic equation of a cause-and-effect relationship between intercession and heavenly assistance, since supplication for needs like good crops, safety from attack, and an end to epidemics was not always answered in the time and manner desired.

The understanding of providence underlying devotion to patron saints in New Spain was a fluid theology that was adaptable to devotees' physical environment, economic conditions, racial mixing, longing for security, and aspirations for social advancement, particularly in settlements like Béxar where isolation and the quest for survival bound residents more closely to one another and to their celestial helpers. In the shifting terrain between belief in a divinely ordained plan for the world and the possibilities of human initiative and divine intervention, New Spain residents like those at Béxar forged, fostered, and refashioned a theology of divine providence through their daily struggles and their collective and individual interactions with their patron saints.

Patron saints varied from place to place depending on the particular historical circumstances of a given settlement and its residents, but the complex contours and processes of adapting the theology of divine providence to specific local conditions were relatively consistent. In the case of Béxar, only Guadalupe's feast coincided with the break between the late maize harvest and the early-year preparations for planting, amplifying the duration and significance of annual festivities in her honor. Furthermore, as the only New World image among Béxar's four primary patrons, the morenita Guadalupe more aptly reflected an emergent and relatively homogeneous regional identity among the town's mixed population of mestizos, other castas, Canary Islanders, Native Americans, and eventually Anglo Americans. Though subsequent urbanization diminished the importance of Guadalupe's feast as a harvest festival, her role as a communal symbol intensified after the political separation of Texas from Mexico begot abrupt demographic and social changes in San Antonio.

Defender of *Dignidad*, 1836–1900

During August 1840 Father Jean Marie Odin, the future first bishop of Texas, visited San Antonio, the name bestowed on Béxar when leaders of the recently established Republic of Texas officially incorporated it as a municipality. Born in the wake of the French Revolution in Hauteville, a small village near Roanne, Odin studied with the Jesuits and at the Sulpician major seminary of Lyon, volunteered to work in the United States, and in 1823 was ordained as a Vincentian priest in the Barrens, Missouri, south of St. Louis. This was a combative era for the French church, and a time during which seminaries stressed ascetic discipline and the noble dignity of the priesthood. Shortly before departing for the Barrens, the young Odin wrote that his future mission field contained "millions of idolators and Protestants." He continued, "Every day these wretched souls fall into hell, and only fifty priests can lend them any assistance."[1]

Odin's approach to church discipline and Protestants led to conflict shortly after his arrival at San Fernando parish, at the time still San Antonio's only congregation. Citing the dictates of Catholic canon law, he refused to allow the tolling of the church bells for the funeral of Colonel Henry W. Karnes, a hero of the war for Texas independence from Mexico, who was of Protestant background. San Antonio mayor John Smith and other Anglo American residents held a meeting to express their indignation. They publicly denounced Odin and his support of a church "principle which twangs more of the age of the inquisition than the liberality which characterizes the present era." San Antonians of Mexican heritage, or Tejanos,[2] neither participated in the meeting nor publicly responded to the vilification of the French clergyman. After a century in which nearly all disagreements among town residents had been between Spanish-speaking coreligionists, the acrimonious denominational and ethnic conflict unfolding before their eyes was no doubt a bewildering spectacle.[3]

The 1840 bell-ringing controversy illuminated the growing diversity of San Antonio's population and the corresponding increase in the complexity of the town's social dynamics. Though decades of collective struggle for survival and perceived group commonalities such as language, customs, behavior patterns, patron saints, devotional practices, and political and economic interests had shaped a sense of Tejano ethnicity, increased interaction with European clergy, Anglo Americans, and other groups induced Tejanos to overcome "pluralistic ignorance," heightening their sense that their traditions and heritage were distinct from those of others. The prejudice, conflict, and unequal distribution of power that characterized the contact between Tejanos and the Anglo Americans who wrested control of San Antonio's political, economic, and social life from them further accentuated perceptions of Tejanos' ethnic distinctiveness. Although Germans, other European immigrants, and African Americans also interacted with Tejanos, their influence on ethnic Mexicans was not nearly as substantial as that of the more dominant Anglo Americans.[4]

After the political separation of Texas from Mexico, San Fernando congregants continued their Guadalupan devotion on the contested and uneven terrain of ethnic and denominational rivalries. The year after the bell-ringing incident, Odin returned for another pastoral visit and noted that "on the 12th of December, the feast of Our Lady of Guadalupe, the patroness of Mexico, and of all the Spanish colonies, the inhabitants of San Antonio, who, in more prosperous times, solemnized this day with great rejoicings, felt their ancient zeal for the veneration of Mary revived." Impressed with the congregation's exuberant devotion, he also asserted that he had "seen few processions more edifying."[5] Though Odin's claim that this celebration rejuvenated a dormant Guadalupan devotion is not consistent with evidence from other primary documents, his vivid description of the Guadalupe processions through the town streets and plazas includes striking features like the firing of guns and cannons as a sign of devotion, practices not mentioned in extant accounts from the Spanish and Mexican periods. For Odin, this celebration represented an admirable expression of Marian piety; for San Antonio Tejanos, the Guadalupe celebrations clamorously expressed their faith, dignity, and ethnic pride, symbolically contesting Protestant and Anglo American presumptions of superiority. As huge crowds moved through the public spaces of the town carrying candles and intermittently praying the rosary, singing hymns to their Guadalupan patroness, and firing devotional gunshots and cannon blasts, the enduring presence and traditions of Mexican-descent Catholics were palpable.

Over the following decades Guadalupan devotion continued to shape and express—at first boisterously, but gradually in more stifled tones—San Fernando devotees' piety, heightened sense of their distinct heritage and ethnic identity, class and gender divisions, and resistance to Anglo American efforts to alter, prohibit, or supersede ethnic Mexican traditions and feasts. The turbulence of this era in which San Antonio shifted from Tejano to Anglo American control, from an overwhelmingly Mexican Catholic to a polyglot population, and from a rural settlement to an urban center facilitated significant transformations in the lives of Mexican-descent San Antonians and their expressions of Guadalupan devotion.

Conflict and Change

San Antonio was frequently beset with violence and bloodshed during the struggle for Texas independence (1835–1836) and its aftermath. Combatants engaged in two major battles of the Texas Revolt at San Antonio: the Texas army's siege and conquest of the city in December 1835 and Mexican forces' reconquest at the famous Alamo battle on 6 March 1836, six weeks before Texas won independence from Mexico at the battle of San Jacinto. Conflicts with Native Americans in and around San Antonio, which had occurred intermittently since the settlement's foundation, continued during the period of the Republic of Texas (1836–1845). These conflicts were most conspicuous in the "Court House fight" at San Antonio on 19 March 1840, when representatives of the Comanches and the Texas government disagreed on an exchange of prisoners and a violent confrontation erupted that left thirty-five Comanches, six Anglo Americans, and one San Antonio Mexican dead. In 1842 Mexican forces occupied San Antonio on two separate occasions, although in both instances they withdrew from the city shortly after seizing it.[6]

The threat of attacks by Native Americans and Mexican forces was all but eliminated after U.S. annexation of Texas in 1845 and the arrival of U.S. military forces, which led to a rapid expansion of the Anglo American and European (especially German) population. Though some Mexicans from south of the newly established border migrated to San Antonio even after annexation, the proportion of ethnic Mexicans in the town's population decreased. The 1850 census showed that 42 percent of San Antonio's 3,488 residents had Spanish surnames, 25 percent were Anglo American, 16 percent were of German birth or parentage, 7 percent were African American, 3 percent were French, and the remainder were largely immigrants from other European countries; Spanish-surnamed residents thus constituted less than half of San Antonio's population for the first time in the settlement's history. This ethnic pluralism is illustrated in an 1853 newspaper report: "We strolled into a Justice Court the other day, and were reminded of the time when God smote the children of men with a confusion of tongues. A German was complained of by a Mexican, and a Frenchman was the witness. Each one spoke his native tongue only, and yet there were no interpreters. Both Justice and Attorneys understood the four languages [including English]."[7]

A year later, a visitor noted that the city's most striking characteristic was its "jumble of races, costumes, languages and buildings," particularly the city's distinct German, Mexican, and Anglo American neighborhoods and the mix of architectural styles around the central plaza. Clusters of entries in the 1850 and 1860 census records confirm perceptions of separation between Spanish-surnamed residents and other groups in San Antonio neighborhoods. Noting this physical proximity, as well as commonalities of language, culture, religion, and low socioeconomic status, many antebellum observers at San Antonio referred to Tejanos and newly arrived residents of Mexican descent as a single group, usually calling them Mexicans. Similarities in the composition of immigrant Mexican and native Tejano families, as well as their strong tendency to intermarry with one another but rarely with European immigrants or Anglo Americans, confirm perceptions of their strong affinity and willingness to forge ethnic Mexican social alliances.[8]

Not surprisingly, the influence of Mexican-descent residents diminished as the city's demographic profile shifted. During the nine years of the Republic of Texas only one Tejano was elected mayor of San Antonio, though Tejanos retained control of the city council; in the first fifteen years after U.S. annexation, there were no Tejano mayors, and the number of Tejanos elected to the city council decreased threefold. Five of the eight city council members were Tejanos in 1845, but by 1860 not a single Tejano served in that capacity. In the economic realm, despite San Antonio's growth as a mercantile center, after Texas became a state the predominantly agricultural Tejano population lost most of its landholdings and became a working underclass. Visitors to the city during the mid-1850s noted of the Tejanos that "only 4 or 5 are received into the circles of the elite" and observed that "by far the most numerous class of Mexicans" were those of the "lower order." These observations reflect some degree of anti-Mexican bias, but census figures confirm that Tejano economic fortunes were decidedly on the wane, even with regard to indicators like the ownership of slaves. The census conducted just before the Civil War revealed that Spanish-surnamed residents owned 3 percent of the slaves in San Antonio. This figure reflects both the Tejanos' diminished economic status and their reported "abhorrence" of slavery. Tejanos were notorious among Anglo Americans for helping slaves escape and for freely associating and intermarrying with them: visitors to San Antonio like abolitionist Benjamin Lundy noted "no difference made here on account of colour" between Mexicans and Blacks.[9]

The case of native San Antonian Juan Nepomuceno Seguín illustrates the loss of Tejano political and economic power at San Antonio during these years. Seguín was a celebrated veteran of the Texas Revolution, represented San Antonio in the Republic of Texas Senate from 1838 to 1840, and became mayor of his hometown in January 1841. However, the following April he resigned the mayoral office when he was forced out of Texas by enemies he described as "straggling American adventurers," who threatened and murdered Tejano families in order to steal their land. After the U.S. war with Mexico (1846–1848), he returned and was elected justice of the peace in 1852 and 1854. He was also president of his electoral precinct and was influential in the founding of the local Democratic Party. But the former mayor and senator never regained these more influential offices after his return from exile. He lamented that the Anglo American takeover had left him "a foreigner in my native land."[10]

As it had for Spain and Mexico in previous eras, San Antonio served as a military base for the United States. At the outset of the war with Mexico in 1846, the immense U.S. force quartered in San Antonio and its environs eclipsed the local civilian population in size. After the war the city began its long tenure as a major military center and depot for the U.S. Army; in the 1850s as many as eighteen frontier posts received supplies from the San Antonio base. While this military presence provided some civilian jobs, it was also a visible symbol of the new regime that ruled San Antonio.[11]

The local parish of San Fernando also changed during this turbulent period of transition. In 1840 Pope Gregory XVI removed Texas from the Mexican diocese of Linares and declared it a prefecture apostolic (a mission territory led by a priest with certain episcopal powers) under the diocese of New Orleans. He appointed Vincentian priest John Timon as prefect apostolic. Since Timon was unable to assume the responsibility personally because of other duties within his religious order, his confrere Jean Marie Odin assumed the leadership of the church in Texas as vice prefect apostolic. Seven years later Pope Pius IX established Galveston as the first Texas episcopal see and named Odin the first bishop of Texas. Shortly after his 1840 arrival in Texas, Odin removed San Antonio's two native-born priests, Refugio de la Garza and José Antonio Valdéz, claiming that their ministry was ineffective and that they had broken their priestly vows by having wives and children. He replaced them with his Spanish confrere Miguel Calvo, initiating a long series of European-born pastors at San Fernando, the vast majority of them French during the second half of the nineteenth century.[12]

Some foreign priests assigned to San Fernando, such as Emanuel Domenech, described Texans of Mexican descent as lacking instruction in the faith, claiming that "the religion of the great majority is very superficial, the great truths of the faith are overlooked, and the most essential duties of a Christian neglected." Yet other clergy assigned to San Fernando, like pastors Calvo (1840–1852) and Claude Marie Dubuis (1852–1858) consistently offered their ministrations in Spanish, participated in established devotional and ritual traditions, and energetically promoted Tejano allegiance to Catholicism. Dubuis founded the parish's first known pious society, the Archconfraternity of the Immaculate Heart of Mary, to strengthen young Catholics "against Protestantism and against moral laxity." Though the archconfraternity did not attain the long-term popularity at San Fernando that it did in Dubuis's native France, the steadfast efforts of Dubuis and other San Fernando clergy to promote Catholic devotion and allegiance coalesced with Tejano efforts to continue practicing their Mexican Catholic traditions.[13]

Tejanos' hegemony in their hometown's religious life and public celebrations dissipated as Anglo Americans' population growth facilitated the formation of their own congregations and public festivities. San Fernando was the city's only church in 1845; by 1860 a second Catholic parish had been formed, along with Presbyterian, Episcopal, Lutheran, Baptist, and Methodist congregations. After annexation Anglo American newcomers increasingly organized festivities for occasions like U.S. and Texas independence days, Washington's birthday, Thanksgiving, and the observance of May Day, a Protestant tradition that included a public procession, awards ceremony, and picnic for Sunday school students. They also promoted the participation of Mexican-descent, German, and other residents in the parades and ceremonies for their "American holidays." Their sentiments were reflected in a *San Antonio Ledger* editorial after Fourth of July celebrations in 1851: "We have many foreigners among us who know nothing of our government, who have no national feeling in common with us. . . . Let us induce them to partake with us in our festivities, they will soon partake our feelings, and when so, they will be citizens indeed."[14]

Many Anglo Americans attributed the changes in Texas to divine providence and not only encouraged Tejano Catholics to embrace patriotic allegiance to the United States, but also urged them to convert to Protestantism. One 1851 editorial in a San Antonio newspaper claimed that the U.S. takeover of Texas had occurred "thanks to the Almighty Being who has so powerfully wrought in our favor." Reverend A. B. Lawrence opined that the political separation of Texas from Mexico was "an indication of Providence in relation to the propagation of divine truth in other parts of the Mexican dominions" and "the beginning of the downfall of Antichrist, and the spread of the Saviour's power of the gospel." Presbyterian minister William L. McCalla, who visited San Antonio in 1840, decried the local customs of holy day festivities and *fandangos* (dances) as evidence of Catholicism's corrupting influence and prayed that Protestant emissaries would reclaim Texas from "the mother and mistress of all churches." Despite such admonitions, or perhaps in part because of them, only a handful of Mexican-descent Catholics joined the city's newly established Protestant congregations. An 1860 Baptist visitor to the city summarized Protestant frustrations at the resilience of Tejano Catholic allegiance, noting that "The Mexican population is Catholic. There has never been a convert from Catholicism to Protestantism, except a few cases owing to intermarrying."[15]

The negative attitudes some Anglo Americans held about the Tejano population undermined the newcomers' efforts to sway Tejanos' national and denominational loyalties. Even the local press referred to Tejanos with the racist slur *greaser*.[16] Commenting on people of Mexican heritage, one Anglo American stated that they "are as bigoted and ignorant as the devil's grandchildren."

Another described San Antonio Tejanos as "ignorant, cunning, treacherous, thieving, bigoted, superstitious, . . . [and] infamously cowardly." Contemporary Protestant newspapers added to the wholesale attack on the Tejano character. In 1848 the *Texas Presbyterian* quoted an Anglo American correspondent who described persons of Mexican descent as "useless, worthless, abandoned, yet with a happy self-sufficiency that renders them blind to every disgrace and indifferent to every disaster." Racial tensions led to potentially volatile situations, as on one occasion when the lynching of a Tejano accused of horse theft nearly resulted in a riot involving Anglo Americans and San Antonio's Tejano population, or during the 1850s when a series of violent attacks on Tejano laborers who transported goods drew a formal response from the Mexican consulate in Washington, D.C., and the intervention of Texas governor Elisha M. Pease to end the "Cart War."[17]

Tejanos sought to defend their rights and customs in elections and public debates. In 1854 the anti-Catholic, anti-immigrant Know Nothing Party achieved their first Texas victory in the San Antonio municipal elections, gaining control of the mayor's office and the city council. During their first weeks in office they repealed a law requiring the city secretary to translate ordinances and other documents into Spanish and banned Mexican fandangos. In response to the Know Nothing threat, San Antonio Tejanos forged political alliances with Anglo Americans and Germans in the Democratic Party and waged a vigorous organizing effort for the statewide elections the following year. Tejano leaders formally declared their opposition to the Know Nothings and accused them of condemning Tejanos to "political slavery" solely because they chose "to worship God according to the dictates of our conscience and the rituals of our ancestors." Local leader José Antonio Navarro wrote an open letter to his fellow citizens of Mexican-Texan heritage that was read publicly and later published in both the English and Spanish press. Navarro reminded his listeners that his people's Hispano-Mexican ancestors had founded their city and had built the parish of San Fernando in which they worshiped God. Citing the anti-Catholic attitudes of the Know Nothings, he proclaimed that "the Mexico-Texans are Catholics, and should be proud of the faith of their ancestors, and defend it inch by inch against such infamous aggressors." Democrats won the 1855 state elections, besting their Know Nothing opponents by almost three to one in the San Antonio area.[18]

Despite such efforts, Tejano success in political activism was relatively rare. When San Antonio elected officials decreed in 1858 that public funds would be available solely for English-language schools, local newspaper editor José Ramos de Zúñiga contested their decision, but to no avail. José Antonio Navarro, the only Tejano elected as a Texas state senator during the first century after annexation, made various legislative attempts to protect the ancestral lands of Mexican Texans, but all of them failed. The extent of Tejano political frustrations was evident in Navarro's status as the sole Tejano representative at the 1845 constitutional convention for the state of Texas. Navarro's struggle to merely prevent the passage of an "odious" and "ridiculous" law that would have restricted suffrage to the "free white population," though successful, illuminated the drastic decline in ethnic Mexicans' political influence under U.S. rule.[19]

Enduring Traditions

In the face of Tejanos' declining influence in political, economic, and civic life, their public display of unabashedly Mexican Catholic traditions and festivities provided an ongoing means of expressing communal identity, group pride, and enduring faith and vitality. One visitor to the city noted the physical markers of faith and identity with which Tejanos adorned themselves: "Every Mexican professes to be a Catholic and carries about his person the crucifix, the rosary, and other symbols of the mother church." Funeral processions for deceased infants at San Fernando wound through the streets and included children dressed in white, fiddlers, gun salutes, and crowds of family and friends. Reflective of the community's faith response to high infant mortality rates, these festive elements expressed confidence in the Catholic belief that a baptized child who dies is sinless and therefore goes directly to heaven.[20]

Processions on other solemn occasions also elicited Mexican devotional fervor. When the San Fernando church bell signaled that the priest would be taking the consecrated communion host to the home of a dying person, "the people hastened to the holy place in order to accompany Our Lord through the streets." For the nine days preceding Christmas, Mexican-descent San Antonians lit lamps and placed them on their homes "in remembrance of the 'Light of the World.'" They began Noche Buena, or Christmas Eve, with a dance that was followed by midnight Mass. Afterward the people filed to the front of San Fernando church and kissed the feet of el Santo Niño, the Holy Child. Outside the church building gun salutes, cannonades, and ringing bells noisily announced Christ's birth. On Holy Saturday (the day before Easter), Tejanos paraded a rag-man figure of the traitor Judas Iscariot through the streets, threw sticks and

"Entierro de un ángel" (funeral of an angel), a painting of a child's funeral procession by Theodore Gentilz, c. 1840s. The San Fernando church tower is in the background. Courtesy The Daughters of the Republic of Texas Library, San Antonio. Gift of the Yanaguana Society in memory of Frederick C. Chabot.

stones at the image, shook makeshift rattles, and created a deafening bedlam with their shouts and screams. Feast days for San Fernando, San Antonio, and San Juan included Mass and other religious ceremonies, as well as dances and festivities like a sport called El Gallo Corriendo, "the running rooster," in which a contestant attempted to ride his horse while bearing a brightly decorated rooster—or sometimes, in its place, a watermelon—over a given route through the town and across a designated finish line. His opponents rode alongside him and employed almost any means imaginable in their attempt to take the rooster.[21]

The frequency, fervor, and festive ambiance of San Fernando's antebellum feast-day celebrations made them one of the most memorable features of life at San Antonio during this period. Well into the following century, area residents like native San Antonian and San Fernando parishioner Enrique Esparza recalled wistfully that "we had many saint days. Then we would visit with relatives and friends . . . [and] join in the fiesta around San Fernando." Sarah French, who settled at San Antonio with her family in 1846 when she was a young girl, remembered that during her early years in the town local customs included "the observing of certain Saints' days." Prominent among these days was the December feast in which "the image of a woman, Saint Guadalupe, the patron saint of Mexico, was carried around the streets."[22]

The annual rituals and festivities in honor of Our Lady of Guadalupe continued to be San Fernando's most conspicuous feast-day celebration. Announced a day in advance with extensive cannonading and bell ringing, Guadalupe feast-day processions flowed out of San Fernando parish into the city's plazas and streets and featured colorful pageantry, vivid religious imagery, lively devotional expressions, enthusiastic participation, and an unmistakably Mexican ambiance. The principal ritual object was a "richly and gorgeously dressed" image of Our Lady of Guadalupe that devotees "loaded with all the necklaces and jewellery [sic] of the town" and "placed upon a bier elegantly adorned." Young girls dressed in white and bearing candles and flowers served as the immediate attendants of the Guadalupan image. Fiddlers and other devotees holding up a cross and Marian banner also participated, along with the parish clergy, large crowds of devotees, and men carrying rifles and pistols for devotional salutes. As they proceeded along their route, members of the entourage intermittently prayed the rosary, sang hymns in honor of their patroness, and acclaimed her with gun and canon tributes. The church bells pealed loudly as they arrived at the doors of San Fernando, where in preparation for this feast local women had generously provided "their most valuable ornaments for the decoration of their temple." Congregants then enshrined the Guadalupe image on its appointed altar and joined in Spanish and Latin services: Mass, vespers, and further recitations of the rosary. The exuberant public rituals revealed Guadalupe's continuing role as the local Mexican Catholic community's primary patroness; even Anglo American newcomers recognized that these devotions were "intended to do honor to Our Lady of Guadalupe, who is supposed to take San Antonio under her special protection."[23]

The persistence of traditions like the Guadalupe feast required sustained Tejano initiative. European clergy assigned to San Fernando may have been familiar with Our Lady of Guadalupe because Pope Benedict XIV had officially declared 12 December her feast day in 1754, but many local practices in celebrating her feast were new to them. Moreover, the practice of the town council overseeing feast-day celebrations had abruptly ceased under the governments of Texas and

Artist Dean Cárdenas's 1995 depiction of 1840s San Fernando Guadalupe processions, based on eyewitness accounts. Courtesy the author.

the United States, as Anglo American newcomers objected to elected officials organizing religious events. Because the poverty and meager population of the settlement during the Spanish and Mexican periods had precluded the formal establishment of a pious society to organize the Guadalupe feast, the sudden collapse of the customary planning structures for the event placed its very existence in jeopardy. After the removal of San Fernando's Mexican priests, Tejano and Tejana devotees demonstrated their dedication to Guadalupe and their communal traditions as they took it upon themselves to raise funds, organize processions, adorn the church and the Guadalupe image, lead the rosary and other prayers, and invite the new European clergy to offer Mass for the occasion and participate in their patroness's feast.[24]

As they had since the previous century, Mexican-descent residents implored their Guadalupan patroness as an agent of divine providence, particularly as a celestial protector who could bring about the climatic conditions needed for agricultural pursuits. Irish Ursuline sister Mary Patrick Joseph, one of the first women religious to serve in San Antonio, wrote an account of "a good simple woman" who reportedly held a Guadalupan image over the San Antonio River and induced floodwaters to recede. Another local woman prayed to Guadalupe when rain was needed and annually had a Mass offered and the church bells rung to honor her patroness. Although the woman was poor, she went from house to house with the Guadalupe image collecting donations to cover the expenses of her celebration. The editor of a San Antonio newspaper wrote in 1854 that he had seen a Marian image in a tree near a *jacal* (hut). Upon inquiry, he discovered that the image had been placed there to intercede for rain. He commented that it was "deplorable to think that human beings will place their dependence on an image for the necessaries of life." However, he also admitted with amazement that "it actually did drizzle a little"! Another San Antonio resident later recalled that

> The gardens or farms were so close to the city that if we listened at the first streak of dawn we could hear the laborers going forth to work and humming a song of praise to María Santíssima [sic], protectress of the field:
>
> Thou art the Shepherdess,
> Lovely and fair,
> The sun that surpasseth
> The moon and the stars.[25]

Confident assurance in the providential assistance of celestial figures led some devotees to expect reciprocity from Guadalupe and other patrons. One female supplicant reportedly sought the favor of rains from Guadalupe, and "if the rain do [sic] not come, she beats the image of Our Lady." Other devotees wondered why their patrons had not defended their honor and dignity more adequately during the turbulent transition to U.S. rule, or even prevented the U.S. takeover and Tejanos' subsequent political and economic displacement. In the most extreme case, in September 1854 a Tejano reportedly went into San Antonio's Mission San Juan (then a mission station that San Fernando clergy occasionally visited) and began to destroy the images of Jesus and the saints. After some Tejana women stopped his destructive spree, the man explained that "the Mexican Gods could neither eat, walk or talk, and were no Gods at all, consequently he wanted to put them out of the way." He added that "if the Mexicans had worshipped the true and only God, the 'gringos' could never have taken Texas." Although the precise reasons for this man's agitation remain unclear, his observations reflect the conviction that the faith and traditions of Mexican-descent San Antonians, especially their trust in patron saints and divine providence, were false religion; Anglo Americans, on the other hand, worshiped the "true" and all-powerful God, who was the reason for their ascendance.[26]

The association between Guadalupe and agriculture began to wane as San Antonio expanded, fewer residents engaged in farming, and the advent of U.S. rule brought new challenges to the forefront of Tejano concern. Over time the sight of farmlands in the distance grew increasingly rare along the Guadalupe procession route, as did the food booths and games on the plazas that had previously distinguished the Guadalupe feast as a harvest festival. Instead, devotees encountered physical reminders of the sanguinary episodes associated with San Antonio's shifting national allegiances. The processions went around the town's two main plazas, passing houses and other buildings that still bore signs of violence, such as the courthouse across from San Fernando church, where a fierce conflict between Texas officials and the Comanches had erupted in 1840. One contemporary visitor noted that the two plazas surrounding San Fernando had, at various times, been "heaped with the slain. The houses that surround the square, and the church, which occupies the center are perforated by hundreds of musket and cannon shot." Another visitor remarked that he had met several Comanche children among San Antonio families and that when he asked "a boy who was assisting a stone mason in the Plaza, how and when he came there, he replied, pointing to the Court House, 'My father was killed there.'" Participants in the Guadalupe processions included relatives and former companions of those killed in battle; like this child, they were reminders of past combat at San Antonio and of the loved ones who no longer took their place among their fellow devotees at the annual Guadalupe feast.[27]

Changes in the physical setting and experience of celebrating the Guadalupe feast, along with San Antonio's increased ethnic diversity, facilitated Guadalupe's rising significance as a marker of Mexican Catholic distinctiveness, particularly as some Anglo American newcomers criticized and attempted to alter or suppress established local practices and feast-day celebrations. Cannonading and bell ringing for the 1852 Guadalupe celebration took place on Friday rather than Sunday, the actual day of the feast. This was done in order "not to disturb" the Sunday "methodistical devotion" of the Anglo American population. On other occasions, Guadalupe processions were reportedly canceled because Anglo Americans found them uncivilized. The writer of an 1853 letter to the editor of the *San Antonio Ledger* deplored the Tejano practice of funeral processions with open coffins, deeming it "a heathen or Indian practice" that "has been very offensive to a larger portion of our community, and should be prohibited by the city authorities." Another Anglo American remarked that during the early 1850s the local Mexican Catholic celebration of Christmas "was carried out in a semi-barbaric style." After a visit to San Antonio, Baptist minister Z. N. Morrell stated that Tejano Catholics' religious practices exemplified "the blindest superstition."[28]

The most protracted Tejano-Anglo conflict regarding Tejano festivities was the battle over the fandangos that were usually part of Guadalupe's and other feasts. One resident noted years later that "there was a great deal of dancing—even on Sunday—for the Mexicans argued that God gave them legs and arms to use as well as heart and soul and that there was no sin in gaiety and pleasure." But many Anglo American newcomers condemned the fandangos. One opponent went so far as to deem them "nothing but a heterogeneous mass of rottenness" and requested that the city council abolish them. Continuing conflicts resulted in the passage of numerous city council ordinances, and at different times during the antebellum period fandangos were taxed, restricted, banned, and then reinstated again. Tejanos used legislative means to defend the practice of holding fandangos, and sometimes they simply ignored municipal statutes aimed at regulating their dances. On at least one occasion, though, Tejano resistance reached the point of violence, when two men of Mexican descent reportedly assaulted a local constable who appeared at their dance after a municipal ban on fandangos was enacted.[29]

Prolonged clashes over fandangos, public processions, bell ringing, cannonading, and other Tejano practices hardened perceptions of difference and lines of separation between Tejanos and other San Antonio residents, a segregation symbolically embodied in the shift of the Guadalupe feast from a community-wide to a strictly Tejano celebration. Editors from local newspapers seemed at a loss even to identify what San Fernando congregants were doing around 12 December, once mistaking their cannonading as a tribute to the editor of a local paper upon his marriage, another time speculating that bell ringing on the days before 12 December was because Christmas and the mayoral elections were imminent. Although Anglo Americans attended San Antonio Guadalupe celebrations during the early 1840s when Tejanos still formed the overwhelming majority of the population, all reports of the celebrations from 1845 to 1860 mention only the participation of Mexican-descent residents.[30]

The case of the Samuel and Mary Maverick family, Protestants who settled at San Antonio in 1838, illustrates the shift in the Guadalupe feast from a town-wide to an ethnic celebration. Before Texas statehood, the Mavericks attended Guadalupe festivities and exchanged social calls with prominent Tejano families. But Mary Maverick's memoirs record no instances of attendance at Guadalupe celebrations or other Tejano events after U.S. annexation, as Anglo Americans were now sufficient in number to establish their own congregations and social circles. Various observers noted the social breach illuminated on occasions like the Guadalupe feast. During an 1859 visit to the city Methodist bishop George F. Pierce wrote that "the old and the new live side by side—different races, unlike in origin, government, education, religion, domestic habits and national destiny, constitute the population—neither materially affecting the other; each perpetuating the customs peculiar to them while separate."[31]

The association of Guadalupe with an emergent ethnic identity in a contested urban environment was also evident in the physical appearance of San Fernando parish. The parish's few sacred images included the *morena* Guadalupe and a "wooden figure of a Mexican representing Christ on the cross." These representations symbolically reinforced Mexican-descent congregants' dignity and connection to celestial beings. Moreover, the church building, which had been the symbolic center of communal life and activity for over a century, retained its prominent location between the two central plazas of the city, a silent reminder of enduring Tejano presence and vitality. As one contemporary Anglo American visitor to San Antonio noted: "Around the plaza are American hotels, and new glass-fronted stores, alternating with sturdy battlemented Spanish walls, and confronted by the dirty, grim, old stuccoed stone cathedral, whose cracked bell is now clunking for vespers, in a tone that bids us no welcome, as more of the intruding race who have caused all this progress, on which its traditions, like its imperturbable dome, frown down." The enduring Tejano flavor of San Fernando was further confirmed by the actions of San Antonio's English- and German-speaking Catholics, who, after temporarily attending the Tejano parish of San Fernando, decided to build St. Mary's Church in the mid-1850s so they could have "a building in which the word of God may be constantly expounded in their own tongue."[32]

Although San Fernando parish and its Guadalupe feast-day celebrations often united congregants as they defended their dignity and collective identity, as during the Spanish and Mexican periods, at times they reinforced internal divisions like the class distinctions among Tejano parishioners. During the early 1840s the general populace participated in religious ceremonies, but afterward "the more prominent families taking the Patroness along with them . . . danced most of the night" in the homes of elite Tejanos. Thus the upper class reinforced their status by transporting to their exclusive festivity the principal ritual object used in religious services. For the 1841 Guadalupe celebration an elderly man and some of his friends purchased 150 pounds of powder for cannon and gun salutes; their donation reflected the long-standing custom of male elite sponsorship for Guadalupe's and other feast days.[33] After annexation a decline in Tejano economic fortunes, even among those few families who had previously been relatively prosperous, mitigated the class divisions evident in San Fernando's Guadalupe celebrations. No extant description of the Guadalupe feast from the 1850s mentions upper-class participants exercising prerogatives over less prominent devotees, as the downward trend in Tejanos' economic situation increasingly put them in a common disadvantaged position in relation to the Anglo American and German populations.

Women's leadership roles in Guadalupe celebrations contrasted with their subordinate social position, but also reinforced conventional views about ideal womanhood. Though Spanish law allowed women more expansive property rights than U.S. codes that were based on England's legal system, under Spanish and Mexican rule women endured inequalities in political affairs, the judicial system, and family life. Texas independence and U.S. annexation did not substantially alter the social and legal restrictions that kept Tejanas subservient. Advice columns that emerged in Spanish-language newspapers throughout the Southwest promoted piety, nurture, domesticity, and moral propriety as feminine ideals; in the words of one male editor, "the mother is the priestess, the mother has a great mission to fulfill on earth, to form souls through her virtue." The expectation that they embrace these ideals also shaped the lives of single women, such as San Antonio–area resident Adina De Zavala, who at age twenty wrote in her journal: "My life is only for my family. My whole life shall be worth while if I can render happy and comfortable the declining years of my parents and see my brothers safely launched on life's troubled seas." But not all girls and women embraced the expectations placed on them. In a complaint that in part reflects a generational difference, De Zavala's *ahijada* (goddaughter), who lived on the outskirts of San Antonio, lamented bitterly in her diary the double standard that kept her secluded in her home—"I don't go anywhere"—while her brother enjoyed the freedom of riding in the countryside and going into town.[34]

In this context, women's roles in planning Guadalupe celebrations, directing recitations of the rosary and other prayers, and accompanying their patroness as attendants provided them with rare opportunities to exercise public community leadership. At the same time, these leadership roles were limited. They reflected an extension of domestic responsibilities into ritual, reinforced the notion that piety was primarily the responsibility of women, and symbolically linked the purity of young girls dressed in white with the Virgin Mary, a communal accentuation of feminine chastity in the absence of a corresponding association between young boys and Jesus.

Reconstruction and Increased Mexican Immigration

After the Civil War, Tejano political clout diminished further. Mexican-descent electees accounted for fewer than 3 percent of city council members from 1865 to 1900, a sevenfold reduction from their already low representation during the twenty years following U.S. annexation. Their lack of power in local affairs was clearly evident in 1896, when San Antonio political leaders T. J. McMinn and Jack Evans sought to legally block the naturalization application of Mexican immigrant Ricardo Rodríguez, a maintenance worker for the city who had resided in San Antonio for thirteen years. Though McMinn and Evans were unsuccessful, their contention that Rodríguez was not "a white person, nor an African, nor of African descent" and was "therefore not capable of becoming an American citizen" intended unmistakable consequences for all San Antonio residents of Mexican descent, none of whom were among the "friends of the court" advising Judge T. S. Maxey on his decision. Judge Maxey eventually ruled in Rodríguez's favor, but Mexican-descent residents' ongoing battles to merely retain basic suffrage and citizenship rights illustrate their precarious position in political and social life. Furthermore, they were not equally protected by the criminal justice system: white assailants frequently went unpunished for violence against people of Mexican descent, such as the brutal 1896 murder of Aureliano Castellón, whose tormenters shot him eight times and then burned his body after he allegedly displayed romantic interest in a white woman.[35]

Despite numerous signs of modernization and economic development—such as a new city hall and county courthouse on the plazas on either side of San Fernando, as well as the city's first steam fire engine, railroad lines, electric street lights, water-pumping stations, faucets in private homes, telegraph line, telephone exchange, chartered banks, and streetcars—ethnic Mexicans' socioeconomic status continued to lag far behind that of Anglo Americans and European immigrants. Mexican-descent residents were concentrated in the barrios just west of San Fernando church. Commonly known by names like "Laredito" and "Chihuahua," these were ethnic enclaves that one traveler described derisively as a "collection of hovels, built of logs, stones, and dried mud, and thatched with

Mexican family in front of their *jacal* on the west side of San Antonio, c. 1880s. Courtesy Witte Museum, San Antonio.

brush or straw," where "the life of the eighteenth century still prevails, without taint of modernism."[36]

The development that most dramatically changed San Antonio was the arrival of the railroad; the first train reached the city on 19 February 1877. An 1866 newspaper article had argued defensively that San Antonio was "no quiet country village, sleeping in the sunshine till some invading railroad wakes it into existence," but twenty-five years later a different observer boldly claimed that "the railroads, indeed, have been the making of San Antonio" into a contender aspiring "to be known as the Texas City of Progress." The railroad accelerated population growth and accentuated San Antonio's prestige as a trade center. Far from closing the income gap between ethnic Mexicans and Anglo Americans, however, the arrival of the railroad decimated the Tejano-dominated trade of transporting goods by cart and horse, which in 1850 had supplied jobs for one-fourth of the local labor force.[37]

San Antonio's racial and ethnic diversity increased further and became even more visibly evident in the city's public festivals. According to municipal records, in 1876 ethnic Mexicans were fewer than one-fourth of the city's 17,314 residents; both Germans and Anglo Americans had eclipsed them in numbers. As

Judith Berg Sobré has shown, the distinct groups vied for civic eminence by organizing events that celebrated their heritage and enabled "outsiders to see, hear, and taste what they had preserved from their 'old country' way of life." Public festivals included German Volksfests, the African American celebration of Juneteenth to commemorate emancipation in Texas, Italian festivities for Columbus Day, the resurgent observance of Mexican Independence Day, expanded festivities for the Fourth of July, and the Battle of Flowers Parade—the founding event of today's internationally renowned Fiesta San Antonio—which prominent Anglo American women initiated in 1891 to commemorate the Texas victory over Mexican forces at San Jacinto. Reflecting national trends like the development of town and municipal festivals and the nascent pageant movement, the expanding list of civic ceremonies at San Antonio illuminated an ethnic competition in which the promotion of U.S. patriotic sentiment gained ascendancy.[38]

Immigration from south of the border increased during the long rule of Mexican president Porfirio Díaz (1876–1911), whose repression of his political adversaries, promotion of agribusiness to the detriment of village land ownership, and expansion of rail transportation induced and facilitated the relocation of many Mexican nationals. During the last decades of the nineteenth century, these newcomers formed a recognizable group of citizens from the Republic of Mexico in San Antonio, founding newspapers, *mutualistas* (mutual aid societies), and social clubs. In 1879, Dr. Plutarco Ornelas became the first resident consul for the Republic of Mexico in the city. Though most Mexican nationals in San Antonio were at the lower end of the socioeconomic ladder, wealthier immigrants were sufficient in number to unite with a small but persistent group of leading Tejano figures to form associations like the Mexican Social Club, an organization that comprised San Antonio's elite Mexican-descent population.[39]

Organizations like the Sociedad Benevolencia Mexicana (Mexican Benevolent Society), Sociedad Mutualista Benito Juárez (Benito Juárez Mutual Aid Society), and Sociedad Beneficia de Señoras y Señoritas (Benefit Society of Married and Single Women) revived local Mexican Independence Day celebrations, which attracted sizeable crowds from San Antonio and the environs, including some Anglo American politicians and other non-Mexicans. The Mexican consul's prominent participation in the celebrations symbolized the growing presence of Mexican immigrants, who joined with Tejanos to organize festivities that included parades, patriotic orations, the grito of independence, the singing of the Mexican national anthem, fireworks, gun salutes, and dances. Social-class di visions among ethnic Mexican participants were evident in the festivities, as in 1878 when an organization comprising twenty-four day laborers planned civic ceremonies and a celebration for the general populace, while "only the very best of our Mexican citizens, with their friends, attended" a formal ball. Reflecting the anticlerical trends in Mexico that gave rise to the 1859 Reform Laws under Mexican president Benito Juárez, both Catholic services like the Mass and the public role of priests were conspicuously less prominent or completely absent, in sharp contrast to Independence Day celebrations at San Antonio (and in Mexico) earlier in the century. Instead, participants honored Guadalupe's civic role as the banner for Mexican Independence, raising cheers for Our Lady of Guadalupe, the independence of Mexico, and the heroic Father Miguel Hidalgo, who had led the independence struggle.[40]

Newcomers to San Antonio influenced developments at San Fernando church, which congregational leaders renovated and enlarged before Pope Pius IX declared it a cathedral in 1874. Like most San Fernando clergy during the second half of the nineteenth century, as well as women religious who established schools and hospitals within the parish boundaries, the architect for the project, François Giraud, was French. The construction included a new nave built over the existing structure, which itself was renovated for ongoing use as a sanctuary. About a third of the previous church was removed, and a new bell tower replaced the original one. According to scholar of church architecture Willard B. Robinson, the resulting edifice, with its stark verticality, "is essentially a French design transplanted to Texas." A few new saints' images that adorned the cathedral, such as the statues of the Virgin Mary and St. Joseph donated by wealthy Catholic citizens Joseph E. Dwyer and Honoré Grenet, enhanced the effort to transform the Spanish colonial church into a contemporary cathedral in the neo-Gothic French style.[41]

With its new status as a cathedral, San Fernando hosted rites like the installation and ordination of bishops, the celebration of a papal jubilee, ceremonies for the 1892 Columbian anniversary, and visits from ecclesiastical dignitaries like Cardinal James Gibbons of Baltimore and Archbishop Francis Satolli, the pope's first apostolic delegate to the United States. The observance of Tejano feasts diminished. Bishop Anthony Dominic Pellicer, the first bishop of the new San Antonio diocese (1874–1880), prohibited the traditional Christmas eve celebration of midnight Mass with adoration of the Holy Child "because of the intrusion of improper and disorderly persons with the vast throngs of all classes, races, and religions, who poured into the cathedral" on that occasion. An 1869 newspaper

San Fernando Cathedral, c. 1880s. Due to a shortage of funds, the second bell tower was not added until 1903. Courtesy Center for American History, University of Texas at Austin, Prints and Photographs Collection, CN#04656.

report related that on the feast of San Juan "troops of boys and men rode through the city on horseback" all day, but travelers who visited the city in the early 1880s observed that a city ordinance had at last banned such displays, ending the Tejano practice of spending feast days "galloping through the streets" after "devoutly attending church."[42]

As certain established practices at San Fernando declined or were even prohibited, some Mexican Catholic religious traditions thrived apart from the parish center. On several occasions San Fernando parishioners reportedly enacted the *pastorela*, a dramatic proclamation of the shepherds who worshiped the child Jesus, but at some point the parish no longer hosted these rites. The first dated report of a pastorela presented in a private home was from 1881, the last year of the episcopal ban on San Fernando's Christmas Eve rites. Thereafter devotees celebrated the festive pastorelas in homes, public halls, and private shrines throughout the Christmas season, but not at San Fernando Cathedral. In 1894, the local community flocked to see Don Pedro Jaramillo, a renowned figure in the healing tradition of *curanderismo* who ignited such a dramatic response in San Antonio that even Anglo Americans and other city residents waited in the long lines to see him. Mexican-descent residents also exhibited

Earliest known photograph of San Fernando church interior, 1877. Courtesy San Antonio Conservation Society. Photo from University of Texas Institute of Texan Cultures, San Antonio.

their religious fervor at La Capilla de Nuestro Señor de los Milagros (the Chapel of Our Lord of the Miracles), a private shrine that reportedly housed a crucifix rescued from a fire or other disaster at San Fernando church during the early nineteenth century. Members of the Ximénez and Rodríguez families, who were joined by marriage, had founded and served as caretakers of the chapel, which, it was said at the time, "always has devotees within it whenever it is open." To this day the chapel attracts supplicants from near and far.[43]

Despite changes at the parish and in the rituals, devotions, and civic ceremonies practiced in San Antonio, San Fernando remained an ethnic Mexican congregation. Texas-born Mexicans made up more than two-thirds of the 4,041 parishioners listed in a 1901 parish census, while an additional 26.6 percent were born in Mexico. The triumphant assertion of Catholic clergy that "Mexicans

Participants in the *pastorela* enactment of the shepherds coming to worship the infant Jesus, San Antonio, 1893. Courtesy University of Texas Institute of Texan Cultures, San Antonio, #68-533.

shall never become Protestants" proved false over the following century: Methodist preachers of Mexican descent ministered in the city by the 1870s— Reverend Jesús Martínez was even arrested for allegedly interfering with a Catholic religious service—and Protestant congregations numbered at least nineteen by the 1890s. Still, throughout the nineteenth century the participation of ethnic Mexicans in Protestant denominations continued to be relatively sparse, enhancing the perception that San Fernando was overwhelmingly San Antonio's Mexican religious enclave. One observer wrote that many members of the cathedral congregation were descendants of the original parishioners. Another described San Fernando as "an old, venerable Spanish cathedral, where dark-brown penitents kneel on cold stones, saying their beads." Yet another stated bluntly that "San Fernando Cathedral is Mexican Catholic."[44]

Some San Fernando celebrations and traditions confirmed perceptions about the parish's Mexican Catholic character. At Christmastime parishioners' residences were "decorated and illuminated by numerous candles," and after Bishop Pellicer's successor, Jean Claude Neraz, lifted the episcopal ban on Christmas Eve rites at San Fernando, "Christ in the manger was represented before the altar, where all had an opportunity to kneel and kiss the infant Saviour." Visitors to the city noted ethnic Mexicans' practice of removing their hats and facing San Fernando while the church bells tolled at the noon hour, an audible reminder for Catholics to recite the Marian prayer of the Angelus. In 1897 La Sociedad Católica de San Fernando, which cathedral congregants had recently formed, solemnized the feast of San Fernando. They organized a procession from the bishop's residence on nearby Dwyer Avenue to the cathedral, where the prelate presided over a sung Mass. Participants included priests, Incarnate Word sisters who served in the parish, children from the parochial school and a neighboring orphanage, and members of the Sociedad de las Madres Católicas (Society of Catholic Mothers) and the Hijas de María (Daughters of Mary), the San Fernando chapter of a young women's pious society inspired by the Marian visions of French sister Catherine Labouré (1806–1876). Groups like the Hijas reflect the French influence on congregation members, but the pious societies' and foreign priests' and sisters' involvement in patronal feasts like that of San Fernando reveals their adaptation to local religious traditions.[45]

San Fernando parishioners also continued to celebrate the Guadalupe feast, though far less conspicuously, particularly during the 1870s, when the proportion of ethnic Mexicans in San Antonio's population reached its low point and San Fernando became the cathedral of the city's first resident bishop. An 1868 newspaper report stated that during the week of the feast the bells at San Fernando "kept up an incessant ringing" and "services of some kind or other seem to be going on all the time." But over the following decade San Fernando congregants reduced their commemoration of the Guadalupe feast to Mass and other prayer services offered within the confines of their parish church, in what one observer described as solemn, "befitting ceremonies." One elderly San Antonio resident, identified as Don Pablo, reportedly bemoaned the decline of feast days like Guadalupe's, which had previously been "celebrated with their ancient splendor" at San Fernando church, accompanied by "the annual Fairs on the Plaza ... illuminated with rockets and fireworks, and echoing the sound of drums and violins." Faced with the lack of such festivities, numerous ethnic Mexicans returned to Mexico for the Guadalupe feast. By the 1890s as many as eight hundred San Antonio passengers rode in train excursions to the border town of Nuevo Laredo for the "bull fights and fiestas" connected with Guadalupe celebrations there.[46]

The Guadalupe celebrations brought San Antonio Tejanos together in worship even amidst the political factionalism of Reconstruction. Most Tejanos were pro-Union before the Civil War, but with the outbreak of hostilities several joined their Democratic allies from the 1850s Know Nothing political controversies and enlisted in the Confederate forces. In the tumultuous decade following the war some Tejanos, particularly members of the older and more influential families, aligned with the ex-Confederate Anglo Americans who dominated the Democrats. Others joined the Radicals, who advocated for African American voting and citizenship rights. Each group of Tejano activists formed its own political club and had its own Spanish-language newspaper. In 1868, the conflict between the two factions was so pronounced that they organized opposing celebrations for Mexican Independence Day. Both Democrats and the San Fernando clergy denounced the Radicals as anti-Catholic. Nonetheless, on the Guadalupe feast three months after the divisive Mexican Independence Day celebrations, the Radicals, whose differences with the clergy allegedly had been resolved, "in uniform, marched to the old Catholic Cathedral" and participated in services with their coreligionists.[47]

Newly arrived Mexican immigrants had divergent attitudes toward Guadalupan devotion that reflected the brewing church-state tensions in their homeland. Catholic officials in Mexico had developed a tacit understanding with President Porfirio Díaz regarding church educational and construction projects, easing decades of conflict between Díaz's predecessors and the Catholic hierarchy. Bishop Neraz, a popular pastor whom many ethnic Mexicans welcomed as a successor to the sterner Bishop Pellicer, celebrated Mass for the San Fernando Guadalupe feast in 1883, after which "a deputation of gentlemen for the [predominantly immigrant] Mexican Benevolent Association, presented the bishop with a handsome and costly chair." On the other hand, some Mexican immigrants who resettled at San Antonio, particularly many elites, were both estranged from the church and disaffected by the policies of the Díaz government. Two 1895 editorials in San Antonio's *El Regidor* newspaper accused Mexican officials like Díaz of using Guadalupan devotion to distract and appease the Mexican masses. Commenting on the highly publicized coronation of Guadalupe at the Guadalupe basilica in Mexico City during October of that year, the editorialist asked rhetorically about the numerous pilgrims who journeyed to Mexico City for the coronation ceremonies: "But what does all this prove? Only that there are fanatics who spend on pipes and flutes significant sums of money that could serve the poor and the public good." He urged his readers to forget "superstitious practices" and foster "honorable sentiments of human dignity and justice." Significantly, these pointed criticisms represented the first recorded public rift among ethnic Mexicans at San Antonio regarding the advisability of Guadalupan devotion.[48]

Primary sources for Guadalupe celebrations in the latter decades of the nineteenth century are limited and do not indicate what roles women and men exercised in organizing and enacting the community's Guadalupan devotion. Intentionally or not, however, the reduction of San Fernando's Guadalupe feast-day celebrations to church services eliminated the leadership responsibilities women and girls had previously undertaken for public Guadalupe processions. The influx of a number of more elite Mexican immigrants, which facilitated the class divisions evident in Mexican Independence Day celebrations and organizations like the Mexican Social Club, also influenced Guadalupan festivities. After one feast-day ceremony at San Fernando, male and female residents named Guadalupe celebrated the feast "as their saint's day with suppers, balls, and receiving numerous presents and well wishes according to their social standing."[49]

Faith, Ethnicity, and Survival

Scholars of the nineteenth-century Southwest, such as Arnoldo De León, have shown that the history of Mexicans who were incorporated into the United States during U.S. territorial expansion "is not solely a story of people victimized by oppression. It is much more the history of actors who have sought to take measures in their own behalf for the sake of a decent living." Along with armed resistance, political activism, the establishment of ethnic associations, participation in unions, the ongoing use of the Spanish language, and the authorship of writings that recorded and defended their historical legacy, Mexicans embraced public ritual and devotion as one such measure "in their own behalf." Many ethnic communities were struggling for survival, of course, and in places like Nacogdoches, Texas, and Santa Barbara, California, "some cultural activities disappeared altogether." Nonetheless, throughout the Southwest many Mexican-descent devotees sustained and adapted traditions such as patronal feast days, la pastorela, pilgrimages, Holy Week, and the feast of Corpus Christi. As Guadalupe's popularity continued to expand after Mexican independence, celebrations of her feast multiplied and became noteworthy events in places like Monterey, California; Santa Rita, Texas (near Brownsville); and Conejos, Colorado.[50]

In the face of tumultuous changes and pressures like those that San Antonio Tejanos endured—military takeover, political and economic displacement, rapid demographic change, violence and lawlessness, ethnic rivalry, the erosion of cultural hegemony, the negative attitudes of some European Catholic clergy toward their faith expressions, Protestant critiques, and attempts to ban, replace, or curtail their traditions—the enactment of Mexican Catholic feasts and religious practices took on heightened significance as public expressions of faith, identity, and resistance. As Bishop Henry Granjon of Tucson observed, in the Southwest the initiatives of Mexican-descent Catholics "to observe their own traditions and customs as they did before the annexation of their lands by the American Union" enabled them to "maintain the unity of the Mexican population and . . . resist, to a certain extent, the invasions of the Anglo-Saxon race."[51]

Guadalupan devotion at San Fernando illustrates a transformation that was common in the former Mexican territories: the evolution of community-wide religious traditions like patronal feasts into markers of group identity within a culturally and religiously diverse milieu. No longer revered as the primary patroness of all San Antonians, Guadalupe became a guardian of ethnic Mexicans within a multiethnic urban landscape. Guadalupe feast-day celebrations complemented traditions like the Christmas devotions practiced at San Fernando and the pastorelas and other devotions enacted in private shrines and homes; together these formed a symbolic array of Mexican Catholic faith expressions. Along with resurgent civic ceremonies for Mexican Independence Day, which included acclamations of Guadalupe as Mexico's national symbol, these ritual expressions differentiated Mexican-descent San Antonians from other city residents, reflecting and shaping an emergent ethnic identity among San Fernando congregants and other residents of Mexican heritage.

Mexican Catholic traditions were not merely one set of practices in a pluralistic, egalitarian society, however. Rather, these traditions expressed the faith, identity, struggle for dignity, and defensive posture of a community under siege. The significance of traditions like Guadalupan devotion for their practitioners is evident in their survival despite sweeping changes like the removal of San Fernando's native clergy and the termination of the town council's organizing role in the Guadalupe feast. Far from eradicating parishioners' devotion, these actions fueled a fear and anger at their economic and political displacement that impelled Mexican-descent Catholics to continue their faith traditions despite the loss of established support structures. As ethnic and denominational pluralism generated group rivalries and Anglo Americans sought to symbolically express their dominance by establishing a prevalent annual cycle of "American" holiday festivities, Mexican-descent Catholics proclaimed their ethnic legitimacy through Guadalupan devotion and other religious and cultural traditions. In the midst of the racial slurs and subordinate social status they endured, devotees' acclamation of their patroness affirmed the honor of their Mexican heritage and the dignity they possessed as children of the brown-skinned Guadalupe.

But if nineteenth-century Guadalupan devotion at San Fernando confirms the insight of scholars and pastoral leaders like Bishop Ricardo Ramírez that faith expressions can engender believers' instinctive reaffirmation of their God-given human dignity and serve as "a defense and protest against the demands of the dominant culture,"[52] it also illuminates the potential limitations of this symbolic resistance. Shifting social conditions, group interactions, and the exploits of historical actors can thwart the effectiveness of collective ritual action. This was evident in the decline of ethnic Mexican traditions at San Fernando due to changing demographics, public criticism and pressure, legal proscriptions, the hegemony of religious professionals like foreign bishops and priests, the privatization of many religious practices, competition from civic ceremonies, and the anticlerical attitudes of some Mexican émigrés. Commenting on Guadalupe celebrations in their homeland, immigrant editorialists even argued that Guadalupan devotion hindered the promotion of equality, human dignity, and social well-being. This critique was reflected in San Antonio before Emancipation and during Reconstruction, when Guadalupan devotion united Tejanos and their political factions but did not play a conspicuous role in their debate about extending the rights of full citizenship to African Americans.

Class and gender divisions within San Fernando Guadalupe celebrations weakened the potential of Guadalupan devotion to mediate group solidarity, demonstrating that the capacity of a religious tradition to unite a group for collective protest and defense does not always lead to a corresponding examination of inequalities in its own ranks. Indeed, these inequalities are sometimes deemed inconsequential compared to the "larger" concern of uniting to defend group honor and interests, and they are sometimes even sacralized in ritual events as a supposedly necessary component of group cohesion. As new generations arose who had no personal memory of the San Fernando Guadalupe festivals and processions during the Spanish, Mexican, and antebellum periods, Guadalupan devotion came to express a multifaceted and fractured struggle for dignity and survival rather than serving as a unified representation of symbolic resistance. Still, ongoing commemoration of the Guadalupe feast and the popularity of December excursions to Mexico revealed that the desire for Guadalupan festivities was not quenched, nor was the capacity of Guadalupe to shape devotees' faith and express their ethnic affirmation. Accelerating Mexican immigration during the first decades of the twentieth century exponentially increased the connections between San Antonio and Mexico, rejuvenating San Fernando's public Guadalupan devotion and reshaping its links to devotees' congregational life, collective identity, and sense of the sacred.

CHAPTER 4

Companion in *el Exilio*, 1900–1940

The disturbing headlines of the 15 December 1931 *La Prensa*, San Antonio's leading Spanish-language newspaper and the most prominent publication of elite Mexican exiles in the city, revealed the mix of anguish and jubilation that marked celebrations of the four hundredth anniversary of Our Lady of Guadalupe's apparitions to Juan Diego. Announcing the "threat of a new religious conflict," *La Prensa* reported that Mexican government officials had condemned as an "affront to the Mexican Revolution" the celebrated quadricentennial festivities at Mexico City's Guadalupe basilica. Prominent government leaders had called for punitive actions against the clergy, civic functionaries who attended ceremonies at the basilica, and journalists who reported favorably on the celebrations. Catholic leaders offered more strident views on church-state relations in Mexico; from exile in San Antonio, Bishop José de Jesús Manríquez y Zárate wrote a pastoral letter that claimed the church in Mexico suffered "a true Babylonian captivity" and turned to Our Lady of Guadalupe as the sole "liberator and defender of our faith and nationality."[1]

For thousands of Mexican citizens who, like Bishop Manríquez y Zárate, migrated to San Antonio during and after the Mexican Revolution (1910–1917), smoldering church-state conflicts in Mexico exacerbated their anguish for their afflicted and war-torn homeland, intensifying their religious devotion and provoking them to "vie with their compatriots across the Rio Grande in doing honor to their queen and patroness." In sharp contrast to commemorations of the Guadalupe feast at San Fernando Cathedral during the late nineteenth century, massive public Guadalupe processions were conducted around San Fernando Cathedral and around new parish churches, such as Our Lady of Guadalupe, which was constructed by Mexican Catholics on San Antonio's west side who "could find neither peace nor happiness until they could kneel down and pray at the feet of la Virgen de Guadalupe in her own church." Spanish-language media seemed to compete with Catholic parishes in fostering Guadalupan devotion, with an all-day radio broadcast of the 1931 feast-day events at the Guadalupe basilica and various newspaper articles attesting to Guadalupe's numerous miracles and narrating her apparitions to Juan Diego. *La Prensa* dedicated its weekly Sunday magazine to a historical overview of Guadalupe in Mexico and gave front-page coverage to Guadalupe celebrations for four straight days. San Antonio archbishop Arthur J. Drossaerts described the affection of Mexican-descent Catholics for Guadalupe as "deeply ingrained in their soul."[2]

Guadalupe's power to captivate devotees at San Fernando, especially émigrés undergoing the agony of a recent separation from their homeland, was clearly evident in the 1931 feast-day celebrations, the most extensive since the parish's founding two centuries earlier. Parish bulletin announcements accentuated the significance of the celebrations "for all those who feel Mexican blood run through their veins, as well as for native Tejanos." To commemorate the quadricentennial, San Fernando parishioners held a novena, including a daily sung Mass offered in solidarity "for the persecuted church in Mexico." They also donated a replica of la Virgen Morena that was blessed and prominently enshrined in the cathedral, a visual expression of piety that helped refashion San Fernando's relatively barren interior and create a sense of belonging and homecoming among Mexican-descent Catholics. On 11 December, the eve of the feast, a large procession wound through the streets and plazas around the cathedral. For the feast itself, huge crowds attended the five scheduled masses, another evening public procession, and the closing service of the novena. One parish society reported that the congregation celebrated the novena and feast with "extraordinary solemnity"; San Fernando clergy stated that the immense crowds and devotional fervor expressed in the religious services were a fitting tribute to Guadalupe for the countless favors she had granted "her chosen people, the beautiful

Mexican nation." The solemnity of sung masses, the rhythmic hum of devotees responding in unison as they prayed the rosary, the resounding message of Spanish-language sermons on Guadalupe and her covenant relationship with Mexico, and street processions that interwove religious and national symbols attested that, though many Guadalupan devotees at San Fernando had recently left Mexico, dedication to their homeland and its national patroness had not left them.[3]

During the first four decades of the twentieth century, Guadalupan devotion at San Fernando increasingly reflected the conflicting sentiments of exile:[4] hope and fear, patriotism and protest, trust in celestial protection and humble acquiescence to divine reprimand, longing for home and struggles over cultural expectations in a new land. At the same time, in the face of Anglo American hostility and prejudice, the transformation of San Fernando's annual Guadalupe celebrations into intense rituals of exile expressed confident assurance that the despised ethnic Mexican residents were a chosen people; the celebrations invigorated native Tejanos' faith and ethnic pride. Guadalupe was a treasured companion whose faithful encountered her most intensely in the midst of displacement and discrimination; her annual feast provided a ritual arena for devotees to forge and celebrate an alternative world: one in which daily lived realities like exile, racism, and gender and generational differences could be reimagined and renegotiated. Thus even as self-proclaimed exile leaders exerted a conspicuous influence on San Fernando's Guadalupe celebrations, parishioners and other participants engaged Guadalupan devotion as a means to address not only the situation in Mexico but also their own needs and aspirations as residents of the United States. The diverse meanings of Guadalupan devotion at San Fernando cannot be understood without an examination of the shifting urban and congregational contexts in which parishioners enacted rituals and devotions.

The Urban Context: Immigrants, Municipal Growth, and Social Conflict

Demographic changes in San Antonio facilitated the exuberant devotion evident in the 1931 Guadalupe celebrations. Dire warnings from Mexican government officials and popular sentiment about the perils émigrés faced in the United States—one *corrido* (ballad) pleaded "Don't go to the gringo" because he will "beat you like a slave and humiliate your country"—did not deter unprecedented numbers of Mexicans from migrating northward, especially after the out-

break of the Mexican Revolution in 1910. Intermittent periods of relative calm
followed the enactment of the 1917 Mexican Constitution, but spontaneous violence erupted once again in central and western Mexico when President
Plutarco Elías Calles (1924–1928) enforced and expanded the constitution's anticlerical articles. The resulting guerrilla war, known as the Cristero Rebellion
(1926–1929), drove even more émigrés north to the United States. Many were
fleeing religious persecution, and the majority were from the Mexican states
where hostilities raged most violently, such as Michoacán, Guanajuato, and
Jalisco. By 1930 the head of the household in two-thirds of the ethnic Mexican
families in San Antonio was Mexican-born, though indicators such as residential patterns and intermarriage rates continued to blur distinctions between
Mexican émigrés and Tejanos while sharpening the social distance between them
and Anglo Americans. Some Mexican nationals in the city supported revolutionary movements: after fleeing house arrest in Mexico, Francisco I. Madero
launched his successful campaign to overthrow Mexican president Porfirio Díaz
from San Antonio, then served as Mexico's president for two years until his 1913
assassination. But as control of Mexico seesawed among various revolutionary
leaders and factions, Mexican newcomers to the city included growing numbers
of émigrés disaffected with the revolution, including political conservatives who
had supported Díaz.[5]

During the 1930s the Great Depression and an accompanying wave of na-
tivist fever led to the repatriation of numerous Mexicans and the illegal deportation of many Tejanos—native-born citizens of the United States who increasingly identified themselves as "Mexican Americans." Also, Mexican president
Lázaro Cárdenas and Catholic Church officials eased church-state conflicts in
1936, opening the door for some Mexicans to return home. Despite these developments, however, many Mexican nationals stayed and, along with a growing number of Mexican American migrants from rural areas to urban centers like
San Antonio, augmented the city's Mexican-descent population significantly.
The San Antonio Public Service Company reported that in 1900 San Antonio
had 13,722 Mexican-descent residents, just over a fourth of the total population.
For 1940, the same source revealed that some 103,000 Mexican-descent residents accounted for more than 40 percent of the city's total population. In the
meantime, social pressure to prove their allegiance to the United States, as well
as the decline of European immigration, led most of San Antonio's sizable Ger-
man-descent population to amalgamate with Anglo Americans in the wake of
World War I. San Antonio's social dynamics therefore increasingly revolved

around an Anglo-Mexican binary split, as many descendants of European immigrants lost their language and cultural traditions, and African Americans, whose proportion of the population was halved from 14 percent in 1900 to 7 percent in 1940, were segregated on the east side of the city and frequently ignored in municipal life.[6]

Among other changes in San Antonio's urban landscape, the city's expanding population increased the number of churches. San Antonio had more than thirty Catholic parishes in 1940, a threefold increase over four decades. In 1900 San Fernando was the only Catholic parish in which Mexican Americans and Mexicans formed the majority; by 1940 at least ten more parishes served predominantly Mexican-descent congregations. The number of Protestant churches also grew rapidly, as did outreach to Spanish-speaking residents by the Baptists, Presbyterians, Methodists, Lutherans, and Disciples of Christ, all of which had at least one Spanish-language congregation or mission by the mid 1920s. Archbishop Drossaerts expressed alarm about this expansion of Spanish-language Protestant ministries in a 1929 speech: "During some jubilee celebration of the combined Protestant churches of the city some seven years ago, my heart ached sorely when I had to see over one thousand of our Mexicans boldly proclaiming their Protestant allegiance, carrying an enormous open Bible in the parade and singing hymns as they marched, which surely were not the lovely Spanish hymns they learned to sing in their younger days, in honor of the Blessed Mother of God."[7]

During these decades the size of the San Fernando congregation more than doubled, and its composition changed from predominantly Tejano to predominantly Mexican. Annual parish reports from 1911 to 1940 indicate that the combined total of Tejano and Mexican worshipers was at least ten thousand, a figure that is still the largest in the congregation's history. A 1930 newspaper article stated that San Fernando had more Mexican members than any other parish in San Antonio. By 1940 the cathedral was so renowned a home for Mexican-descent faithful that one researcher noted: "All Mexican people who do not belong to any other Mexican parish by right belong to San Fernando parish."[8]

The growth of the San Fernando congregation was accompanied by its increased prestige within the institutional structures of the Roman Catholic Church. In 1926 Pope Pius XI established the archdiocese and province of San Antonio. Bishop Drossaerts, the local bishop since 1918, served as the first archbishop of San Antonio (1926–1940) and metropolitan of the ecclesiastical province, exercising a leadership role among other bishops in dioceses that were now under the San Antonio archdiocese's jurisdiction. San Fernando thus became, in official ecclesial parlance, a metropolitan cathedral, a change that further augmented the prominence of this center of Spanish-speaking Catholicism.

Increasing Mexican immigration exacerbated Anglo American hostility toward both Mexican émigrés and native Mexican Americans. By the 1920s Anglo American students had formed SSS (Stop Speaking Spanish) Clubs at public schools to ensure the enforcement of the Texas legislature's 1918 mandate for English-only instruction. A local Spanish-language newspaper reported in 1923 that "youths of our race have been villainously attacked by some individuals who ran at them in automobiles" and that local authorities arrested the victims rather than those who had assaulted them. In San Antonio's predominantly Anglo American north side neighborhoods, real estate covenants precluded Mexican home ownership and exacerbated residential segregation in the city. Sporadic efforts at union organizing among ethnic Mexican workers often met with vigorous resistance, as in 1938 when Emma Tenayuca and other organizers led thousands of Mexican-descent women pecan shellers in a strike to protest a wage reduction. Police dispersed the pickets with tear gas and clubs, and despite public statements of disapproval by state and federal officials, the San Antonio police chief persisted in his refusal to allow picketing. Sometimes anti-Catholic prejudice united Mexican-descent Catholics in common cause with their Anglo American and other coreligionists, as in 1924 when San Fernando priests announced from the pulpit that all Roman Catholics were "compelled" to cast ballots against a slate of candidates backed by the Ku Klux Klan. In other instances, Spanish-speaking Catholics met hostility and rejection at the doors of their own churches. Older parishioners recall that their people attended San Fernando because they were rebuffed at Anglo American parishes and told to attend the "Mexican church" where they "belonged."[9]

Most San Antonians of Mexican heritage experienced not only hostility but also poverty. To be sure, some benefited from San Antonio's economic boom during World War I and the 1920s as the establishment of Kelly, Brooks, and Randolph fields expanded an already extensive network of military installations. A growing tourism industry provided Mexican-descent residents with some additional economic opportunities. The city's first public library, automobiles, radio stations, movie theaters, and motorbuses were visible signs of success and progress, as were various new multistory buildings that sprouted up along the downtown streets near San Fernando Cathedral. But despite these developments, the emergence of a Mexican American middle class, and the presence of

Workers shelling pecans by hand at the Southern Pecan Shelling Company, San Antonio, 1938. Courtesy San Antonio Light Collection, University of Texas Institute of Texan Cultures, San Antonio, #1759-B.

some wealthy Mexican émigrés, a 1929 report indicated that almost 90 percent of Mexican-descent residents were in the city's poorest economic class. The vast majority of these residents lived in the barrio on the west side of the cathedral and the downtown area. Father Carmelo Tranchese, a Jesuit priest assigned to Our Lady of Guadalupe parish in 1932, described the barrio as "simply terrible. Those long rows of miserable huts in the Mexican Quarter, that exhausting heat, that resigned poverty painted on the faces of the Mexicans. . . . I am familiar with the slums of San Francisco, New York, London, Paris, and Naples, but those of San Antonio are the worst of all."[10]

Economic disparity was accompanied by disparity in political influence. The Texas state legislature instituted a poll tax in 1902 that was roughly equivalent to a full day's pay for an ethnic Mexican worker; until its repeal during the Civil Rights era this tax deterred numerous poor and working-class voters from exer-

In the center of the picture is San Fernando Cathedral with the second bell tower, added in 1903, amidst the growing urban landscape on San Antonio's Main Plaza, c. 1927. The Bexar County Courthouse is to the left of the cathedral, the city hall is behind it, and the Frost National Bank is to the right. Courtesy San Antonio Express News Collection, University of Texas Institute of Texan Cultures, San Antonio, #83–514.

cising the franchise. In 1923 the state legislature formally established the so-called White Man's Primaries, which had already been active in San Antonio for nearly five decades, further undermining the political representation of Mexican-descent people. Not surprisingly, from 1900 to 1940 citizens of Mexican heritage held fewer than 4 percent of San Antonio's city council posts.[11]

The debilitating influence of racism and poverty on Mexican-descent residents' sense of dignity and personhood was strikingly evident in Spanish-language newspaper advertisements for a color-altering cream that could "whiten the skin" in "three days." This product purportedly relieved ethnic Mexicans and other users from the "humiliation of dark and ugly skin." Implicitly drawing a connection between dark skin, poverty, and social status, the ad went on to declare that people with white skin "have greater success in business, love, society."[12]

Despite such signs that Mexican-descent San Antonians at least partially internalized the prevalent racist ideology, in some instances they struggled to promote their interests and to combat prejudice and oppressive social relations. Mexican Americans who were armed with the rights of citizenship sometimes led these efforts. A 1908 U.S. government report stated that in San Antonio, "There is usually a Mexican member—an American-born citizen of Mexican descent—on the school board to represent the Spanish-speaking people of the city." In a 1933 book published in San Antonio, World War I veteran J. Luz Sáenz stated that although Mexican Americans were honorable citizens who had "contributed with their blood" to the U.S. cause, their "worst war" was not against the Germans in Europe but against injustice "in the bosom of our native land."[13]

As more immigrants arrived and Anglo-Mexican ethnic tensions mounted, some Mexican Americans found it politically expedient to distinguish themselves from their Mexican counterparts. Various organizations that established San Antonio chapters during the 1920s, most prominently the League of United Latin American Citizens (LULAC), restricted their membership to U.S. citizens of Latin American descent. Though primarily an attempt by a nascent Mexican American middle class to promote "Americanization," good citizenship, and the use of the English language, LULAC also focused considerable attention on issues like school reform, increased Mexican American representation on juries and for other public duties, and an end to discrimination. Their promotion of what Richard García has called a "consciousness of duality"—the retention of elements from their Mexican heritage and the simultaneous adoption of the U.S. political and civic ethos—frequently pitted them against Mexican exile elites in a struggle to define the collective identity of the people of San Antonio's west side, which "was teeming with Mexicans of different social groupings, classes, and political ideas, as well as different levels of acculturation."[14]

Newcomers from Mexico also combated racism and discrimination. In 1916 the editors of *La Prensa*, the most prominent among some two dozen Spanish-language newspapers founded in San Antonio, published a series of articles on public education that persuaded the school board in nearby Austin to end segregated education for Mexican-descent children. Fourteen years later an editorialist for the paper complained bitterly that a "campaign dominated and controlled by the Anglo-Saxon element of America" was using the new medium of film to "project racial superiority" and stereotypically portray "the villain" as "a Mexican with long mustache, wide sombrero, and a pistol in his belt." He called on Spanish-speaking artists to combat these racist depictions by making movies that more accurately represented their people. In 1920 another San Antonio newspaper, *El Imparcial de Texas*, defended two Mexicans condemned to death by U.S. courts. *El Imparcial* was founded by Mexican émigré Francisco A. Chapa, a noted figure in the state Democratic party, who as editor often aired his political views in its pages. One *Imparcial* editorial presented a stinging rebuttal to negative pronouncements on Mexicans' character by former governor of Texas James Ferguson, denouncing Ferguson's conception of an allegedly "inferior race" as a "clamorous injustice." Mutualistas in San Antonio, which attracted numerous immigrant members as well as some native Mexican Americans and doubled in number to about twenty-five during the first decades of the twentieth century, also acted in the public arena to promote the concerns of the ethnic Mexican population. While focused primarily on immigrants' acute need to foster reciprocal relations of ethnic and economic solidarity, local mutualistas extended their practice of mutual support to struggles to desegregate swimming clubs and movie theaters, ban films that depicted Mexicans in derogatory and stereotypical ways, and defend the rights of compatriots incarcerated in U.S. prisons.[15]

Separate efforts to combat racism reflected antipathies, misunderstandings, and tensions between Mexican immigrants and native Mexican Americans. In his landmark 1926–1927 study of Mexican immigrants, Manuel Gamio concluded that the differences between the two groups were "purely superficial" and that they were drawn together by their common language, low social status, needs, ideals, tendency to intermarry, and the plight of enduring Anglo American prejudice. Nonetheless, he noted that "Mexicans who are American citizens . . . sometimes speak slightingly of the immigrants (possibly because the immigrants are their competitors in wages and jobs), and say that the immigrants should stay in Mexico." Gamio also opined that immigrants considered "the American of Mexican origin as a man without a country. He reminds him frequently of the inferior position to which he is relegated by the white American." Though his views reflected biases like his encouragement of repatriation, which George Sánchez and other scholars have critiqued, Gamio accurately depicted the tensions that arose among many ethnic Mexicans in San Antonio.[16]

Not surprisingly, differences between Mexicans and Mexican Americans were also evident in the immigrants' greater concern about events in Mexico. Mutualistas fostered Mexican nationalism, particularly through their ongoing organization of patriotic celebrations like the popular festivities for Mexican Independence Day. One immigrant stated bluntly, "I would rather cut my throat before changing my Mexican nationality," while a corrido attested that "he who denies his race is the most miserable creature. There is nothing in the world so vile as he. . . . A good Mexican never disowns the dear fatherland of his affections."[17]

The most influential voice shaping Mexican national consciousness in San Antonio was *La Prensa*. Founded by émigré Ignacio E. Lozano, the paper was run by Mexican elites whose expressed purpose was "to serve Mexico and Mexicans and to honor our native land whenever we have the opportunity to do so." They accomplished this by developing and propagating the ideology of *El México de Afuera* (literally, "Mexico abroad"), which depicted Mexicans in the United States not primarily as immigrants seeking economic opportunities or other personal gain but as exiles who had fled repressive conditions at home in order to preserve their national patrimony, and who awaited the opportune moment to return and initiate national reconstruction. The advocates of El México de Afuera explicitly promoted an unyielding dedication to a nationalistic spirit, Mexican national heroes, the Spanish language, Mexican citizenship, and a Catholic faith rooted in devotion to Mexico's national patroness, Our Lady of Guadalupe. *La Prensa*'s view of the exiles and their world resonated with many San Antonians and with others well beyond the city limits. While financial difficulties limited many Spanish-language newspapers' life span—fewer than half of those established at San Antonio lasted more than two years—*La Prensa* struck such a chord in readers that it endured for nearly five decades. Significantly, its circulation peaked at over thirty-two thousand in 1930, just after many exiles left Mexico during the Cristero Rebellion.[18]

As Juanita Luna Lawhn has shown, the patriotic exile vision of *La Prensa* and some other émigré newspapers encompassed promoting "traditional" roles and values for women, advocating both domesticity and the importance of "proper" behavior among single and married women alike. Kathleen May Gonzalas, a teacher in San Antonio's west side schools, concluded from her 1920s research on local Mexican family life that the husband "dictates to his wife what she is to do at all times and in all matters," but reportedly Mexican immigrant males also frequently complained about "the 'Americanized' Mexican women who dress like Americans and have the customs and habits of American women." As Mexican wives and daughters adapted to life in the U.S. milieu, particularly the increasing number of women who settled in urban environments like San Antonio and worked outside the home to support their families, they demanded greater autonomy in their private and public lives. Women's steadily expanding leadership in business, radio broadcasting, and organizations like LULAC, mutualistas, and unions—along with the tensions and disagreements that accompanied their rising prominence—illuminates this trend of Mexican-descent women asserting themselves and pursuing their aspirations.[19]

Clashes over women's behavior were particularly severe regarding the dating and courtship practices of younger women. Though generational conflicts between fathers and sons also occurred—in one corrido a father speaks for many of his compatriots when he says, "This I will never tolerate . . . that instead of being a cowboy [my son] goes out with writers"—attempts to direct the lives and actions of young women were far more intense. The primary means to achieve this control was through the practice of chaperonage, which, "though conjuring images of patriarchal domination," as Vicki Ruiz has insightfully noted, "is best understood as a manifestation of familial oligarchy whereby elders attempted to dictate the activities of youth for the sake of family honor." A young woman's purity influeced not only her own reputation, but that of her entire family. Often older women rather than men expressed concerns about feminine decorum, reflecting their primary responsibility for enforcing such expectations. One immigrant mother in San Antonio avowed that she "doesn't like the American customs in the matter of the liberty and way of behaving of the young women of this country—customs and ways of being by which her daughters have been influenced and which greatly concern her." Catholic leaders reinforced such convictions; in a 1926 pastoral letter Bishop Drossaerts decried the "unchaperoned automobile parties, . . . indecent dances, suggestive moving pictures, and . . . immodesty in dress" among young women and called on them to embrace "Mary Immaculate" as "the ideal of maidenly modesty and purity."[20]

Mexican-descent young women alternately responded to the practice of chaperonage with acceptance, rebellion, and circumvention or compromise. Faced with cosmetics, new styles in dress, images from advertising and popular culture, the greater freedoms many of their Anglo American female counterparts enjoyed, and in some cases their own status as wage earners whose financial contribution to family life seemed inconsistent with strict behavioral codes, numerous young women felt the expectations placed on them were unjust. Many especially resented the double standard they perceived in these expectations: reflecting on her first kiss, poet Bernice Zamora addressed the boy who had kissed her, "My mother said shame on you, my teacher said shame on you, and I said shame on me, and nobody said a word to you." Still, a number of young women conformed to family and church expectations. One immigrant man concluded that "when one falls in love with a girl one then wants to see 'if one can do something,' but if the girl won't let one" because she is Catholic or under the counsel of her elders, "then one has to be married by the church if one really cares for her."[21]

The Parish Context: Congregational Leadership and Devotional Piety

During the first decades of the twentieth century, exiled Mexican bishops and clergy assisted at San Fernando and influenced the life and devotion of the cathedral congregation. Their presence and influence were particularly evident during the Mexican Revolution and the Cristero Rebellion. For example, in 1914 five Mexican archbishops and eight bishops resided in San Antonio, awaiting a change in the political climate so they could return to their dioceses. Though not formally assigned to the cathedral, exiled bishops and priests were the first Mexican clergy to offer consistent service at San Fernando since the removal of Fathers Refugio de la Garza and José Antonio Valdéz in 1840. Apparently the San Fernando congregation appreciated their presence, as parish records frequently indicate high attendance at services led by the exiled clergy. When Bishop Maximino Ruiz of Chiapas preached at the triduum (three services) to Our Lady of Guadalupe in 1915, the parish chronicler for that year noted that "there was a great assemblage of faithful at all of the rites during these days." He went on to praise "the fervor and pious sentiments that they manifested."[22]

New clergy who were formally assigned to the cathedral also energetically promoted the spiritual growth of the congregation. Bishop John Anthony Forest, San Antonio's bishop from 1895 to 1911, invited priests and brothers of the Missionary Sons of the Immaculate Heart of Mary, or Claretians, to establish their first community house in the United States at San Fernando. Founded in 1849 by the Spaniard St. Anthony Claret (1807–1870), the Claretian missionaries had established a strong reputation for their preaching, as well as for their capacity to foster a lived Catholic faith through frequent reception of the sacraments and participation in pious societies. Bishop Forest invited them to San Fernando because he was impressed with the preaching missions that Claretians based in Mexico were conducting at various locales across the Southwestern

United States. Their seventy-six years of service at San Fernando commenced with the 1902 arrival of Fathers Bernabé Marinas, León Monasterio, and Camilo Torrente. Significantly, unlike the diocesan clergy they replaced, most of whom had been French during the last half of the nineteenth century, the Claretians were largely of Spanish origin and thus were native Spanish-speakers.[23]

The Claretians assigned to the cathedral congregation reported that Mexican-descent Catholics suffered from "religious ignorance" and required "much attention" to keep them "constant in the practice of their religious duties; otherwise, Protestants who are zealous here will get them." Today older parishioners recollect that the Spanish clergy were occasionally impatient and overbearing with their Mexican and Mexican American congregants. However, the same parishioners recall the tireless dedication of the Claretians in revitalizing San Fernando's sacramental and devotional life. While the size of the congregation did not change significantly from 1915 to 1930, for example, the number of communions received more than doubled. Extant primary sources confirm the priests' extensive ministrations in preaching and leading devotional services and in enriching the devotional space of the cathedral by procuring more than a dozen new statues, new stations of the cross, stained-glass windows, and a *nacimiento* (crib scene) for the Christmas season, adornments that transformed a liturgical space left relatively barren by the Claretians' predominantly French predecessors. The Spanish priests and brothers also fostered congregants' faith by collaborating with the religious orders that staffed the parochial school and the lay leaders and women religious who offered catechetical instruction.[24]

Parishioners launched and sustained efforts to ensure that their own sacred images were prominently displayed at the cathedral, and some acted on their own to procure new images, as María Jackson did in 1930 when she donated a new statue of St. Anthony in honor of her deceased mother, Francisca Luna. In other cases members of pious societies acted collectively, as during 1931 when members of the Asociación Nacional de los Vasallos de Cristo Rey (National Association of the Vassals of Christ the King), which Mexican exiles organized in both women's and men's sections at San Fernando in 1925, worked with their Claretian spiritual director to procure a Cristo Rey (Christ the King) statue. Despite the economic woes of the early Depression years, they raised $150 in less than five months. The image was blessed at San Fernando in January 1932, just three years after the end of the Cristero Rebellion, in which Mexican Catholics had fought under the banner of Cristo Rey and had declared him and Our Lady of Guadalupe the only legitimate rulers of their nation.[25]

The process of procuring Immaculate Heart of Mary and Our Lady of Guadalupe images in the early 1930s further illuminates the laity's influence on decision-making processes in the parish. In April 1931 the Claretians launched a campaign for donations to purchase a statue of their order's primary patroness, the Immaculate Heart of Mary. By the following week only twenty dollars had been collected, and the front page of the parish bulletin lamented that the "beloved of the Virgin seem to be very slow in . . . offering their generous cooperation to remedy this necessity." But over the next five weeks there was little improvement. The Claretians put the project on hold for six months, then renewed their plea for donations on 15 November as the parish prepared for the four hundredth anniversary of the Guadalupe apparitions. Again, however, the response to their appeal was minimal; over the following month they received a mere sixteen dollars. It took another two years to raise enough money for the statue. Significantly, in the midst of the first two faltering fund drives for the Immaculate Heart statue, congregants presented the parish with both the Cristo Rey statue and a Guadalupe *cuadro* (picture). Parish records mention no collections or other fundraising activities for the Guadalupe image, which devotees apparently secured on their own to mark Guadalupe's quadricentennial. According to the parish bulletin, a group of unnamed *padrinos* and *madrinas* (donors or "sponsors") presented the image for blessing and enshrinement at the cathedral during the novena of Guadalupe celebrations held that year.[26]

Parishioners exerted their strongest leadership and influence at San Fernando through the numerous parish societies and associations they helped establish and develop. By 1930, there were at least eighteen such organizations, twice as many as there had been three decades earlier. As elsewhere in the United States and throughout Latin America, pious societies at San Fernando served multiple purposes. Their explicit purpose was primarily religious, with membership requirements for observing codes of conduct, practicing specific devotions, and participating in sacramental celebrations like corporate communion (the group reception of communion by the members of a parish organization). In addition, these associations provided social networks and activities, communal support during time of illness or other critical need, the consolation of collective presence and prayer at funerals for deceased members, and a fundraising source for the parish. Moreover, as Edmundo Rodríguez has shown, in the face of growing urbanization pious societies enabled congregations like San Fernando to engender "a sense of belonging to human-size communities" despite many congregations' increasingly unwieldy size. However, in almost all cases the "communi-

Entrance procession for Mass at San Fernando Cathedral during Christmas season, c. 1950. The Guadalupe image that devotees presented and dedicated at the parish in 1931 is enshrined prominently at the right side of the sanctuary. Courtesy Esther Rodríguez.

ties" formed in pious societies were exclusively for members of a particular age group and gender.[27]

From the outset the Claretians praised the pious societies as the "principal supporters of the cathedral's worship life." They sought to animate and guide these societies by providing them with spiritual directors, endorsing association activities in bulletin announcements, and attending society-sponsored events, all as part of an effort to strengthen parishioners' faith and allegiance to the church. The cathedral clergy also enforced their conviction that worthy reception of holy communion required that members of parish associations be married within the church.[28]

Claretians' participation in the pious societies afforded parishioners their most frequent opportunities to interact with their pastors and spiritual directors and to influence decisions that shaped parish life. One clear example of lay initiative was the founding of the Asociación Nacional de los Vasallos de Cristo Rey. In August 1925 Mexican émigré Félix V. García and a group of compatriots organized the first parish-based women's and men's sections of the Vasallos. This exile association addressed the violence and political upheaval in their native Mexico by fostering the resurgence of religious practice among Mexicans, in the belief that this was "the most effective means to achieve the national reconstruction of our country."[29]

The Vasallos' first major project was to advance the goal of reviving Mexico's religious spirit by raising funds for a statue of the Sacred Heart of Jesus, an image they associated with Christ's kingship, near Cubilete, in the Mexican province of Guanajuato—significantly, at a mountaintop site located in the Cristero Rebellion's most embattled region, which the Vasallos claimed was "the geographic center of the Republic of Mexico, indeed, the heart of the entire nation." Members were to recite their commitment formula daily and proclaim it publicly at society events: "For the honor and glory of the Sacred Heart of Jesus, perpetual king of Mexico, I submit myself voluntarily as his vassal, promising to promote his interests and work until death to extend his sovereignty in my native land, always under the mantle of my holiest mother of Guadalupe, queen of the Mexican people." Both the society banner and the member medallion reinforced their dedication to the "true" king and queen of Mexico: the Sacred Heart of Jesus appeared on one side of the society's insignia, and Our Lady of Guadalupe on the other side. After establishing their pious society, the San Fernando Vasallas and Vasallos organized a monthly Hora Santa Nacional (National Holy Hour) and an annual Cristo Rey novena and feast-day celebration, gathering together other organizations and congregants from throughout the parish in public processions and intercessory prayer for their beleaguered homeland.[30]

Because lay leaders in organizations like the Vasallos addressed the specific concerns of Mexican exiles, the participation of Mexican Americans was relatively sparse. Nonetheless, pious societies at San Fernando facilitated Mexican–Mexican American interaction and collective initiatives. The growing number of parish societies and associations provided ample opportunity for them to interact at monthly corporate communions, devotional services, meetings, social gatherings, and joint fundraising efforts for cathedral projects such as the 1930 construction of a new San Fernando school.

In several cases immigrants and native Mexican Americans worked collaboratively within a single parish association, such as the Hijas de María, which parish leaders and their Claretian pastors rejuvenated after a gradual decline following its founding at the parish during the late nineteenth century. The San Fernando Claretians saw this pious society of *señoritas* (unmarried young women) as a potent defense against "the dangers that surround and assault" young women, as well as a source of spiritual life that helped them preserve "the incomparable beauty . . . of chastity." For the young women themselves, the organization provided numerous opportunities for social gatherings that their parish priests publicly endorsed as "most wholesome amusement" and as occasions on which "parishioners get to know one another and interact as family members, taking on the parish's interests as their own." Given the disagreements over social activities and chaperonage between young Mexican-descent women and their parents, the participants no doubt valued highly this endorsement from San Fernando clergy.[31]

The Hijas were among the most active devotional groups in the cathedral congregation, as evidenced by their leadership in annual parish Marian devotions like those to honor the month of May (which in Catholic devotion is dedicated to Mary), the Assumption (15 August), and the feast of the Immaculate Conception (8 December). The Hijas also far surpassed all other pious societies in organizing plays, concerts, parties, dinners, picnics, booths for parish festivals, and other fundraising events. Unlike most other parish groups, they did not limit the site of their social and fundraising activities to church facilities, but held several events at local social centers such as Beethoven Hall and the San Pedro Park Auditorium. In their first annual variety show, held at the outset of the triduum for Our Lady of Guadalupe in 1923, the Hijas played to a full house of about a thousand attendees at the Ursuline Academy; the local press reported the event as "a brilliant artistic, social, and financial success." While the popularity of the Hijas' events and their status as one of the largest pious societies within the cathedral congregation necessitated the use of these larger gathering spaces, clearly the Hijas worked to ensure that their association fulfilled their religious as well as their social needs. Festivities for parish events like the Guadalupe feast provided opportunities for young women to organize the social activities they desired while simultaneously demonstrating to their parents and themselves that they had not lost their faith, traditions, and sense of proper feminine decorum.[32]

Pious societies were so important in the life of the parish that even children had their own association, the Sociedad del Niño Jesús (Society of the Child Jesus). Founded in 1925 with strong Claretian support, this society initiated chil-

Hijas de María with their spiritual director and a statue of the Immaculate Conception, San Fernando Cathedral, c. 1920s. Courtesy San Fernando Cathedral.

dren into practices like corporate communion, Marian devotion, processions, singing at Mass and other services, and participation in catechesis and parish missions—all with the hope and expectation that they would continue these activities and participate in pious societies throughout their lives as adults. The desire of parents that their daughters and sons learn Mexican Catholic devotions and Spanish prayers and hymns was not without ambiguity, however, as the children were required to speak only English at the San Fernando parochial school, which large numbers attended. Nonetheless, nearly all San Fernando children joined the society at least initially because the induction ceremony accompanied a procession, short devotional service, and group photo session on the afternoon of their First Holy Communion day, an important rite of passage in Mexican-descent families.[33]

Though frequently successful in shaping and enacting a distinct organizational vision, female and male leadership efforts in groups like the Hijas and Vasallos were not always marked by harmony. After a contentious meeting about low attendance and inadequate recruitment of new members, in June 1928 Macario Guzmán, the president of the Vasallos, quit the organization. In other instances, controversy arose between groups: in the case of the 1927 Guadalupe celebration, the Vasallas (the Vasallos' women's section) successfully contested their male counterparts' presumed prerogative of carrying the society banner in all association events and processions.[34]

The Vasallas' protestation of male privilege and the Hijas circumvention of parental restrictions on single daughters' social activities confirm Yolanda Tarango's claim that church volunteer work and associations facilitated some degree of female autonomy by providing "an opportunity for women to work in an area outside of the home at a time when patriarchal structures did not allow other spaces for women to develop." For many ethnic Mexican women, church activities afforded "the only arena in which they could legitimately, if indirectly, engage in developing themselves." Yet the emancipation from gendered expectations that this allowed was far from complete. Often it was the mothers, aunts, or *madrinas* (godmothers) who enforced the practice of chaperonage. Significantly, though young single men at San Fernando participated actively on parish sports teams and in the popular San Fernando Band, energetic Claretian efforts in 1931 to address the "great necessity" of establishing a pious society for them—after all, every other age and gender group had an association—met with limited success. The double standard of not requiring male chaperonage thus diminished the importance of parish institutions for young men's social life.[35]

The varied purposes and motivations that coalesced in parish associations did not extensively undermine the societies' core goal of fostering devotional life and activities. Lay initiatives to promote pious societies and their accompanying devotions complemented the Claretian pastoral strategy of augmenting Catholic faith and allegiance through extensive spiritual exercises. The common emphasis on an expansive network of devotions enabled lay leaders to help shape and enlarge San Fernando's annual calendar of liturgical and devotional celebrations. By 1930 San Fernando held novenas, triduums, and feast-day celebrations nearly every week of the year. Parishioners often spilled out into the city plazas and streets in processions for celebrations like El Santo Entierro (the entombment service for Jesus on Good Friday), the entrance rite for the Mass at which young children received their first communion, and the feasts of Christ the King and Our Lady of Guadalupe.[36]

The Symbolic World of Guadalupan Devotion

The extensive and ardent devotional piety of the San Fernando congregation encompassed a resurgence of its public Guadalupan devotion. With the support

of Spanish Claretians and exiled Mexican clergy, along with the frequent symbolic presence of San Antonio's bishop or, after 1926, archbishop, the growing
San Fernando congregation expanded their annual Guadalupe celebrations and
revivified their tradition of acclaiming their patroness in public ritual. An annual
triduum with solemn feast-day rites began in 1914, expanding on the practice of
holding services solely on the feast day. By the following decade, Guadalupe processions were held on two nights: the procession of roses on 11 December to
commemorate the roses Juan Diego gathered as a sign from Guadalupe, and the
procession of lights on 12 December. Devotees bore roses and candles in these
respective processions, and members of pious societies were prominent as they
walked in unison under their society banners, wearing their society uniforms or
medallions. The annual Guadalupe triduum now also included daily masses, as
well as evening services for recitation of the rosary and various other prayers, the
hearing of sermons, the singing of Guadalupan and other Marian hymns, the
benediction of the Blessed Sacrament, the distribution of commemorative holy
cards, and the panegyric, an oration extolling the honors of the community's patroness. In some years parishioners further expanded these festivities with varying combinations of an all-night vigil service before the Guadalupe feast, a corporate communion of all pious societies, or a dramatic reenactment of the
apparitions to Juan Diego. They also organized social events to accompany religious services. San Fernando's fervent Guadalupe celebrations drew huge
crowds and on several occasions even attracted groups of pilgrims who had
walked as far as thirty miles to the cathedral from Poteet and other nearby
towns.[37]

The primary reason for this resurgence of Guadalupan devotion and public
ritual was the participation of Mexican émigrés at the cathedral. San Fernando's
first recorded Guadalupe triduum, in 1914, followed closely upon the mass ex-
odus at the outset of the Mexican Revolution; more than a hundred exiled bishops and clergy, along with hundreds of Mexican faithful, attended the Guadalupe
feast-day celebration that year. Similarly, the reanimation of religious processions through the city streets and plazas coincided with the Cristero Rebellion,
an era when numerous exiled bishops, priests, and lay Catholics formed part of
the San Fernando congregation, which frequently offered Mass and prayers for
the peace and well-being of Mexico. Significantly, in the late 1920s and early
1930s participants in the Guadalupe processions bore torches decorated with the
green, white, and red colors of the Mexican flag, while members of the various
parish associations marched under their respective banners and the Mexican flag,
and occasionally the U.S. flag. Devotees also decorated the cathedral in the Mex-

Our Lady of Guadalupe procession flowing out of San Fernando Cathedral, 1933. The Mexican flag and Guadalupe image are above the main entrance of the cathedral. Members of the Hijas de María are dressed in white and processing behind their society banner. Courtesy San Antonio Light Collection, University of Texas Institute of Texan Cultures, San Antonio, #0140-F.

ican tricolors for the Guadalupe feast. Although all pious societies participated in Guadalupe celebrations, the most conspicuous group, and the group that attended the Guadalupe image in feast-day processions, was the Vasallos de Cristo Rey, which had a pronounced exile identity and forged a strong link between religious devotion and the national reconstruction of Mexico. As the urban skyline arose around San Fernando and overshadowed the cathedral edifice, the throngs of devotees praying and singing in Spanish and proudly displaying their Guadalupan patroness, Mexican national colors, and society banners proclaimed the Mexican presence in a public space stamped with the architectural markers of U.S. modernization and progress.

The juxtaposition of religious and national symbols embodied the famous words of Mexican novelist and journalist Ignacio Manuel Altamirano, which *La*

Pilgrimage participants and other devotees assemble in front of San Fernando Cathedral for the Guadalupe feast, c. 1930s. At the center of the photo next to the furled U.S. flag is a banner from a parish Guadalupana society. Courtesy Felipa Peña.

Prensa paraphrased and reprinted several times during this period: "The day that the cult of the Indian Virgin disappears, the Mexican nationality will also disappear."[38] Essayists for *La Prensa* frequently echoed these sentiments. One writer confessed that although he had become a religious skeptic as an adult, in exile the celebration of Guadalupe's feast engulfed his "entire soul . . . in a prayer of grand and sorrowful memory" and transported him and others "a little bit closer to our beloved, lost homeland." Drawing on central themes first articulated in nineteenth-century Guadalupe sermons and writings in their native land, exiled Mexican prelates in San Antonio also highlighted the intrinsic connection between Guadalupe and the Mexican nation. In a 1914 sermon for the Guadalupe feast at San Fernando, for example, Archbishop Francisco Plancarte y Navarette of Linares reportedly urged "the people of Mexico to return to an adoration and supplication of Our Lady of Guadalupe as a means of obtaining peace in their country." Two decades later Archbishop Leopoldo Ruiz y Flores, the ordinary of Morelia and the pope's apostolic delegate to Mexico, issued a press release from San Antonio on Guadalupe's feast day, assuring his fellow exiles that Guadalupe "will save Mexico from the claws of atheism, the plague of materialism, and the hate of Bolshevik socialism." Similarly, Claretians assigned to San Fernando assured their flock that "if Mexico is faithful to the Virgin . . . there will be days of peace and prosperity for the Mexican people." Such statements illuminate that San Fernando Guadalupe celebrations included a sense of protest—sometimes implicit, sometimes explicit—against political and religious conditions in Mexico.[39]

Conversely, some exiled commentators used the feast day to claim that Mexico's social upheaval was a divine punishment for national infidelity to the covenant God had enacted with the Mexican people through Our Lady of Guadalupe. Just as the "Virgin of Guadalupe rose up terrifyingly" to champion Mexican independence and castigate Spanish subjects who refused to fulfill "the civilizing mission that had been entrusted to them," so too this loving mother now permitted, in the words of one exiled priest, "tribulations" among "the Mexican people who had not shown themselves suitably fervent" in their faith and devotion. Another exiled clergyman contended that the Mexican government had brought a "severe and just punishment" down from heaven by its misguided efforts to banish God from schools, persecute the church, profane sacred temples, and mock the clergy in press reports that fomented paganism. To remedy the horrific conditions in Mexico, he called his compatriots to a spiritual renewal that included the rich sharing their goods with the poor, a return to mutual love as the basis of social life, parents' insistence on religious instruction in their children's schools, greater respect for the things of God, and the clergy's diligence in fulfilling their duties of propagating Christian doctrine and consoling the afflicted. Such proclamations added the theme of covenant renewal to San Fernando's multivocal commemorations of Guadalupe.[40]

For the editors of *La Prensa* and other elite exiles who propagated the ideology of El México de Afuera, Guadalupe represented even more than a national symbol and special protectress of the Mexican people. These enthusiasts, many of whom worshiped at San Fernando, did not merely claim that they remained Mexicans because they retained their language, culture, religious and patriotic spirit, longing for the homeland, and Mexican citizenship. Rather, they boldly professed that they were the true Mexicans because they embodied these core elements of Mexican nationality more faithfully than their compatriots who remained at home. Indeed, as Juan Bruce-Novoa has observed, these exiles pointed to conditions in their homeland as a betrayal of the Mexican Revolution and contended "that they were right and justified in choosing exile, because exile was the only place the true Mexican could morally exist." In 1940, exile Federico Allen Hinojosa wrote from San Antonio that members of El México de Afuera distinguished themselves by maintaining "their unbreakable religious spirit, their firmly grounded Catholicism that reflected especially in their love and veneration of the Virgin of Guadalupe." Moreover, he said that the exiles even achieved "a reconquest of the lost lands" that the United States had taken from Mexico. This reconquest entailed a physical repopulating of the former Mexican territories, but was at its core "vigorously spiritual." Thus, from the México de Afuera perspective, while Mexicans at home despoiled the national heritage and patrimony, the exiles' propagation of Guadalupan devotion in the United States was an integral part of their success in keeping Mexico alive and even recreating it in conquered territories.[41]

Though prominent exiled clergy and lay leaders like the Vasallos and the *La Prensa* writers fashioned the strong exilic messages associated with Guadalupe at San Fernando and in San Antonio more generally, not all émigrés agreed with their political convictions. One immigrant asserted during the Cristero Rebellion, "I was educated in a Jesuit School but I am not a fanatic. I have always taken part in the liberal struggles and although I have nothing to do with the actual religious conflict I think that the Government [of President Calles] more or less is right in the measures which it takes." Numerous immigrants were more concerned with day-to-day survival than with the political situation in Mexico. A woman who came to San Antonio after divorcing her husband in Mexico City described the difficulties encountered "when one is a woman alone and everyone wants to take advantage of one." She confessed that "the Virgin of Guadalupe will help me to get along well for I always pray to her in my prayers at night and on Sundays when I go to Mass." The primary basis of Guadalupan devotion for many immigrants was their straightforward and steadfast conviction that Guadalupe "continues to perform miracles." Advertisements in local Spanish-language newspapers appealed to their strong faith in Guadalupe as a protectress and healer. One ad for "Té Guadalupano Purgante" (Guadalupan Purgative Tea) described Guadalupe as the "queen of the infirm" and extolled the powers of this tea made from "herbs, flowers, tree bark, seeds, leaves . . . that grow in the environs of Tepeyac, where Our Lady of Guadalupe appeared." Though no devotees publicly protested the strong exilic overtones of San Fernando's Guadalupe feast-day celebrations, their supplication to Guadalupe for assistance with their everyday needs, anxieties, and concerns undermined the strong focus on the homeland in exilic Guadalupan devotion.[42]

Not surprisingly, even as their public Guadalupan devotion was reinvigorated with the initiatives of the newly arrived Mexican émigrés, native Mexican Americans found that the links between Guadalupe's celestial aid and their life situation in the United States resonated more profoundly for them. Religious and cultural traditions had weakened as San Antonio's Mexican-descent residents were numerically overwhelmed during the latter decades of the 1800s, but ongoing feasts like Guadalupe's presented the newcomers with familiar symbols and rituals that united the émigrés in worship with San Fernando parishioners. Thus, like San Fernando's pious societies, the cathedral congregation's Guadalupe celebrations fostered ethnic cohesion and blurred the distinctions between Mexican-descent devotees from either side of the border.

Mexican émigrés' conviction that Guadalupe had elected the Mexican people as her "chosen race" contrasted sharply with Mexican Americans' experience of being relegated to secondary status during U.S. territorial expansion. Mexican editorialists in *La Prensa* expressed their solidarity with people of Mexican ancestry born "in distant lands that were at one time Mexican." One writer opined that although Mexicans born in the United States might be "enmeshed in the contradictory intermingling of Anglo-Saxon education and Latino thought" and might consequently lose touch with their ancestral heritage, in spirit they remained Mexican because they had not forgotten how to "pray in Spanish and worship the Virgin of Guadalupe." Echoing an audacious claim that had emerged in Mexico during the late nineteenth century, another essayist contended that only Guadalupe had prevented the United States from taking all of Mexico. The essayist argued that the consequences of the 1846–1848 war between the two nations would have been "100 times" worse if the "invader" had not made the fatal error of negotiating peace terms at a site near the basilica of Our Lady of Guadalupe, who consequently protected her children's dignity and won them an unexpected diplomatic victory! One immigrant women's group, the Club Mexicano de Bellas Artes (Mexican Fine Arts Club), gathered annually during the Guadalupe triduum at San Fernando to offer a Mass and to further their objectives of conserving "Mexican traditions and customs" and "the Castilian language."[43] The immigrants' esteem for their heritage and confidence in their dignity as Guadalupe's favored daughters and sons animated the México de Afuera exile mentality, and it also provided an impetus for Mexican Americans to renew their own ethnic pride and sense of dignity as the children of a heavenly mother. In an era of rising ethnic prejudice in San Antonio, Mexican émigrés' assurance of their celestial election and rich cultural patrimony fortified both Mexican Americans and the immigrants in their resistance to discrimination.

Seen in this light, San Fernando's Guadalupe celebrations were a sacred realm in which cathedral congregants were valued and respected, in striking contrast to the racism they encountered in the world around them. While Mexican-descent residents continued to struggle for equal rights in schools, courtrooms, and the work place, at San Fernando they instilled in one another a sense of dignity and pride as children of a loving mother. While racism in movies and other areas of social life was so strident that even Spanish-language newspapers advertised "whitening" cream, Mexican-descent devotees acclaimed the brown-skinned Morenita, displaying her image in public processions and enshrining it prominently in the cathedral. While their representation in government bodies like the city council was minimal, San Fernando congregants exercised their leadership in their many pious societies, organizing communal events like the annual Guadalupe triduum and processions. While the Spanish language was officially banned in public schools, Guadalupan devotees marched through the city plazas and streets singing the praises of their patroness in their native tongue. While the threat of repatriation hovered ominously, especially during the Depression, familiar devotions like those to Guadalupe made San Fernando a spiritual home that provided solace and reassurance. While they were frequently rebuffed at Anglo American parishes, San Fernando congregants celebrated their patroness's feast in the company of archbishops, bishops, and priests whose presence confirmed the value of their language, cultural heritage, and religious traditions.

Dramatic reversals of lived realities in ritual enactments did not substantially alter the systemic racism that beset ethnic Mexicans. Nonetheless, whether or not this was the intended result of the enactments, San Fernando's reanimated Guadalupe rituals fortified devotees and counteracted the hostility and rejection they often met in the wider church and society. As one devotee remarked in acclaiming Guadalupe's compassion for the poor and downtrodden: "Because the Virgin is Indian and brown-skinned and wanted to be born in the asperity of [Juan Diego's] rough cloak—just like Christ wanted to be born in the humility of a stable—she is identified with a suffering, mocked, deceived, victimized people." Another enthusiast opined that la Morenita was nothing less than a "symbol" of "our race" and contended that "if it had been a Virgin with blue eyes and blonde hair that appeared to Juan Diego, it is possible that she would have received a fervent devotion, but never as intense, as intimate, nor as trusting as that which the multitudes offer at the feet of the miraculous 'Guadalupita.'"[44]

San Fernando Claretians pursued yet another vision for Guadalupan devotion, engaging it as a means to entice ethnic Mexicans into active participation in the parish and the sacraments. Perceiving Mexicans and Mexican Americans as lax Catholics and easy prey for Protestant proselytizers, the Claretians strove to link the vast force of Guadalupan devotion with Catholic identity and full involvement in the life of the Catholic Church. One parish bulletin announcement proclaimed that "it is not enough that the image occupies a preferential place in your home and that you invoke her with devotion in all your perils; you must also proclaim your love for Mary in public." All the faithful were exhorted to honor her by "approaching the eucharistic banquet with souls purified through a sincere confession." When some devotees failed to participate in the sacraments and other church services for the Guadalupe feast, the San Fernando clergy decried the "unpardonable indifference" in hearts so devoid of devotion and patriotism that they "palpitate not a drop of blood for the Virgin of Guadalupe nor for Mexico."[45]

Guadalupe's importance in the lives of Mexican-descent women and their families is confirmed by their individual devotion and by the presence of Guadalupe images in their homes, where "the feast day of the patroness of Mexico was observed by religious and civil exercises." At San Fernando women's initiative extended beyond their traditional role as leaders of familial piety to leadership in the congregation and even to demands for parity with their male counterparts. For example, Elena Lanzuri, who had previously led the choir at the Guadalupe basilica in Mexico City, directed a group of more than fifty singers at San Fernando in the 1935 celebration of Guadalupe's feast; younger-generation women from the Hijas de María organized social gatherings in conjunction with the Guadalupe feast; and various women's groups, most notably the Vasallas de Cristo Rey, participated in the preparation of Guadalupe celebrations and walked together in the processions. Beginning in 1927 the Vasallas insisted that they be allowed to alternate turns with male Vasallos in carrying the society banner for events like the Guadalupe procession, an action that reflected their equal and often greater contribution of hard work and financial support for Guadalupan festivities.[46]

Yet the longstanding Catholic association of Mary with what Elizabeth Johnson has called the "male projection of idealized femininity" clearly influenced Claretian and parental visions for the Hijas de María and shaped the San Fernando clergy's and some lay leaders' efforts to promote Marian devotion more generally. Both priests and parents—in many families mothers more than fathers—counseled young women to embrace Guadalupe as a model of purity. Beatriz Blanco, an Hijas de María member who played a prominent role in organizing the social events that single women so enthusiastically supported, edited *La Prensa*'s "Página del hogar y de las damas" (Home and Ladies Page) and was the only woman credited with publishing a Guadalupan reflection in *La Prensa* during this period. Significantly, this leader who helped create and expand a social life for herself and other young women was also the only editorialist who opined that Guadalupe "personifies our native land, religion, and home." She went on to warn that "whoever tries to destroy the Guadalupan Virgin will have committed a crime" against "the sacred laws of the home, love and unity, the foundations of the family." These statements say at least as much about *La Prensa*'s editorial policies as they do about women's perspectives on Guadalupe: the invocation of Guadalupe's authority buttresses the paper's insistent endorsement of female domesticity. From this perspective, women should forego activist, political, or other public roles because as homemakers they are already the foundation and binding force of society and their community in a far more fundamental sense. Their Guadalupan devotion was to build the nation by building the home, while men's devotion was to directly shape the contours of political and civic life.[47]

The strong ethnic solidarity evident in Guadalupan devotion in this period also did not preclude differentiation between worshipers of different social classes, national origins, and age groups. One Claretian parish chronicler noted in 1926 that "the most prominent Mexican families attended this [Guadalupe] triduum by invitation," although there is no indication that the rich received any special recognition or other prerogatives in worship services and other festivities.[48] While the Vasallos de Cristo Rey did not exclude Mexican American members, their frequent prominence in Guadalupe celebrations reflected a predominant focus on Mexico and the views espoused by Mexican clergy and proponents of the México de Afuera mentality. More strikingly, Guadalupe processions, like pious societies and spiritual exercises such as Lenten missions, generally divided devotees into separate groups, with children leading the entourage, followed by young women, older women, and then men. This arrangement was consistent with Archbishop Drossaerts's pastoral letter on feminine modesty, the Claretians' vision for the Hijas de María and other parish associations, and the practice of keeping a proper distance between unmarried women and men through chaperonage. Thus the high point of Guadalupe celebrations symbolically represented and reinforced a hierarchical vision of the world, with assigned roles and places based on age, gender, and, to some extent, national origin.

A Theology of Exile

The potent combination of displacement, fervent devotion, robust nationalism, longing and distress for their native land, and the need to survive in a new country induced numerous Mexican émigrés in the Southwest and Midwest to establish parishes and chapels dedicated to Our Lady of Guadalupe during the first four decades of the twentieth century. During the short span of the Mexican Revolution and the era of the Cristero Rebellion alone, Mexican nationals dedicated houses of worship to Guadalupe in such diverse places as Los Angeles, Houston, Dallas, Kansas City, Milwaukee, St. Paul, and Toledo.[49]

Guadalupe celebrations with "strong Mexican nationalistic overtones" abounded, and they were so conspicuous that occasionally they led to open conflict between devotees and Mexican consulate officials. In Los Angeles leaders of a 1934 public Guadalupe procession held in the wake of renewed religious persecution after Mexican president Cárdenas's election announced that the event was "a memorial service for those who had suffered persecution in Mexico." The Mexican consulate urged all "real Mexicans" to boycott the procession, but forty thousand people reportedly took part, some bearing placards that read "atheism reigns in Mexico City and Moscow." A week later the Mexican vice consul in nearby San Bernardino unsuccessfully petitioned local officials to cancel the parade permit for a similar event. He then published a letter in a Spanish-language newspaper calling for a boycott. Mexican Catholics bought or stole all the copies of the paper they could find and burned them. Lay leaders then wrote President Franklin D. Roosevelt, accusing the Mexican consuls of attempting to deny their constitutional right to freedom of religion; subsequently Mexican officials reassigned the consuls stationed at Los Angeles and San Bernardino to posts outside the United States. At the same time, however, as George Sánchez reveals in his study of 1900–1945 Los Angeles, such conspicuous debates about Mexican national issues and identity did not restrain "the complex process of cultural adaptation" that was unfolding among ethnic Mexicans in the Southwest and Midwest.[50]

As in other U.S. locales affected by the growing Mexican diaspora, Guadalupan devotion at San Fernando during the early twentieth century was complex and multilayered. One conspicuous element of the devotion was that it illuminated the faith and search for meaning of émigrés who sought to reconstitute their lives in a new land. Bishops, priests, and lay leaders with a pronounced exile mentality exercised an influence disproportionate to their numbers in the preaching, symbolic representations, and intercessory focus of San Fernando's Guadalupe feast-day celebrations. As Tom Tweed's study of diasporic religion shows, exponents of exilic faith frequently engage in "theologizing about dominant symbols" like Guadalupe as a means to "focus on the community's past and the homeland's fate. They also become more concerned than ever to define the tradition doctrinally as the group struggles to maintain a national identity in the face of a host culture that appears to threaten it."[51] The heightened concern for collective history, the homeland, theological orthodoxy, and national identity and pride was clearly evident in Guadalupan devotion at San Fernando: in the preponderance of the Mexican flag and its tricolors during feast-day processions, in the Vasallos' plea for spiritual renewal as the only means to reconstruct the homeland, in sermons that called for a return to virtuous living and the propagation of authentic church teaching, in interwoven expressions of collective intercession and protest, in bold articulations of Guadalupe's central role in Mexican history, and in the insistent and pervasive claim that Guadalupe is the Mexican national emblem. Even the separation of devotees according to age and gender in Guadalupe processions reflected a desire to reestablish order and decorum amidst the chaos of social unrest at home and the potentially splintering effects of exile.

Clearly one of the most striking features of exilic theologies mediated in faith communities like San Fernando is their lack of ambiguity. There is no room for compromise or conspicuous gray areas in a perspective that dichotomizes authentic history and falsehood, religious truth and heresy, patriotism and traitorous subversion. When religious practitioners with a pronounced sense of group identity perceive that their well-being and way of life are under attack, they tend to demand conformity in their ritual and belief systems as a means of establishing, in the words of Mary Douglas, "strong boundaries between purity and impurity . . . where all moral failings are at once sins against religion and the community."[52] For devotees in a world of upheaval, Guadalupe feast-day celebrations at San Fernando shaped and transmitted their unwavering convictions that ungodly forces had defiled their homeland's sacred patrimony, that the present turmoil was a time of purification and grave moral responsibility, and that their destiny was intrinsically linked to Guadalupe and their dedication to her. Drawing on foundational themes of the Christian tradition, such as justice, mercy, and covenant, devotees posited that both Mexico's historical trajectory and their own lives were at a critical juncture in which their right conduct and belief held the future in the balance.

But not all San Fernando parishioners and clergy embraced the exilic mentality to the same degree. Claretians supported exiled bishops and other coreligionists and endorsed the strong exilic messages in Guadalupe celebrations, but primarily employed Guadalupan devotion as a means to foster Catholic allegiance, faith development, and worthy reception of the sacraments. Through their leadership initiatives and demands for parity, some women contested the notion that remaining faithful in exile entailed their acquiescence to expectations of female domesticity or to the corollary belief that women's public roles threatened their foundational purpose of anchoring community and society through homemaking and maternal nurture.

For both male and female émigrés, particularly those of the poor and working classes, who were the vast majority of Mexicans in San Antonio and at San Fernando, the more immediate concerns of surviving and starting anew meshed with and often surpassed concerns for the homeland. As San Fernando congregants struggled to forge a life in the United States for themselves and their children, Guadalupan devotion, like émigré life itself, reflected Devra Weber's insight that "the importance of reciprocity" in any society is even "more powerful among immigrants."[53] Just as economic reciprocity and ethnic solidarity were the foundation of mutualistas and reciprocal intercessory prayer and mutual support were central to pious societies, Guadalupan devotees perceived their relationship with Guadalupe as one of mutuality. In exchange for their fervent prayers and reverence, devotees relied on Guadalupe to preserve their health, shield them from discrimination, watch over their children, and provide for their needs, as well as renew their homeland. In this exchange of devotion and favors, Guadalupe's supplicants strove to raise their fallen nation by reinvigorating religious practice, while also acknowledging that divine judgment was fitting and just because the nation had sinned by failing to fulfill the duties imposed by a covenant relationship with celestial beings like their patroness. But on a more personal level, their prayers for healing, protection, and sustenance reoriented the publicly acclaimed link between Guadalupe and the Mexican nation toward her reciprocal relationship with immigrants and their families and loved ones as they struggled to make a life in a new land. The interplay between divine justice and human pleas for relief, God's mercy and devotees' acceptance of suffering and rightful judgment—both in everyday life and in the fate of the Mexican nation—constituted the porous boundaries of the divine-human reciprocity embodied in Guadalupan devotion.

Attraction to exilic themes had less direct appeal among Mexican Americans. The exiles' claim that Guadalupe had made Mexicans her chosen people resonated with them, but this assertion had more significance in elevating their dignity and honor in a hostile U.S. environment than in explicating Mexico's current plight and reassuring them about its destiny. The claim of El México de Afuera advocates that Guadalupe was leading a spiritual reconquest of the Southwest may have exaggerated Mexican exile influence in the United States, but it accurately reflected Guadalupe's bearing on the group pride of U.S.-born ethnic Mexicans who had survived the difficult half century following the 1840s war between the United States and Mexico.

Still, exilic theology was both conspicuous and influential in San Fernando's public Guadalupan devotion, as is evident in the ways that Mexican Americans, Spanish Claretians, and women and men émigrés responded to the presence and insights of exiled leaders and devotees. Intentionally or not, while some of Guadalupe's followers developed an exilic theology primarily focused on their Mexican homeland, many others embraced the elements of that theology that were most conducive to the process of sustaining their dignity and establishing a life for themselves in the United States. The efforts of the Hijas de María to engage Guadalupe and other parish celebrations as a means to address their own social needs indicate that Mexican émigrés, especially of the younger generations, adapted to their new life circumstances even as they supported and actively participated in feast-day rituals with strong exilic overtones. As émigrés forged communal bonds with Mexican Americans and one another, la Morenita's devotees invigorated their confidence that they were heirs to the dignity she personified. Long after the intensity of the exile experience faded, the exiles' core belief that they were Guadalupe's privileged sons and daughters endured, strengthening succeeding generations as they continued to negotiate the transition from being El México de Afuera to being Mexican Americans.

CHAPTER 5

Celestial *Mestiza*, 1940–2003

My most vivid memory of Guadalupan feast-day celebrations at San Fernando is from 1992, the first time I participated in the serenata. A friend and I arrived more than an hour before the 11:00 p.m. celebration to ensure that we could be seated. The festivity and fervor of the event inundated the senses—bright colors, the aroma of countless fresh flowers, the infectious excitement of the crowd, and the hour-long service of emotive singing by both local singers and internationally acclaimed musicians. But the most impressive moment was the reenactment of Guadalupe's apparitions to Juan Diego. True to this foundational narrative of Mexican and Mexican American faith, the reenactment portrayed the first bishop of Mexico, Spaniard Juan de Zumárraga, as skeptical when he first heard Juan Diego's message that Guadalupe wanted a temple built in her honor. The scoffing *rechazos* (rejections) by the bishops' assistants elicited agonizing winces from some onlookers, stony silence from others. Finally, the doubting bishop comes to believe when the stooped indio stands erect, drops from his tilma roses that have grown out of season, and presents the image of Guadalupe that has miraculously appeared on the rough cloth of his garment. As the re-

Juan Diego reveals the Guadalupe image on his tilma in dramatic reenactment at the San Fernando *serenata*. Courtesy Mario and Guadalupe Mandujano.

pentant bishop and his assistants fell to their knees in veneration before Juan Diego's tilma, sustained applause erupted from every corner of the cathedral.

Though the faces around me reflected the Indigenous ancestry of many parishioners, the congregation was composed not of Native Americans but of predominantly ethnic Mexican worshipers in blue jeans and evening dresses, business suits, Mexican-style *guayabera* shirts, and fancy hats and bandanas. Their pastor at the time, renowned theologian Virgilio Elizondo, asserts that they are mestizos born from two dramatic clashes of peoples: first the Mesoamericans with the conquistadores of sixteenth-century Catholic Spain, and then, in the century and a half following the U.S. takeover of northern Mexico, Tejanos and immigrants from Mexico with U.S. Protestants and Catholics of European ancestry. What Elizondo articulates as the painful historical process of their double *mestizaje*—the dynamic and often violent mixing of cultures, religious systems, and races[1]—is echoed in many San Fernando congregants' stinging memories of the polite disdain or outright hostility they have met in their dealings with sales clerks, bosses, coworkers, teachers, police officers, health care providers, social workers, government employees, professional colleagues, and civic and church leaders. Thus it is not surprising that the liturgical drama of the lowly indio Juan Diego's rejection, his encounter with a loving mother, and his final vindication before the ecclesiastical leader of the Spanish conquistadores resonates with them.

Celebrating the story of Guadalupe's maternal care and Juan Diego's struggle and triumph does not obliterate the painful daily realities faced by San Fernando congregants; despite noteworthy advances in leadership roles and economic well-being, many parishioners still endure low wages, unemployment, inadequate health care and educational opportunities, ethnic stereotypes, putdowns, and, especially among professionals, an inordinate pressure to prove they are on a par with their non-Latino colleagues. But San Fernando parishioners find solace in Guadalupe's election of the unexpected hero Juan Diego, as well as hope in his unwavering faith and *aguante* (unyielding endurance). Though they recognize that their Guadalupan devotion does not eliminate all the rechazos and social ills that beset them, most congregants do not consider themselves a dominated people, and they ardently attest that Guadalupe uplifts them as she did Juan Diego, strengthening them in the trials and difficulties of their daily lives. In a word, they confess that the Guadalupe narrative is true—it reveals the deep truth of their human dignity and exposes the lie of social inequalities and experiences that diminish their fundamental sense of worth.

During World War II and the half-century that followed it, the extension of Guadalupe's protective mantle to new generations of Mexican Americans overshadowed earlier devotees' association of Guadalupe with exilic Mexican nationalism and helped facilitate their adaptation to U.S. society. Through fervent appeals for Guadalupe's protection of Mexican American soldiers during war, massive archdiocesan public processions and outdoor masses at San Fernando during the 1950s and early 1960s, annual parish celebrations like today's internationally televised Guadalupe serenata, and personal encounters with their celestial mother, the Guadalupan devotion of ethnic Mexicans at San Fernando shaped and was shaped by their continuing efforts to forge a home and a life in the United States. Demographic shifts and Mexican Americans' national and local struggles for civil rights, as well as the changing leadership and ministerial initiatives at San Fernando, constituted the broad contexts in which Guadalupan devotion evolved.

Mexican Americans and the Demand for Equality

The size of San Antonio's Mexican-descent population, which had been relatively stagnant during the Great Depression of the 1930s, increased anew during World War II and has continued to grow ever since. In 1970, census figures
indicated that about 8 percent of San Antonio's inhabitants were African American, 39 percent were Anglo American, and 52 percent were of Mexican descent,
the first time since the U.S. takeover of Texas in 1845 that a census revealed an
ethnic Mexican majority in the city. According to the 2000 census, Hispanics
made up nearly 59 percent of San Antonio's 1.1 million residents; the vast majority were of Mexican descent, but other Latino groups like Puerto Ricans and
Cubans were represented as well. Significantly, the primary cause of growth in
San Antonio's Mexican-descent population is not immigration but the birth of
second-, third-, and fourth-generation Mexican Americans, along with shifts in
agricultural and other job markets that have increasingly led Texas Mexicans to
resettle in urban locales. In 1960, only 12 percent of the Mexican population in
San Antonio were foreign born; 31 percent were second generation, and 57 percent were of the third or later generations. Despite some ongoing immigration,
the 1990 census showed that the total foreign-born population of San Antonio
was less than 10 percent, a figure that increased only slightly with the 2000 census. Some native-born residents descend from ancestors who first came to San
Antonio in the nineteenth and even the eighteenth centuries, but most are the
children, grandchildren, and great-grandchildren of the numerous émigrés who
arrived during the Mexican Revolution and its aftermath. The rise of these generations reared in the United States is the most important demographic shift in
San Antonio from the time of World War II until the present.[2]

Changing demographics, along with the return to Mexico of many bishops,
priests, and exiled lay leaders as decreasing church-state tensions abated even
further after the 1940 election of Mexican president Manuel Avila Camacho,
contributed substantially to the demise of the local Spanish-language press. By
1940 *La Prensa* was San Antonio's only remaining Spanish-language newspaper,
although its increasing presentation of U.S. and local news, stories on Holly-
wood stars, translated U.S. literary works, and bilingual advertisements signaled
that its editors were adapting to the shifting needs and perspectives of its read-
ership. Four years after the 1953 death of the newspaper's founding editor, Igna-

cio E. Lozano, his widow, Alicia, announced that publication would be discontinued due to rising costs and declining circulation, a decline she attributed to "the younger generation of Latin Americans being able to read English and the dwindling of the non-English reading generation." Efforts to reestablish *La Prensa* as a weekly continued until its definitive discontinuance in 1962. Though local publisher Tino Durán revived *La Prensa* as a weekly community newspaper in 1989, to date San Antonio has not had another major Spanish-language paper.[3]

Changes also occurred within the civic and political organizations that Mexican-descent residents founded and supported. The mutualistas that had been so popular among immigrants declined sharply during the economic hard times and accompanying deportation threats of the Depression; after World War II only a scant few mutualistas continued to provide services, such as burial insurance and emergency assistance, and to host family festivities. Meanwhile, Mexican American leaders of groups like the League of United Latin American Citizens (LULAC) became more conspicuous in their efforts to promote their people's general welfare and to oppose segregation, restrictive housing covenants, and racial prejudice. LULAC leadership also helped sharpen Mexican American identity by continuing the organization's founding vision of promoting U.S. citizenship. Though by the 1970s its leaders publicly categorized immigration as a human rights issue that influenced immigrants and U.S.-born Mexican Americans alike, during the 1940s and 1950s LULAC had maintained an official position against the bracero guest-worker program and had even endorsed U.S. Immigration and Naturalization Service (INS) repatriation campaigns like the infamous "Operation Wetback" of 1954.[4]

Mexican Americans' participation in World War II—both in the armed forces and on the home front, where women and men worked in factories and in homes and aided efforts to support the troops—accelerated the process of adaptation to U.S. society that had begun before the war and invigorated even further the resolve to combat segregation and discrimination against citizens of Mexican descent. In the wake of the war Mexican Americans frequently buttressed their protests with the argument that soldiers who fought tyranny abroad should not return to the prejudice they and their families often endured at home. One leading figure in this struggle was attorney Alonso S. Perales, a native Texan, World War I veteran, cofounder of LULAC, and columnist for *La Prensa*. Perales published a voluminous 1948 book that documented more than four hundred instances of discrimination against veterans, their families, and other

Mexican Americans in Texas. Leaders like Perales frequently united to decry instances of discrimination as a "disgraceful blight on our way of life." In 1954 San Antonio attorneys Gus García and Carlos Cadena became the first Latinos to win a U.S. Supreme Court case, successfully arguing against the exclusion of Mexican Americans from jury duty and, by extension, their segregation in housing and in schools and other public facilities. Mexican American veterans of World War II enhanced such efforts with their own demands for equality, especially through the American G.I. Forum. Founded in 1948, the forum played a major role in the Mexican American struggle for equality and civil rights, particularly during the anti-Communist scare of the 1950s, when their status as war veterans made them less vulnerable than other activists to accusations of disloyalty.[5]

The widespread agitation for social change throughout U.S. society during the 1960s included the Chicano movement, which was most visible to the general public in the efforts of César Chávez, Dolores Huerta, and the United Farm Workers, but also encompassed the efforts of national and regional activist groups such as three renowned organizations founded in San Antonio: the Mexican American Youth Organization (MAYO), the Mexican American Legal Defense and Education Fund (MALDEF), and the Southwest Voter Registration and Education Project. Mexican American leaders also initiated numerous local and statewide efforts to advance community concerns and issues. For example, Veronica Salazar, María Antonietta Berriozábal, and Luz M. Escamilla were key leaders in establishing a chapter of the Texas-based Mexican American Business and Professional Women's Association (MABPWA) at San Antonio during the early 1970s. MABPWA emphasizes the goals of "women's career development, involvement in civic issues, and attention to cultural heritage."[6]

The organization that is most acclaimed for its political and social influence on San Antonio itself is Communities Organized for Public Service (COPS). Lay leaders like founding president Andrés Sarabia, professional organizer Ernie Cortés, and priests such as Edmundo Rodríguez and Albert Benavides collaborated in the 1974 effort to establish COPS among six ethnic Mexican Catholic parishes on San Antonio's west side. Their first major issue was the horrendous drainage and frequent flooding in their neighborhoods, which had resulted in school closings, accidents, damaged homes, impassable roads, bridge collapses, a dearth of business establishments, and even deaths. When COPS members discovered that many drainage projects had actually been authorized in bond issues approved as far back as 1945, they filled city hall during a council meeting to voice their outrage. Stunned by the crowd and the overwhelming evidence presented, Mayor Charles Becker ordered the city manager to devise a drainage project implementation plan; COPS then took the lead in the passage of a $46.8 million bond issue for fifteen west side drainage projects. Led primarily by Latina leaders like Beatrice Gallego, Carmen Badillo, Beatrice Cortés, Sonia Hernández, Patricia Ozuna, and Virginia Ramírez, the organization subsequently won more than one billion dollars in infrastructure improvements for primarily low-income and working-class neighborhoods, as well as significant advances on community issues like education reform, job training, economic development, and a living wage. Members attest that "the most positive change has been in the attitude of our people. Twenty-five years ago, we couldn't imagine that a city council member would attend our meetings, now we know that with the power of educated, organized people, anything is possible."[7]

Mexican Americans also increasingly won political office. Not a single Mexican American had served on the San Antonio city council during the 1940s, but they won 18 percent of city council elections in the 1950s, and 27 percent in the 1960s. During these decades nearly all council electees had the endorsement of the Good Government League (GGL), an organization of prominent business leaders who exercised almost absolute power over city government. The GGL's increasing nomination of Mexican American and, starting in 1965, African American candidates for city council was in large part due to the 1959 establishment of the Bexar County Democratic Coalition, a joint effort to contest the GGL's hegemony that was led by Mexican Americans, African Americans, organized labor, and Anglo American liberals and activists.[8]

During the 1970s community pressure finally brought the rule of the GGL to an end. With the legal leverage of a MALDEF brief presented to the U.S. Justice Department, their efforts culminated in a 1977 city council decision that mandated the end of all at-large districts for municipal elections. The new geographical "single-member" districts created in their place facilitated the election of Mexican American and some African American candidates. Three years later Henry Cisneros was elected San Antonio's first Mexican-descent mayor since Juan Seguín fled the city under threat of Anglo American violence nearly 140 years earlier. The number of ethnic Mexican council members continued to increase steadily; during the 1990s they accounted for nearly half of city council electees, and in 1997 they formed a majority on the council for the first time since 1845. Reflective of Mexican American women's long-standing leadership in community activism, as well as their involvement in the political campaigns of Mexican American men dating back to the early 1950s, in the past twenty-five years the first Mexican American women electees have served on the council: Yolanda Vera, Helen Ayala, Debra Guerrero, and the first Latina electee, María Antonietta Berriozábal, who served five terms as a council member before narrowly losing a bid for the mayoral office in 1991.[9]

The life and career of Henry B. González, San Antonio's most renowned national political leader, clearly illustrate the shift from émigré to Mexican American concerns among the generations of Mexican-descent residents born in the United States. His father, Leonides González, was a Mexican émigré from a prominent family in Mapimí, Durango, where he had served as the *jefe político* (political chief) until the outbreak of the Mexican Revolution. Soon after his 1911 resettlement in San Antonio, the elder González began a forty-year tenure as managing editor and business manager of *La Prensa*, joining the effort of the newspaper's founder, Ignacio E. Lozano, who was an acquaintance from his hometown. While his father was part of the exile group that established and developed *La Prensa*, Henry González, a San Fernando parishioner who was born in San Antonio in 1916, focused his life work on the needs and civil rights of U.S. residents, particularly ethnic Mexicans. He was elected to the San Antonio city council in 1953, and in 1956 became the first Mexican-descent state senator since José Antonio Navarro served over a century earlier. Then in 1961 González became the first Mexican-descent Texan elected to the U.S. House of Representatives, where he was widely acclaimed during his thirty-seven years in office as one who "championed the rights of common people."[10]

A growing number of Mexican Americans have succeeded in business and professional life—many, for example, at the expansive South Texas Medical Center, one of several economic catalysts on the north side of the city, a section that is still predominantly Anglo American but now has some ethnic Mexican residents. Other Mexican Americans have benefited from employment at one of the five major U.S. military installations in the metropolitan area, installations that accounted for one-third of San Antonio's employment during the 1950s. Even after the 1995 announcement that federally mandated military base closures would include San Antonio's Kelly Air Force Base, the largest single employer in the city, the influence of the military on the local economy and job market remained substantial. For many Mexican Americans, employment at a military base represents an economic passage out of the working class. Meanwhile, tourism has expanded dramatically in San Antonio, particularly after local leaders organized the 1968 HemisFair, a world's fair that marked the 250th anniversary of European settlement in the area. Internationally renowned for the Alamo, the River Walk, and other attractions, San Antonio now has a tourism industry that rivals military bases as the city's primary generator of economic activity, though the employment opportunities generated by expanding tourism are largely low-wage service jobs.[11]

Some prominent ecclesial leaders supported the Mexican American struggle for advancement and rights and even fostered that struggle within the church. San Antonio's second archbishop, Robert E. Lucey (1941–1969), is widely acclaimed as a tireless advocate for social action, labor unions, and civil rights. He was the first Catholic bishop in Texas to mandate the desegregation of parochial schools, doing so six weeks before the famous 1954 Supreme Court decision in *Brown* v. *Board of Education*. Subsequently he established the Archdiocesan Department of Social Action, which collaborated with African American and other leaders and played a key role in the successful 1960 effort to desegregate San Antonio's Majestic Theater and later numerous other public facilities. In 1966, when farm workers marched from the Rio Grande Valley in south Texas to the state capital in Austin under the banner of Our Lady of Guadalupe, Lucey celebrated Mass with them at San Fernando Cathedral and demanded that their employers "behave like human beings and grant you steadily increasing wages." Within the church, Lucey was instrumental in 1945 in the establishment of the Bishops' Committee for the Spanish Speaking, the U.S. bishops' first collaborative effort in Hispanic ministry. Shortly after his arrival in San Antonio he had noted that many Catholic pastors induced Spanish-speaking Catholics who lived within their parish boundaries to attend San Fernando. He deemed this a segregationist practice, called it his "special headache," and subsequently fought to integrate parishes.[12]

Lucey's progress toward securing first-class status in the church for ethnic Mexicans fell short of Latino Catholics' growing aspirations for equality. In 1969, Father Ralph Ruiz, priest-director of the Inner City Apostolate for the San Antonio archdiocese, led the Chicano priests' support group that founded PADRES (Padres Asociados por los Derechos Religiosos, Educativos, y Sociales, or Priests Associated for Religious, Educational, and Social Rights) as a national association of Chicano priests dedicated to addressing the struggle of their people in both church and society. PADRES was inspired by the Vatican II worldwide council of Catholic bishops (1962–1965), the 1968 Latin American episcopal conference at Medellín, Colombia, the emergence of Latin American liberation theology, and the activism of the civil rights and Chicano movements.

It called for societal changes but focused even more attention on intrachurch concerns, such as the promotion of native Spanish-speaking pastors, liturgical expressions that respect Latino cultures, an equitable distribution of church resources, and most prominently, the appointment of more Chicano and other Latino bishops. By 1974 at least five national or regional offices associated with the apostolate to the Spanish-speaking were located in the San Antonio archdiocese: PADRES, the Mexican American Cultural Center, the National Foundation for Mexican American Vocations, the Southwest Regional Office for the Spanish Speaking, and Las Hermanas, the first national organization of Chicana and other Latina Catholic women.[13]

Ruiz and the founders of other church organizations were part of an increase in the number of Chicano ecclesial leaders that paralleled the rise of Mexican American leadership in political and civic life. Most notably, in 1970 PADRES member Patricio Flores became the first Mexican American bishop in the United States. Flores served as an auxiliary bishop in San Antonio from 1970 to 1978 and as San Antonio's first Mexican American archbishop from 1979 until he reached the mandatory retirement age of seventy-five and was succeeded by Archbishop José Gómez in February 2005. His renowned role as an outspoken advocate for Mexican American and other Latino Catholics is illustrated in his closing address to a 1977 Encuentro Nacional (National Encounter) of Hispanic Catholics. While Flores applauded Latino advances in both church and society, he also called for "25 times more representation and participation at all levels of life."[14]

Despite advances in leadership and ministerial initiatives within Roman Catholicism, Protestant outreach efforts and a history of Roman Catholic institutional neglect have helped facilitate increased Latino participation in Protestant churches, particularly Pentecostal and evangelical congregations. Some Latinos maintain dual or multiple denominational attachments; they may attend a Protestant church regularly for Sunday worship but celebrate occasions like baptisms and funerals in a Catholic parish. Others return to the Catholic fold, such as San Fernando parishioner Mary Navarro Farr. After eight years in an evangelical church, she became upset with the "anti-Catholicism" in her congregation and was drawn to San Fernando by "the treasure of the Eucharist, the maternal care of Our Lady of Guadalupe, and the music and sacred imagery" she remembered from her childhood. Nonetheless, though no demographic study has indicated how many San Antonio Latinos claim a Protestant affiliation, their growing numbers are confirmed by the scores of Latino congregations listed in the city telephone directory, such as Iglesia Pentecostal Unida Hispana, La Puerta Abierta, Iglesia Bautista Nueva Esperanza, La Roca Centro Cristiano, San Esteban Lutheran, El Divino Salvador United Methodist, Iglesia Rios de Amor, El Divino Redentor Presbyterian, and Iglesia Evangelica Cristiana Espiritual.[15]

The lives of Mexican Americans have changed in other ways as succeeding generations have adapted to life in the United States. Marriages between Mexican-descent residents and Anglo Americans, a rare occurrence during the late nineteenth and early twentieth centuries, began to increase after World War II. In 1960, 10 percent of all Spanish-surnamed San Antonians who had married were in mixed marriages, and 20 percent of the Spanish-surnamed persons who married in that year had non-Spanish surnamed spouses. National and regional studies reveal gradual changes in Mexican American family structures, such as noteworthy decreases in the number of extended-family households and in the strength of *compadrazgo*—the relationship between parents and the godparents of their children that in traditional Mexican Catholic understanding is a lifelong familial bond of mutual support and affection.[16]

By the early 1990s more than half of Mexican-descent women in the United States worked outside the home, part of a growing trend that reflects both economic necessity and opposition to restrictive views on women's domesticity and their singular role as homemaker. Employment outside the home led a growing number of women to seek greater mutuality in household and child care duties. They used tactics such as praise, instruction on tasks, attempts to reformulate gender roles from previous generations, work slowdowns or stoppages, and even open confrontation to dispel the expectation that in the home a man "no levanta ni una cuchara" (doesn't even lift a spoon). Beatríz Pesquera has concluded that, particularly among women in the professions and in blue-collar positions, "employment generally does bring about greater male involvement in household labor, but it does not lead to an egalitarian redistribution of tasks." Among younger women, the decline of the chaperonage system has provided greater opportunities for dating and other social activities. The lives of both females and males in younger generations are increasingly shaped by influences such as clothing fashions and public schools, mass media and youth culture, work experiences and peers, musical trends and the Internet.[17]

Changes that tend to facilitate integration into U.S. life, society, and cultural norms are counteracted by ethnic Mexicans' ongoing struggles with discrimination and economic hardship. Improvements in leadership representation, critical infrastructure, and civic life have not eradicated all social ills; according to a

1993 study San Antonio is still one of the most residentially segregated cities in the Southwest, and Mexican Americans disproportionately bear the burden of poverty. The city's long-standing lack of industrial growth and unionism have facilitated the expansion of its low-wage workforce, relegating many Mexican-descent San Antonians, particularly women and their dependent children, to poor and working-class income levels. The 1990 census indicated that 29 percent of Mexican Americans in San Antonio lived below the poverty line, an improvement from their 42 percent poverty rate in 1960, but still nearly twice as high as the poverty rate for Anglo Americans in the city. The 2000 census figures for Bexar County, where San Antonio is located, reveal that although overall poverty rates in the county are somewhat lower, more than three times as many Hispanics live in poverty than their white, non-Hispanic counterparts. There are also persistent income disparities between Mexican Americans and Anglo Americans with equivalent education levels. In the face of continuing inequality and discrimination many Mexican Americans band together for mutual support and resist the embrace of a U.S. national identity through countless daily acts, such as speaking Spanish or "Spanglish," a combination of Spanish and English; retaining ethnic Mexican customs and eating Mexican foods; protesting the policies and actions of U.S. officials; and articulating memories that contradict the U.S. and Texas history often taught in schools.[18]

Various observers have opined that Mexican Americans suffer the plight of oppressed, second-class citizens. Shortly after World War II an Anglo American writer went so far as to claim that people of Mexican heritage "have a tendency to look on San Antonio as an occupied city. They feel much the same bitterness about . . . San Antonio . . . that Poles felt about Warsaw during the Nazi occupation." Commenting more that five decades later on the contrast between the political and economic advancement of some San Antonio Mexican Americans amidst the ongoing, debilitating poverty of many others, Professor Rodolfo Rosales of the University of Texas at San Antonio argued that contemporary political life in the city is marked by the "illusion of inclusion," that is, increased Chicana and Chicano political representation but little or no change in business leaders' unparalleled capacity to impose their vision of growth and development as the priorities of the city and its elected officials. Significantly, San Antonio's Mexican history and ambiance are both a source of pride for many Mexican American residents and the city's primary source of tourist appeal. Professor Antonia Castañeda of San Antonio's St. Mary's University points out the irony in this juxtaposition, averring that "we Latinos have contributed to our own demise" by promoting major tourist attractions like the annual Fiesta San Antonio, which celebrates an 1836 military victory and the independence of Texas from an allegedly inferior Mexican nation.[19]

Parish Leadership and Public Ritual

World War II helped facilitate a shift at San Fernando from an immigrant parish marked by strong pious societies to an increasingly Mexican American congregation that accentuates public ritual and worship. Parish organizations like the Asociación Nacional de los Vasallos de Cristo Rey illustrate the transition from Mexican national to Mexican American consciousness and identity, even among immigrants. By the 1940s the Vasallos were focusing considerable attention on the concerns of a Mexican-descent community that was establishing roots in the United States—to the detriment of their original purpose of fostering their Mexican homeland's national reconstruction. Though they initially offered their annual Cristo Rey novena as an intercessory prayer solely for Mexico, during World War II the organization dedicated the novena to prayer for the protection of U.S. soldiers and even "por Dios y por mi patria" (for God and my country)—the latter from an oration during the 1944 novena, for which the commemorative card depicted an image of the Sacred Heart of Jesus and the colors of the U.S. flag. The Vasallos also dedicated their monthly Holy Hour to intercession for the safe return of "our soldier parishioners." Though they initially raised money for projects in Mexico like the statue of the Sacred Heart of Jesus near Cubilete, Guanajuato, the Vasallos increasingly used their funds for the funerary and other needs of their members and to support parish projects like the 1943 construction of an altar for Our Lady of Guadalupe. In June 1951 a letter from the Vasallos organizational headquarters in León, Guanajuato, officially excused the San Fernando Vasallos from sending any further donations to Mexico and encouraged them to continue their work of fostering devotion to Cristo Rey in the United States.[20]

Several pious societies waned despite such efforts to accommodate their members' increased focus on life in the United States. By the late 1950s more than half of the eighteen parish organizations that had been operating in 1930 were no longer active in the parish. When Dolores Trippe, the founding president of the Vasallas, who had held her office for forty-five years, died in 1970 at the age of ninety-three, no new leadership arose to help the organization achieve its earlier prominence as an association of exiles. The diligent work of the Clare-

Commemorative card for the 1944 Cristo Rey novena at San Fernando Cathedral.
Courtesy Josefina Rodríguez.

tians helped sustain parish associations like the Vasallos as members began to age and decrease in number, and when the Claretians left San Fernando in 1978 the Vasallos and several other remaining pious societies dissolved. The Hijas de María is the only pious society that has continuously existed at San Fernando since before World War II, though as young women increasingly had opportunities for social activities outside church auspices, the extent of the organization's social events decreased considerably, as did the number of young women who participated. Indeed, although traditionally the Hijas was an organization of señoritas, in 1987 San Fernando leaders founded a section of the Hijas for señoras, providing ecclesial sanction for married women to continue in the organization. According to Carmen Cedillo, who has been associated with the Hijas at San Fernando since 1954, this adaptation played a significant role in the organization's longevity, as it enabled the Hijas to engage both Mexican immigrant women and their Mexican American daughters and granddaughters in common devotional and social activities.[21]

As pious societies popular among immigrants began to fade after World War II, parishioners founded some new associations to animate the congregation's faith and piety. In 1959 the San Fernando gymnasium was the site for the San Antonio archdiocese's first *Cursillo de Cristiandad* (Brief Course in Christianity), a lay-run retreat movement that trained participants to actively live and spread their Catholic faith. Over the next two decades the Cursillo enlivened the faith of many San Fernando parishioners and formed them as leaders in congregational life and beyond. One prominent pious society is the Guadalupanas, which women parishioners established in 1949 to provide a distinct association for promoting devotion to Our Lady of Guadalupe and organizing her feast-day celebration, a task for which the Vasallos de Cristo Rey had previously taken primary responsibility. Though separate organizations, at first the Vasallas and Guadalupanas had virtually the same membership; they even conducted their monthly meetings one right after the other in the same room. However, according to Josefina Rodríguez, a long-standing member of both organizations, a split between Vasallas president Dolores Trippe and younger parish leaders eventually drove the two societies apart.[22]

The Guadalupanas have enabled women parishioners—and beginning in 2002 a few men inductees as well—to develop their capacity as leaders and organize devotional activities like the Guadalupe triduum or novena. They also sought to enhance devotion by securing a Guadalupe statue for the parish in 1957,[23] replacing the image previously enshrined during the 1931 quadricentennial Guadalupe celebrations. Like other Guadalupe representations at the cathedral, this statue quickly became the object of widespread devotion, as in 1961 when, parish reports indicate, "throughout the day people came here to the cathedral to prayer [*sic*] before the altar of Our Lady of Guadalupe" on her feast day. The Guadalupanas in the parish still promote devotion to their celestial mother; many continue the custom of wearing the society insignia—a golden Guadalupe medallion with attached streamers in the tricolors of the Mexican flag—and even request that the insignia adorn their corpse at their funeral.[24]

Despite the emergence of the Guadalupanas and the ongoing efforts of the Hijas de María, today the San Fernando congregation does not have nearly as many novenas and similar devotional services as it did during the 1920s and 1930s, when the predominantly immigrant congregation formed numerous parish associations with their accompanying pious traditions. In some ways the liturgical reforms of Vatican II inadvertently abetted this decline. During the 1970s when San Fernando clergy instituted evening masses as authorized in new liturgical guidelines, the Hijas de María reduced their Marian devotions for the month of May from seven to four nights a week because the new Mass schedule conflicted with the customary hour for these observances. Similarly, the alteration of the dates for some liturgical feasts coincided with the diminishment of related devotional practices, such as the novena to Cristo Rey, which dissipated after the Christ the King feast was officially moved from the end of October to the end of November. The advent of television, increased access to entertainment and recreational activities, and the growing number of women with work responsibilities both inside and outside their homes had an even greater influence on the decline of parish associations and devotions among immigrants and nonimmigrants alike. Though some elderly parishioners bemoan these changes, congregants like Rosie Chacón aver that San Fernando is a vital community today precisely because it unifies people in common worship and public ritual but at the same time doesn't "have a lot of parish societies which fracture us."[25]

The rise of Mexican American leadership at San Fernando, which parallels Mexican American advances in other areas of church and society, inevitably shaped all elements of the congregation's day-to-day life, such as observance of religious traditions, the use of English, and the style and content of catechetical instruction, homilies, and pastoral *consejos* (advice). In 1939 the first and only Mexican American community of women religious, the Missionary Catechists of Divine Providence, established a house within San Fernando's parish boundaries and collaborated with lay women colleagues and other women religious to establish catechetical centers for children in neighborhoods throughout the parish. Subsequently the decrees of Vatican II provided for a revived permanent diaconate as an order of ecclesial ministry open to both married and single men, enabling Mexican Americans to exercise greater leadership and ordained ministry in pastoral work such as visiting the sick and imprisoned, preaching at Mass and other liturgies, and presiding at baptisms, weddings, and funerals. Currently there are four deacons at San Fernando, all of them Mexican Americans. Parish lay leaders are also predominantly Mexican American, and the congregation itself is increasingly so, though San Fernando's central location, its ambiance as a venerable cathedral, and its emphasis on Mexican religious traditions continues to attract a disproportionate number of San Antonio's Mexican immigrants, along with a few Latinos of other nationalities and some Anglo Americans.[26]

The departure of the Claretians led to the appointment of San Fernando's first Mexican American rector. Though the official reason for their departure was a "shortage of personnel" elsewhere, long-standing parishioners like Felipa Peña recall that several Claretians felt that archdiocesan authorities had failed to consult them adequately about a renovation of the cathedral in the 1970s, which the archdiocese funded in part with funds from the closing and sale of the San Fernando parish school. The aim of the renovation was to rehabilitate the aging historical structure and update it in accordance with the principles of Vatican II. When the work was completed in 1977, the cathedral was rededicated "to 'La Virgen de Guadalupe' as well as to all parishioners of San Fernando." The following year the Claretians left, and Monsignor Bernard Popp began his service as rector, which continued until he was named an auxiliary bishop of San Antonio in 1983. His replacement, Archbishop Flores's first appointee for cathedral rector, was Father Virgilio Elizondo, San Fernando's first native-born San Antonian pastor of Mexican heritage since the dismissal of Father Refugio de la Garza in 1840. When Elizondo completed the maximum two terms as cathedral rector in 1995, Archbishop Flores selected as his replacement Father David García, another Mexican American and native-born San Antonian.[27]

Elizondo, who is the son of Mexican immigrants, was deeply influenced by Vatican II, especially the conciliar documents' call for a return to the sources of faith; by the advent of liberation theology; and by the Chicano movement, which "forced me and many others to take a much deeper and more critical look at the inner functioning of our church and, even deeper yet, of religion itself." In 1972 he founded the Mexican American Cultural Center (MACC) at San Antonio as a "response to the struggles, frustration, and disappointments" of Mexican American Catholic leaders who contended the "multiple pastoral needs of our people" could only be addressed in the context of a fundamental recognition that "we have a unique identity of our own, for we have maintained our language, religion, and many of our customs and traditions in an English-speaking environment." As its first president, Elizondo helped forge MACC into a national training, advocacy, and research center for Hispanic ministry, rights, theology, and religious traditions.[28]

When Archbishop Flores invited Elizondo to serve as cathedral rector, he specifically commissioned the priest to apply lessons learned at MACC to his ministry at San Fernando: "Now is the chance to prove that what you have been saying needs to be done. Let's show what our people have to offer." The most conspicuous evidence that Elizondo took this commission to heart was his extensive efforts to foster pride in Mexican American heritage and identity, especially through the revitalization and reinvention of public ritual traditions at San Fernando. As sociologist of religion Stephen Warner noted after he first experienced the San Fernando congregation at worship, group traditions and identities are "made, not born," and the public rituals Elizondo shaped are "an assertive educational mission" and "an intentional engendering of religious and cultural traditions that he feels his parishioners have a right to embrace and to pass on to their children."[29]

The language used in San Fernando worship events confirms Warner's observations. When the Claretians instituted the liturgical reforms of Vatican II, such as vernacular celebration of the Eucharist, they did so by establishing a worship schedule that included some masses in Spanish and others in English.[30] Conversely, Elizondo and his successor, García, employ a bilingual style of preaching and prayer leadership that accommodates monolingual Spanish and English worshipers alike. At the same time, by strategically shifting back and forth between the two languages with a minimum of direct translation or repetition, they also keep bilingual worshipers consistently engaged. Their approach enables the various generations of Mexican-descent parishioners to worship together and intentionally fosters bilingualism as a valued expression of Mexican American identity and heritage.

The prominence of bilingual public rituals over the past two decades stems from the conscious desire of Elizondo, García, and other San Fernando leaders to foster ethnic pride, identity, and religious expression in a manner that is harmonious with Catholic liturgy and with teachings about human dignity and

God's presence and action in everyday life. Besides the posadas—reenactments of Mary and Joseph's pilgrimage to Bethlehem—in various parishioners' homes and neighborhoods during the nine days before Christmas, one grand posada is enacted on the streets of downtown San Antonio, with the holy pilgrims denied access at places like the city hall and county courthouse before finally receiving shelter at the cathedral. The proclamation of Jesus' passion and death on Good Friday begins in the public market, winds through the city's downtown streets, and ends with a dramatization of the crucifixion on the steps of the cathedral. In 1985 the San Fernando congregation began celebrating a weekly televised Mass that soon was broadcast internationally. Frequently these Sunday celebrations incorporate Mexican Catholic traditions such as an Epiphany entrance procession with parishioners dressed as the Magi, the blessing of children near the time of the feast of the Presentation of Jesus in the Temple, and the remembrance of the community's deceased heroes and leaders on a Sunday proximate to the feast of All Saints and All Souls, popularly known as *el Día de los Muertos*, the Day of the Dead.[31]

Although successive generations of parishioners have historically altered and molded San Fernando's devotional and liturgical life, like Elizondo and García numerous contemporary Mexican American congregants emphasize the continuity of sacred traditions celebrated at the cathedral. They maintain that these traditions form them as a people by keeping their religious and cultural heritage alive. As parishioner and psychologist Frank Paredes put it: "The public rituals and fiestas at San Fernando strengthen us in our identity by allowing us to pridefully celebrate our culture and faith." Patti Elizondo (no relation to Father Elizondo), a broadcaster, television documentary producer, and bilingual lector for masses at the cathedral, attested that San Fernando ritual events like Guadalupan feast-day celebrations awaken her "sense of community" and enable her "to indulge in the splendor of my rich culture and its infinitely delicate expressions of religious fervor." After a Good Friday procession in which thousands accompanied an enactment of Jesus carrying his cross through San Antonio's downtown streets, parishioner and journalist Victor Landa stated: "Every step down the Via Dolorosa is an affirmation of our past, an understanding of our present, and a courageous entrance into our future. Every year, as the procession winds its way from the Market Square to the cathedral, a community deepens its roots."[32]

The ongoing arrival and involvement of Mexican immigrants at San Fernando fosters the cultural and religious spirit that many Mexican Americans find so attractive. Guadalupe "Lupita" Alvarado came to San Antonio with her family as an early teen and soon began attending San Fernando, where she could "continue the traditions my mother had in Mexico." Her first vivid memory of the parish is the celebration of her *quinceañera*, a traditional celebration of a young woman's maturation to adulthood, which impressed upon her the need "to be like Mary and be strong in faith amidst the challenges of today's world." Subsequently she met another immigrant, Mario Mandujano, when they played the parts of Mary and Joseph in San Fernando's grand posada. Two years later they were married. Today Lupita works as San Fernando's director of religious education, and Mario serves as volunteer coordinator for the Guadalupe apparitions reenactment, the cathedral's annual grand posada, and the Good Friday passion drama and procession. They have three children, Marito, Andrés, and Aimeé, all of whom they have encouraged to participate in these ritual dramas and other religious customs. Like Lupita, Mario stresses his strong desire to "pass on to my children" the traditions that "my mother taught me."[33]

Celebration of major events at San Fernando, such as Pope John Paul II's 1987 visit or the funerals of prominent citizens like Congressman Henry B. González in 2000, further enhances congregants' pride in the prominence and public role of their parish and its members. Parish leaders like Gene Rodríguez are quick to point out that it is San Fernando's ethnic Mexican congregation that plays host on such occasions and welcomes dignitaries and other guests from San Antonio and beyond into their worship and traditions. As Rodríguez puts it, no matter where else San Antonians worship, San Fernando is "everybody's second home." Parishioners and visitors alike assert that the congregation has made the cathedral a sacred place where "lawyers stand in line for communion with day laborers" and an increasingly diverse body unites in worship. Former mayor Bill Thornton, a Baptist who frequently has partaken in cathedral worship and ritual traditions, notes: "I can feel just as comfortable at San Fernando in silk tie and dark suit as the homeless person sitting next to me. We would both be asked to participate. . . . San Fernando is a place where we can all come together as San Antonians."[34]

The weekly televised Mass attracts literally millions of worshipers from various religious, ethnic, and socioeconomic backgrounds, a number of whom send in letters and prayer requests and even visit San Antonio on pilgrimage to attend the Mass after first participating via television. During Elizondo's years as pastor, new celebrations like the citywide Thanksgiving service and the annual Pilgrimage of Hope for those afflicted with HIV/AIDS gathered Hindus, Buddhists, Muslims, Jews, and Christians from various denominations for interfaith services at the cathedral. García has fostered these annual worship events and has revived other traditions like the Spanish colonial practice of asking God's blessing on newly elected city council members, though in the present era this prayer service is interdenominational rather than a Roman Catholic celebration. Such celebrations and the general ambiance of hospitality at the cathedral led newspaper columnist Jan Jarboe to dub San Fernando the "celestial center of San Antonio."[35]

Critics of the cathedral's worship life find fault with the kinds of faith expressions enacted at San Fernando, with the way they are celebrated, or with their prominence (or lack thereof), but even these critics confirm San Fernando's renown as a parish whose leadership prioritizes the promotion of public ritual, particularly devotional traditions rooted in Mexican Catholicism. Some worshipers aver that the television broadcasts detract from the sacredness of their treasured expressions of faith. Parish leaders occasionally conflict over the preparation and performance of certain rituals and devotions: on Good Friday in 1991, for example, when the head of the parish office inadvertently assigned Lupita Alvarado de Mandujano (who was then a parish office staff member) to answer phones at the same time she was to participate in the passion drama, Lupita was dismayed and "shocked that this wasn't a day off" at the parish. Liturgists have commented that the religious traditions and practices of the San Fernando congregation interfere with the sacramental liturgy prescribed by the Roman Catholic Church.[36]

Adherents of other Christian denominations sometimes chide parishioners for their devotional traditions; during some public processions detractors stand on the plaza in front of San Fernando and repeatedly shout things like "You've been deceived! Believe in Jesus Christ and you shall be saved!"—implying that San Fernando congregants engage in superstitious devotions and lack the salvation offered through true biblical faith. Closely scrutinizing congregational involvement in social action efforts like those of COPS, an organization that San Fernando did not officially join until 1997, some observers question how effective the powerful ethnic affirmation of San Fernando's public rituals is in inspiring worshipers to struggle for justice and social transformation. Some Mexican Americans, particularly those who speak English predominantly or are monolingual, prefer to worship at more suburban parishes like those on San Antonio's north side. One young professional whom I met when she visited San Fernando for a family baptism told me that the "Mexican" devotions and celebrations are "good for the *mexicanos,* but not for us who are born here."[37]

New Generations of Devotees

Like other devotions and prayers at San Fernando during World War II, annual Guadalupe celebrations focused on prayers for "victory, peace, and the safety of the men on the battle fronts." Fully one-seventh of the congregation, nearly 1,500 parishioners, enlisted in the armed forces, at least ten times the number who had participated in World War I. Nearly every parishioner had an immediate family member, other relative, or friend in the military. A year after the United States entered the war the congregation reportedly participated in the annual Guadalupe triduum and public candlelight procession "with even greater devotion and solemnity than usual." In recognition of Our Lady of Guadalupe's 12 December feast day, they also united at Mass on the twelfth day of each month to plead that their celestial mother protect *los desaparecidos* (the "disappeared" soldiers—that is, soldiers missing in action). As parishioners risked and sacrificed their lives in the service of the United States, San Fernando devotees instinctively called on their Mexican patroness for protection as they had for generations in times of drought, sickness, exile, and other difficulties.[38]

The emergence of archdiocesan Guadalupe celebrations centered at San Fernando after the war further revealed and mediated Guadalupe's role as the patroness and guardian of Mexican Americans. In 1954, the hundredth anniversary of Pope Pius IX's definition of Mary's Immaculate Conception as a Catholic doctrine, San Antonio's observance of the international Marian Year culminated in an archdiocesan celebration of Guadalupe's feast with public processions and an outdoor Mass on the plaza in front of San Fernando. Two years later the San Antonio archdiocese's Catholic Council for the Spanish Speaking organized an archdiocesan Guadalupe celebration with some thirty-five thousand participants in what the archdiocesan and secular press hailed as the "largest mass religious demonstration in the history of San Antonio." Modeled on the 1954 event, this public display of devotion inaugurated an annual archdiocesan Guadalupe celebration with an outdoor Mass at the cathedral; eight years later inclement December weather led organizers to alter the custom to include an indoor Mass at a site like the Municipal Auditorium or the Convention Center Arena.[39]

The outdoor masses at San Fernando were preceded by massive public processions from other parishes, in most years Our Lady of Guadalupe church to the west of San Fernando, St. Henry's to the south, and St. Joseph's to the east. Significantly the lay planning committee for the archdiocesan Guadalupe feast was typically composed of about ten prominent Catholic men, half of them Anglo Americans and half Mexican Americans. Among the latter group were noted leaders like County Commissioner Albert Peña Jr., prominent businessman and city council member José Olivares, and civil rights activist Alonso Perales. Reflecting the organizers' conviction that Guadalupe extended her patronage to other San Antonians and to all peoples of the Americas, as well as to Mexican Americans, County Commissioner Peña, at the time also the president of the Catholic Council for the Spanish Speaking, remarked before the 1958 celebration: "Our Lady of Guadalupe is not the property of the Mexicans. She belongs to all the peoples of the Americas, and here in San Antonio . . . it is fitting that all Catholics turn out to pay special homage to the Mother of God, best known hereabouts as Our Lady of Guadalupe."[40]

Participants and symbolic representations in the archdiocesan Guadalupe celebrations reinforced the connection between Guadalupe, Mexican Americans, and other U.S. Catholics. Whereas in the 1920s and 1930s Spanish Claretian and Mexican exile clergy had presided over the Guadalupe feast, at these archdiocesan celebrations Archbishop Lucey, auxiliary bishop Stephen Leven, and numerous English-speaking and bilingual priests led a worship assembly that was primarily Mexican American. The honor guard for the archdiocesan celebrations frequently included organizations that were prominent among U.S. Catholics generally, like the Fourth Degree Knights of Columbus, the Holy Name Society, and the Boy Scouts of America, groups that took on a leadership role that pious societies and their predominantly immigrant members had previously held. In Guadalupe processions, the U.S. flag shared, and at times occupied exclusively, the place of honor formerly reserved primarily for the Mexican flag. For the 1960 archdiocesan celebration, organizers formed "Viva María" clubs patterned after the popular "Viva Kennedy" clubs formed during that year's presidential campaign; their efforts to incite greater participation in the Guadalupe celebration through "voter turnout" strategies like the use of posters and telephone committees reflected the pride of numerous Mexican Americans and other Catholics that one of their own had ascended to the highest political office in the United States. A major conference convened in conjunction with the 1963 celebration confirmed the link between Guadalupe and Mexican Americans; its general theme was "The Beauty of Merging Cultures," and it encom-

Priest and male devotees lead procession from Our Lady of Guadalupe parish to San Fernando cathedral, 1954. The U.S. flag is to the left of the Guadalupe image and the Mexican flag is to the right. Courtesy Felipa Peña.

passed workshops that focused on Mexican American efforts to enhance educational opportunities, equal employment, the rights of migrant farm workers, and "community acculturation."

At the same time, Guadalupe celebrations at San Fernando have continued to reflect Mexican piety and devotional traditions. The parish triduum, or in some years the novena, a practice that Mexican exiles and Spanish Claretians instituted at San Fernando during the early twentieth century, was the most consistent element of parish Guadalupe celebrations until the Claretians left the cathedral in 1978. Mexican songs like "Ante tu altar, Virgencita Morena" ("Before Your Altar, Brown-skinned Virgin") continued to evoke heartfelt devotion. In select years parishioners also engaged in established practices like the dramatization of Guadalupe's apparitions to Juan Diego and the corporate communion of parish societies on Guadalupe's feast day. On occasion the archdiocesan celebrations at San Fernando had distinctively Mexican elements, such as the dressing of children in "traditional Mexican costumes" in 1956; the participation of a boys' choir from Ciudad de los Niños of Monterrey, Mexico, in 1962; and the

Guadalupanas' presentation of Mexican "Indian gifts" to Our Lady of Guadalupe in 1963.[41]

Since their foundation in 1949, the San Fernando Guadalupanas have introduced and enacted other practices common in Mexican devotional life, like the formal reception of new members into their society on the Guadalupe feast, a crowning ceremony for Our Lady of Guadalupe, and the early morning song tribute of las mañanitas. To this day devotees like émigré Alfredo Ramírez contend that San Fernando's ambiance and vibrant celebrations of Mexican Catholic traditions like Guadalupe's feast make it "the one place in San Antonio that's still part of Mexico." Contemporary immigrant Guadalupan devotees at San Fernando offer prayers that reflect the homeland and maternal bonds many devotees associate with Guadalupe; one divorced woman who came to the United States "all alone" often asks Guadalupe to watch over her children still in Mexico. She also expresses frequent thanks for the "greatest gift" Guadalupe gave her: a dream in which her deceased mother "told me she would care for me in my struggles and in my problems."[42]

Nonetheless, the shift in emphasis from Mexican national to Mexican American consciousness in San Fernando's Guadalupan devotion is evident in the experience of parishioners like Josefina Rodríguez, a native of Monterrey, Mexico, who immigrated to San Antonio in 1925 and has worshiped at San Fernando Cathedral for most of her ninety years. The first time I visited her home, I was struck by the numerous sacred images and relics of San Fernando's past. Most notably, over her mantel was a huge banner of Our Lady of Guadalupe that she and other members of the Vasallas de Cristo Rey had used in their devotions decades before. When I gazed admiringly at the image and inquired about its association with the Vasallas, Josefina told me the story of her resettlement in the United States: her family's dismay at abandoning their war-torn homeland, their struggle to survive as newcomers in San Antonio, the solace and solidarity they found at San Fernando in Mexican religious traditions and parish associations like the Vasallas and later the Guadalupanas. But her most memorable moment in the parish was the day her son, Alex, left for the Korean War. Like so many times before and since, on that day Josefina prayed before San Fernando's image of Our Lady of Guadalupe. She is deeply grateful that Guadalupe answered her fervent supplications by bringing her son home safely a few years later. Time and circumstances, particularly the experience of bearing and bringing up her son and three daughters in the United States, had transformed Josefina's Guadalupan devotion: what had once expressed the prayers of a young woman longing for a lost homeland became the vehicle of a soldier's mother's intercessory pleas as she adapted with her family to life in a new land.[43]

The written prayer intentions and notes of gratitude that devotees customarily leave before images such as those of the crucified Jesus, Guadalupe, and the saints bear witness to the struggles and afflictions of many as they adapt to life in the United States: a worker pleads that their supervisor will act more charitably; another seeks hope amidst relentless financial and personal challenges; an infirm person offers thanks for healing after medicinal remedies had failed; a young woman begs for help to control her sharp temper and bring her boyfriend back into her life; an elderly person asks that recalcitrant government officials would grant Medicare and Medicaid benefits. One woman writes: "The man I'm living with is no good. He doesn't love my child. Help me to find a man that will love me and my child and if not me, at least my child." On a Sunday afternoon a young couple—the man a Mexican immigrant and the woman a Mexican American—kneel before the Guadalupe image at San Fernando, asking for work and the safe delivery of their second child. A young man in military uniform asks Guadalupe to intercede for him because "the end could come and we need to be close to God," while a mother pleads for her son, whose wife left him after he lost his job. A student from a local college explains that he has lit a candle before Guadalupe out of gratitude for success on his midterm examinations, commenting as many Guadalupan devotees do: "Our Lady of Guadalupe is magnificent; she's everything."[44]

Attempts to conjoin the intercessory prayers and faith expressions of Mexican-descent devotees from both sides of the border are evident in contemporary televised celebrations of the Guadalupe serenata, which parish volunteers like professional producer Homer Villarreal organized for the first time in 1988. The 1989 celebration illustrates the general pattern of the first San Fernando serenatas, which, despite some variation, continues to shape this annual parish event to the present day. Whether by design or not, the 1989 serenata encompassed symbolic juxtapositions that revealed it as a Mexican American expression of a Mexican tradition. Parishioners presented the Mexican-origin ritual dramas of the Guadalupe apparitions to Juan Diego, while San Antonio artists Alex Rubio and Alberto Ramírez complemented this custom by placing five murals in the sanctuary that depicted the apparitions in the contemporary Chicano style showcased on walls and buildings in San Antonio's west side. Famous Mexican stars Tito Guizar, Janice de Lara, and Manuel López Ochoa each offered an emotionally charged musical tribute to an image of Guadalupe in the church sanctuary, as did popular Mexican American singers Patsy Torres, Mario Bosquez, Michael Morales, Ada García, and Johnny Canales, along with San Fernando Cathedral choirs and local mariachi groups like the Rondalla de Mi Tierra. Packing the pews were participants of Mexican heritage from both sides of the border. At the conclusion of the event, the congregation and all the musical groups offered a stirring rendition of mañanitas to Guadalupe as the assembly unfurled colored streamers attached to the Guadalupe image, a ritual innovation that San Fernando leaders employed to symbolically link devotees to one another and extend the protective mantle of their common mother to her children beyond the Mexican border.[45]

At times serenata participants and television viewers have expressed criticism of and even outrage over the interweaving of devotion and popular songs, most notably selections of music such as a 1995 rendition of "Paloma Negra," a song about an unfaithful lover, which many deemed blasphemous in a ceremony to honor Guadalupe. Nonetheless, broadcasts of the serenata enhance perceptions of the San Fernando congregation's importance and credibility, accentuating ethnic affirmation as a central meaning of Guadalupan devotion at San Fernando. As one observer noted: "To watch a dignified usher signal discreetly to a colleague in the back of the crowded nave that he has two seats available halfway to the front—all while the TV cameras are rolling—is to sense the pride that is conferred by the centrality of the cathedral in the public life of San Antonio." Parish leaders are particularly pleased that live telecasts of the San Fernando serenata are usually aired immediately before coverage of celebrations at the Guadalupe basilica in Mexico City, juxtaposing San Fernando with the sacred center of Guadalupan devotion and making it, in the words of one devotee, "el Tepeyac del norte" (the Tepeyac of the north). Congregants have also noted that the serenata spreads Guadalupan devotion to non-Hispanics and, along with weekly broadcasts of the Sunday Mass, has had an evangelizing influence on people from far and near who participate via television. One of Janie García's many ministries at the cathedral has been helping to answer the "100 letters a day" that, she proudly attested, San Fernando's television ministry prompts viewers to send.[46]

Besides highlighting Guadalupe's importance for signifying and promoting their ethnic Mexican heritage, numerous contemporary parishioners emphasize that Guadalupe is an ideal representation of motherhood; many explicitly connect their devotion to her with their affection for their own mothers, grandmothers, aunts, and madrinas. Though parish leaders like Gene Rodríguez at-

Artists Alex Rubio and Alberto Ramírez enshrine one of their five murals depicting the Guadalupe apparitions, San Fernando Cathedral, 1989. Courtesy San Antonio Express-News Collection, University of Texas Institute of Texan Cultures, San Antonio.

test that "women have a sisterhood bond and common maternal experience with Guadalupe that no man can replicate," both male and female devotees acclaim Guadalupe as their mother. Some men come to Guadalupe seeking maternal solace after committing an injustice—at times even a harmful or violent act against their wife or another woman—rightly or wrongly expecting that a mother's love is always accepting. One male parish leader noted, "I've seen more of our men go directly to Our Lady of Guadalupe in church like they would plead before their own mothers. She doesn't always effect good behavior with some of the bad guys. They go to her for forgiveness after they've done their 'delito'"—that is, committed their offense. But men do not see Guadalupe solely as the supreme model of motherhood. Some tattoo her image on their bodies as a protective shield: a soldier bound for Iraq explained that a Guadalupe medal could be lost or stolen, but a tattoo would ensure that "she will always be with me and watch over me." Occasionally Guadalupe tattoos are juxtaposed with tattoos of women who are far more sensual than maternal. Men also honor Guadalupe at the serenata with affectionate songs like those they would typically direct to a wife or lover rather than their mother, revealing how devotees' imaginings of Guadalupe can interweave notions of maternity, romance, the female body, and eroticism in complex and varied formulations of idealized femininity.[47]

For men, however, leadership in San Fernando's public Guadalupan devotion has decreased in recent decades. Though they continue to offer Guadalupe public tributes in celebrations like the serenata, since the establishment of the Guadalupanas, male leadership in organizing the Guadalupe feast is no longer as conspicuous as it was during the colonial and Mexican periods and in subsequent eras when they participated in pious societies like the Vasallos de Cristo Rey and the planning committee for the archdiocesan Guadalupe celebrations after World War II. The increased privatization of devotion reflects a general trend in U.S. religion. It also confirms current parish leaders' claim that during the 1950s and early 1960s "as men had other avenues of [public] expression . . . their leadership in public devotion has lessened."[48]

The extension of Guadalupe's patronage to the lives of Mexican Americans and even non-Hispanics is reflected in claims about her capacity to synthesize diverse peoples and cultures. This had been an important theme in Mexican sermons and writings about Guadalupe since the nineteenth century, and *La Prensa* writers have expounded it in the post–World War II era. Pointing out that in Mexico Guadalupan devotion is common among criollos, Indians, and mestizos, one writer asserted that in that context Guadalupe continues her historical role of "influencing national unity, the spiritual fusion of races, the consolidation of national harmony." He also claimed that "our Guadalupan Virgin is not Spanish, nor is she of any Indian race; she is Mexican, that is, Indio-Hispanic," and thus she gives birth to a new civilization: she is "the synthesis of all that is good and pleasing in both races, the conquerors and the conquered."[49]

Expanding on this theme of synthesis, former San Fernando rector Elizondo proclaims in his preaching and theological writings that Mexican Americans are the dignified bearers of a rich mestizo heritage—neither Spanish nor Indigenous, neither Mexican nor North American, but a dynamic mixture of all these root cultures. In his view, the "mestiza" Guadalupe, "the first truly American person and as such the mother of the new generations to come," provides hope and inspiration for Mexican Americans struggling to embrace their identity as mestizos, synthesize the richness of their parent cultures, and be transformative agents of Guadalupe's power to harmonize diverse peoples. Like Elizondo, contemporary parishioners claim that Guadalupe unites ethnic Mexicans of all ages from both sides of the border, as well as Anglo Americans and other people throughout the Americas. Some devotees have proudly observed that the Guadalupe basilica in Mexico City has a permanent display of the national flags for all the countries in the Americas, a symbolic expression of unity imitated at San Fernando on occasions like the 1991 Guadalupe serenata and feast, when Guadalupe was honored as "the mother of all the Americas" at the outset of the fifth centenary of Columbus's arrival in the "New World."[50]

Celebratory claims about Guadalupe's role of inspiring harmony and creative synthesis are at times tempered with stern warnings about the high expectations and responsibilities these possibilities place on her devotees. While averring that the Guadalupe feast unites not just the different cultural groups in Mexico but also diverse devotees "without distinction of age or class," *La Prensa* editors warned that faithfulness to Guadalupe required an ongoing and urgent struggle for liberation from "a new form of slavery, that of hunger and ignorance that cruelly attacks the Indian races" in Mexico. The most memorable Guadalupan homily I have heard at San Fernando echoed these sentiments. Associate pastor Arturo Molina, a Chicano activist priest, emphatically challenged devotees with the message: "We cannot love Our Lady of Guadalupe unless we love *el pobre* [the poor one] Juan Diego with the commitment of our lives." Similarly, Elizondo opines that at times Guadalupe has been "co-opted and domesticated by the powerful of Mexico, including the church" and has also served to "canonize and maintain [class] divisions among the Mexican American people." Thus he

Devotee offering roses to Our Lady of Guadalupe, 1991. The flags of all the countries of the Americas surround the Guadalupe image. Courtesy San Antonio Express-News Collection, University of Texas Institute of Texan Cultures, San Antonio.

enjoins his fellow Mexican Americans to see in Guadalupe and in their own mestizo identity a calling and a mission, and he urges them to recognize that it is precisely those who know multiple cultures and have borne the pain of rejection who can lead the way in building a society in which the divisive barriers between peoples are broken.[51]

San Fernando leaders thus envision Guadalupe as a powerful symbol of unification, but there are limits to this power. During World War II Guadalupe was transformed from a symbol of Mexican nationalism into a protector of Mexican American soldiers fighting for the United States. She continued to serve in this new role during later conflicts, such as those in Korea, the Persian Gulf, and Iraq; during the Persian Gulf conflict one parishioner excitedly told San Fernando priests that the prayer of the rosary protected her nephew and three sons from harm. No extant records reveal that Guadalupe has ever been engaged at San Fernando as a symbol of protest against war, even during the Vietnam era, when many Chicano activists asserted that the war was unjust and protested the disproportionate Chicano representation in the armed forces and among the casualties of war. Indeed, Chicano antiwar activists in San Antonio like County Commissioner Peña often found that their protestations put them "outside the reality of a [Mexican American] community that historically had been very patriotic" and had frequently supported the military because their family members were enlisted and because it offered a rare opportunity for upward mobility. Thus although San Fernando devotees proudly acclaim Guadalupe as the mother of all, this affirmation does not necessarily lead to an explicit engagement of the gospel call to see one's "enemies" as sisters and brothers.[52]

Guadalupe celebrations at San Fernando do not have a strong ecumenical dimension. Though frequently noted for his ecumenical spirit, in 1947 Archbishop Lucey expressed his outrage at Protestant proselytizers, whom he accused of displaying "a picture of Our Lady of Guadalupe to deceive the unwary" among Mexican-descent Catholics. More recently Roberto Piña, who served as a MACC faculty member for more than two decades and regularly visits San Fernando to worship, attested that a relative who converted to Pentecostalism "sparked a family feud that has pitted brother against brother" when he "started bad-mouthing Catholic symbols such as Our Lady of Guadalupe." With the greater openness to non-Catholics encouraged by Vatican II, the organizers of the 1964 archdiocesan Guadalupe celebration at San Fernando planned to introduce an "ecumenical note," but it is not evident from extant reports what that note was. In 1986 a group of artists from the Methodist, Baptist, Episcopal, and

Photographs of soldiers placed before the Guadalupe image at San Fernando during the 1991 Persian Gulf conflict. Courtesy Virgilio Elizondo.

Catholic faiths presented a hand-carved Guadalupe icon to the cathedral, but apparently this image never gained prominence among San Fernando congregants, as it quickly faded from view and current parish leaders do not recall ever seeing it. Although San Fernando's participation and leadership in interfaith services and ecumenical efforts have increased considerably since Monsignor Popp's first years as rector, collaborative engagement of people from divergent religious traditions is not extensively reflected in the cathedral community's Guadalupan devotion, no doubt due in large part to the theological barriers related to understandings of Mary among Catholics and those of Protestant denominations and other religious groups.[53]

Clearly mestizaje—the blending of traditions, cultures, and peoples—is an ambiguous and complex process. Guadalupan devotees at San Fernando exhibit a wide array of understandings about how Guadalupe accompanies and guides them as they forge their lives in the pluralistic society of the United States. For example, though some community leaders, like *La Prensa*'s writers, continued to promote the "traditional qualities of the Mexican woman," which stemmed from the Guadalupan "Marian cult and her constancy at home," after World War II ethnic Mexican women at San Antonio became increasingly involved in public activism for Mexican American rights, in political campaigns, and later in elective bodies like the city council. A growing number of women at San Fernando, particularly professional women, perceive Guadalupe as a model for and supporter of their expanding public roles and their work outside the home—an understanding of Guadalupe largely absent from the testimonies of male devotees. As parish leader Esther Rodríguez observes, "Guadalupe gives you dignity to go places you haven't been before."[54]

Women like Mary Esther Bernal exemplify this claim. Bernal, who first served as San Fernando's organist in 1950 at the age of fifteen and later was choir director for more than two decades, compiled the first book with Spanish-language songs to be used in Texas public schools, went on to become the director of bilingual education for the San Antonio Independent School District, and subsequently was elected to two terms on the district's school board. She claims that "San Fernando taught me the leadership skills" to enter public life and to work for the reversal of injustices she still remembers from her early years: segregated buses and public facilities, the prohibition of teaching Spanish songs in San Antonio public schools, and the placement of "Be American. Speak English" signs on the walls of parochial schools. Her first memory of Guadalupe is of playing the organ for a Guadalupe celebration at St. Leo's parish, in which "my mother and all the ladies of the parish spoke Spanish" and sang Spanish songs that defied the anti-Mexican bias all around them.[55]

While assisting some Mexican Americans to advance in U.S. life, Guadalupe has also enabled many to sustain, or even rediscover, a sense of connection to their Mexican heritage and family. One young man from Victoria, Texas, about 115 miles southeast of San Antonio, came to the city as a college student and now is a counselor at San Antonio College. He attested that "my sister introduced me to Our Lady of Guadalupe about a year and a half ago" and that now he sees Guadalupe as "our most sacred rock and stronghold." His weekly Sunday routine includes attending Mass at San Fernando and then praying for his family before the cathedral's Guadalupe image—for his parents still in Victoria and his three siblings who are scattered around the country. He explains: "You know how it is. I come here and everyone else has their own family but I'm alone, so I come to pray to her so I can be with my family."[56]

Similarly, San Antonio native Tina Cantú Navarro recalled, "I went to a non-Hispanic school and grew up in a non-Hispanic environment, so I didn't hear of Guadalupe until I was an adult." After she completed a Master's degree in theater design at Yale University and returned home to teach at San Antonio's Trinity University, her sister Mary told her how Guadalupe had "appeared to the Indigenous people, not the haves but the have-nots. That impressed me and made her real to me." Subsequently Tina visited the Guadalupe basilica in Mexico City, where she decided to draw a costume sketch of Guadalupe as a spiritual exercise because "I am a costume designer and when I do that I become one with the person." She attested that she was "deeply moved" by Guadalupe's "countenance" and "her hands with a gentleness but also a tremendous strength," and she avowed that "every time I ask for something for someone I feel like she listens." Tina had been a San Fernando parishioner for about a decade when I interviewed her in 2003. She treasures the cathedral's worship celebrations, and she has designed new costumes for the parish posada and Good Friday procession to help enhance San Fernando's public ritual. In 2000 she became a member of the Guadalupanas. She values learning from the older members, helping in the preparation for the Guadalupe feast, and participating in other Guadalupana activities, like making altars for the parish Día de los Muertos celebration. As one who came to know Mexican traditions as an adult, Tina stated, "I feel maybe a greater need to come in touch with my roots."[57]

Guadalupe's role in Mexican American mestizaje not only animates a sense of devotees' ongoing links to their Mexican origins, but also is a means for ethnic Mexicans in the United States to contest and reconfigure elements of their Mexican background. Chicana writer Sandra Cisneros critically reappraises Guadalupe as an advocate for counteracting the "traditional" gender roles and expectations that she purportedly buttresses. Though Cisneros is far from typical of San Fernando worshipers and is professedly estranged from the Catholic Church, when we conversed several times during the mid-1990s she was holding weekly peace vigils before the Guadalupe image at San Fernando to pray for her friend Jasna in Sarajevo. She had also acclaimed San Fernando in a *New York Times Magazine* article as San Antonio's foremost "sanctuary of the spirit." During her childhood and young adult years in Chicago, Cisneros had learned to perceive Guadalupe as a source of divine sanction for a familial and cultural code of silence about women's bodies and sexuality, as well as for a double standard of feminine purity and masculine promiscuity. Only after a series of experiences like her weekly peace vigils at San Fernando and a visit to the Guadalupe basilica at Tepeyac, Mexico, was she able to reclaim Guadalupe. These experiences and Cisneros's association of Guadalupe with a pre-Columbian antecedent, the goddess Tonantzin, enabled her to embrace Guadalupe as a brown-skinned, feminine manifestation of divine power who dwells "inside each Chicana and mexicana" and can enable them to see the totality of their corporeal existence as created in the divine image. Describing herself as someone "obsessed with becoming a woman comfortable in her skin"—brown skin that she sees reflected in the divine pantheon through Guadalupe—Cisneros sums up her view of Guadalupe by adapting words from the Hail Mary, "Blessed art thou, Lupe, and, therefore, blessed am I."[58]

Still other devotees turn to Guadalupe not as a corrective for perceived deficiencies in their Mexican heritage, but for protection against the pitfalls and evils they see in the United States. Kneeling before the Guadalupe image in the center of the San Fernando sanctuary during the 2003 Guadalupe feast, Peter Paul Ruiz prayed so intently with his gaze fixed on the eyes of Guadalupe that other devotees walked around him rather than obstruct his line of sight. He didn't finish his lengthy prayer until the start of Mass necessitated that he move from the sanctuary. A Mexican American in his late twenties or early thirties who has never spoken Spanish, Ruiz feels a strong attraction to San Fernando and its Guadalupe image, and he has "prayed before her here for years." He offered an extensive, stream-of-consciousness commentary on his prayer intentions that day that reflected his perspectives on a variety of political and societal concerns. Besides interceding for his parents, who had died in recent years, as U.S. forces struggled in Iraq Ruiz came before Guadalupe to pray for

> our soldiers and for peace, . . . for the protection of the Americas and of this nation, because we wouldn't be where we are today without her. Look at all this country has. But now we are threatened by evil. Look at this gay marriage thing. . . . And it's sad to say but this affects even the church lately. And the judges just let them do it. They don't care, as long as they get their money. The same thing they did to us with abortion. That's not right. And it hurts women. They used to have status, now they don't have status. So I pray to her to watch over this country because there's lots of evil now.[59]

Like those of Cisneros, Ruiz's strong views on Guadalupe are not those that most San Fernando devotees express. Ruiz's and Cisneros's sharply opposing views on sexuality and women illustrate the widely diverse—and even contradictory— ways that contemporary devotees engage Guadalupe.

Varied perspectives on the meaning of Guadalupe have not diminished San Fernando devotees' conviction that she strengthens and assists them in their daily lives as U.S. residents; nor has it inhibited them from fostering Guadalupan devotion among the young. Though parishioners have sought to transmit their faith and religious traditions to younger community members for generations, this task has taken on an even more conspicuous and programmatic form as a larger proportion of the children in the parish have been born and raised in the United States. During the 1950s and 1960s the majority of participants in the archdiocesan celebrations at San Fernando were Mexican American children and young adults who joined in the public processions with their classes from Catholic elementary schools, high schools, and colleges. Often one of the choirs for the event comprised students. Because a number of these younger Mexican Americans preferred to speak English while many of their parents and elders preferred Spanish, the sermons, songs, and devotional prayers were usually in both languages. In 1964, the first year in which the Vatican II liturgical reforms allowed for Mass to be offered in the vernacular, organizers chose English rather than Spanish as the language for the outdoor Mass. Floats depicting Guadalupe's four apparitions to Juan Diego circled the plaza prior to the Mass in 1963 and 1964 in a paradelike addition to the annual festivities that was intended as both an expression of devotion and a catechetical lesson to inspire a new generation of Guadalupan devotees.[60]

The Guadalupanas have fostered devotion by enlisting young people to take active roles: participating in Guadalupe processions, crowning her image, presenting flowers to her, and publicly praying the rosary. Father Elizondo introduced the practice of children and young adults offering homage and thanksgiving to Guadalupe with the traditional *matachines* dances, a popular custom from Mexico that enables Mexican Americans to learn the veneration of Guadalupe and to appreciate the Indigenous roots of their mestizo ancestry. During

Float depicting apparition of Our Lady of Guadalupe to Juan Diego circles the plaza in front of San Fernando, 1964. Courtesy Catholic Archives at San Antonio, Chancery Office, Archdiocese of San Antonio.

Mass on special occasions like the Guadalupe feast, he and other San Fernando priests have involved children in various ways, such as inviting them to sit near the altar during the homily or to offer Guadalupe flowers and silent prayers at an appropriate moment during the service.[61]

The objective of fostering Guadalupan devotion among the young was evident in the 2003 Guadalupe serenata, where a group of young women from Irving Middle School came in mariachi uniforms and carried the flags of Mexico, Texas, and the United States in the procession. All stated that either their grandmother or mother had taught them the importance of Guadalupe, whom they viewed as "our mother and the mother of Jesus." A Mexican American young man who attended the feast—a fifteen-year-old dressed in blue jeans, gym shoes, and an Adidas T-shirt—said that Guadalupe is significant because she is "the mother of God and came to bring her son to the Indians of Mexico."[62] Like many other children and teenagers at San Fernando, these observers echoed the lessons they had received: Guadalupe is their mother, someone they can turn to in time of need, and an important figure in the history and the lives of the Mexican people. Their attachment to Guadalupe reflects the efforts of their families and the San Fernando congregation to inculcate in them a corporeal grasp of Guadalupe's significance.

Nonetheless, many parish leaders and Guadalupan devotees express concern, and in some cases anxiety, that younger generations will fail to embrace their Catholic faith and traditions like Guadalupan devotion, particularly as a growing number of young people lack direct links to the living memory of their Mexican heritage. Until recently most Mexican Americans who worshiped and exercised leadership in the congregation had immigrant parents or grandparents, caregivers who often taught them Spanish prayers, Mexican Catholic faith expressions, and a sense of awe and wonder before the sacred. As these vital familial links with Mexico are weakened in generational transition and young people are more fully integrated into U.S. society, the challenge of initiating younger congregants into their elders' spiritual vision and faith expressions intensifies. The concerns of parish leaders are consistent with the research findings of Anthony Stevens-Arroyo, who shows that besides the well-known growth of Hispanic Protestantism, which now encompasses one-fourth of the U.S. Latino population, the percentage of Hispanics in the United States who profess "no religion" doubled to 13 percent during the 1990s.[63]

Longtime parishioner and prayer group leader Zulema Escamilla Galindo speaks for many parents and grandparents when she details the persistent problems she perceives among the young in her neighborhood on San Antonio's west side: drugs, crime, poor education, unemployment, a lack of respect for elders, and the absence of a sense of purpose in life. Her devotion to Guadalupe was most deeply confirmed when she received consolation and hope from being able to "share my pain with the Virgin" during the funeral Mass and other prayers offered for her son. Galindo acclaims the efforts to engage people of all ages in Mexican Catholic faith expressions at San Fernando, and she fosters these expressions among her friends and extended family by organizing neighborhood celebrations of traditions like las posadas and the *levantado del niño* (a prayer service on the occasion of the solemn removal of the child Jesus from the crib to mark the end of the Christmas season). She especially encourages the participation of her grandchildren and other young people in parish events like the Guadalupe feast because "we need these traditions to evangelize our children. . . . We've got to give our *jovenes* (young people) something that can guide them."[64]

Mestizo Discipleship

The shift at San Fernando from primarily exilic to Mexican American Guadalupan devotion does not represent a pattern among all ethnic Mexicans in the United States. Devotion to Guadalupe is more widespread and diverse than ever in U.S. Catholic congregations. Parishes like St. Cecilia in New York, a city whose Mexican population tripled during the 1990s, reflect the ongoing waves of new Mexican immigration in many locales and the primarily émigré focus of an earlier era at San Fernando. Recently Guadalupan devotees in the East Harlem congregation stimulated a "renewed interest in patron saints" when their enshrinement of the Guadalupe image prompted other parishioners to press for public displays of their own sacred patrons: for Blacks the mulatto St. Martin de Porres, for Puerto Ricans Nuestra Señora de la Divina Providencia, for Ecuadorans the Virgin of Cisne, and for Filipinos their customary regal-looking child Jesus. Leaders in other parishes accentuate varied meanings of Guadalupan devotion; for example, they engage Guadalupe to draw her devotees into the sacraments as did the Claretians at San Fernando, to counteract Protestant proselytization as did some nineteenth-century French clergy in San Antonio, to foster social concern and involvement in social action, and to educate devotees in post–Vatican II Catholicism.[65] As in the case of San Fernando congregants, adaptation to life in the United States shapes the varied meanings of Guadalupan devotion in numerous faith communities, as do multiple combinations of other factors evident in San Fernando's historical experience: levels of ongoing immigration, proximity to the border, the political and social situation and the state of Guadalupan devotion in the Mexican region from which émigré devotees originate, the ethnic and racial composition of the U.S. parishes where they worship, their experiences of welcome and rejection in church and society, their socioeconomic status, generational transition, settlement patterns, and the pastoral vision of church leaders they encounter.

Many elements of Guadalupan devotion at San Fernando illuminate congregants' increasing attention to their life concerns as Mexican Americans, from the striking transition of the Guadalupe celebrations' intercessory focus during World War II to the personal prayer intentions and testimonies of contemporary supplicants. Unlike exile leaders of the early twentieth century, Mexican immigrants with prominent ministerial roles at San Fernando today, such as Lupita and Mario Mandujano, are more explicitly focused on helping their children preserve Mexican traditions in the United States than on the social reconstruction and well-being of the country they left behind. Over the past half-century San Fernando's immigrant and Mexican American leaders have employed Guadalupan devotion and other religious practices in an instructional effort directed at both young and adult ethnic Mexicans—mestizos whom Jorge Gracia has rightly deemed the "product of a long, drawn-out gestation that still continues"[66]—so they can draw inspiration from their Mexican traditions and more resourcefully live in the United States on their own terms.

The effort to form mestizo disciples reflects the conviction that mestizaje, particularly that which originates in military conquest rather than mutual choice, is not a process best left to chance and circumstance, but one for which participants must be prepared. More broadly, it is an attempt to address the dilemma that has been present in Guadalupan devotion since its inception: how to reconcile and integrate the Spanish with the Indigenous and, in more recent times, the U.S. North American with the Mexican. Just as Juan Diego was reassured of his dignity by his encounter with the brown-skinned Guadalupe and was enabled to overcome humiliation and deliver Guadalupe's message to Bishop Zumárraga, when devotees acclaim the fundamental goodness of their celestial mestiza and their mestizo heritage, they gain greater confidence to demand unity born of mutual respect in their daily interactions—with bosses and coworkers, strangers and neighbors, spouse and in-laws, elected officials and civil servants, even parish leaders and their fellow congregants. The engagement in San Fernando's public ritual of activists like Alonso Perales, Albert Peña Jr., and Veronica Salazar; artists like Alex Rubio and Patsy Torres; mothers and parish organization leaders like Zulema Escamilla Galindo and Josefina Rodríguez; newscasters and journalists like Patti Elizondo and Victor Landa; elected officials like Henry B. González and Mary Esther Bernal and her husband, former state senator Joe Bernal, along with numerous other professional and working-class congregants, reveal the resonance this educational mission has with many ethnic Mexicans and its multiple links with wider currents in the civic life of San Antonio.

Seen in this light, the assertion of San Fernando leaders over the past five decades that Guadalupe is not merely an ethnic or national symbol but the mestiza mother of the Americas represents simultaneously a call to unity and an affirmation of ethnic Mexican heritage and pride. After all, according to the leaders, it is *their* celestial mother who can bring greater harmony, reconciliation, and equality to a fragmented and divided world. Such acclamations of Guadalupe's international patronage, which Pope John Paul II confirmed in his 1999 proclamation that she is the "mother and evangelizer of America,"[67] reflect the frequent tension in religious traditions between tribalism and all-embracing community, between the particular and the universal. Even as Mexican Americans engaged their celestial mestiza as the special protectress of them as her children striving to forge a new life in a stratified society, they also envisioned an amplified domain for Guadalupe that encompassed other U.S. residents, including the very Anglo Americans against whom Guadalupe purportedly protected them, as well as all the peoples of the Americas and anyone in the process of mestizaje or synthesis.

At San Fernando the two poles of universalism and ethnic affirmation are not equal in strength, however. Along with her maternal care, Guadalupe's association with ethnic pride and group solidarity are clearly the most pronounced collective meanings of public Guadalupan devotion in the history of San Fernando and many other ethnic Mexican communities; her unifying message is a challenging vision that San Fernando leaders have accentuated only recently and that, by their own admission, they and their congregation have yet to fully embrace and live. Moreover, as Arturo Bañuelas has noted, the presumption that Mexican Americans, spurred by their experience of struggle, rejection, and the countervailing collective dignity and pride they receive from Guadalupe, will massively "accept their divine election and mission to forge a new Christian universalism"[68] does not eliminate the possibility that many will ignore or only halfheartedly support pastoral leaders' call to enact that mission. No San Fernando parishioners openly contest their leaders' vision—who would argue against a proclamation that their beloved Guadalupe is the mestiza mother of all? Most are openly pleased and welcoming when non-Mexicans join in their Guadalupan devotion and other celebrations or participate in the events via television and by sending letters to the parish. But for many congregants the ongoing daily struggles for respect, sustenance, familial well-being, health, and a better life make them more likely to seek Guadalupe's maternal aid for their own needs, survival, and sense of dignity than to be her instruments for addressing social fragmentation and other problems in a systematic fashion.

Other barriers further inhibit the capacity for enacting Guadalupe's call to unity, such as the lack of ecumenical participation in San Fernando's Guadalupe celebrations and accusations of Catholic "Mariolatry," or Marian idolatry, from Pentecostal and other Protestant groups. Ethnic Mexicans' history of oppression may also cause, as Bañuelas has warned, "negative manifestations of the very obstacles mestizaje is called to overcome."[69] Distinctions like those between women and men and between devotees of different social classes can lead to harmful interactions and divisiveness, as they have throughout San Fernando's history. Supplicants' pain and disgust at their plight are evident in their prayer intentions, their Guadalupan perspectives on male-female relations, and the pleas of contemporary parish leaders that Guadalupe's unconditional love and transformative presence impel her followers to eliminate disharmony and discrimination, even within their own parish community. A more subtle but potent obstacle to Guadalupe's unifying power is the "illusion of inclusion": the advancement of some Mexican American leaders is taken to represent a formidable transformation in a stratified social order, but their advancement fails to substantially address devotees' and other ethnic Mexicans' aspirations for a more thoroughly egalitarian society. Finally, despite the individual involvement of some parishioners and worshipers, there is a lack of sustained collaboration and engagement between the San Fernando congregation and noteworthy activist groups like LULAC, the American G.I. Forum, MALDEF, MABPWA, and, until recently, COPS. This is yet another area in which the Guadalupan vision of concord and inclusive pluralism could be more fully enacted, a concern parish leaders are currently attempting to address through San Fernando's first community center for parish-based and other community outreach programs.

Like that of many other sacred figures and icons, Guadalupe's adaptability as an ethnic or patriotic symbol is striking. Writing in the mid-seventeenth century, Miguel Sánchez presumed that the Spanish conquest of Mexico was an act of divine providence. He applauded Guadalupe as Spain's "assistant conqueror" and attested that the "heathenism of the New World" was "conquered with her aid." But Sánchez's often-repeated assertion that Guadalupe chose the people of New Spain as her own resounded in the early-nineteenth-century struggles for Mexican independence under the banner of Guadalupe and subsequently in the ways devotees symbolically associated Guadalupe with the Mexican nation.[70] At San Fernando and various other U.S. parishes with sizeable contingents of ethnic Mexican congregants, the link between Guadalupe and U.S. nationalism has never been as pronounced as her association with Mexico—the Mexican flag and tricolors still appear far more frequently at Guadalupe celebrations than those of the United States. But the shift during World War II from Guadalupe as a symbol of Mexican nationalism to her role as a protector of Mexican American soldiers fighting for the United States reflects the long-standing tendency of her devotees to equate their own national sentiments with hers.

One of the greatest potential limitations to Guadalupe's uniting of peoples and cultures is the ambiguity of mestizaje itself. Some scholars and observers dichotomize the possible outcomes of ethnic Mexican contact with the U.S. milieu and a majority-culture Catholicism steeped in European roots, arguing either for assimilation or for resistance and cultural retention. But the recent history of San Fernando reveals a far more complex process of hybridization and mutual influence among varying actors, traditions, and social forces. San Fernando devotees claim that Guadalupe has enabled them to recover, celebrate, reinterpret, reconfigure, and contest elements of their Mexican background in varied and sometimes conflicting ways, as well as to shape their efforts toward advancement, protest, resistance, and adaptation in the United States. Thus, though the engagement of Guadalupe as a help and guide for Mexicans and Mexican Americans is widespread at San Fernando, devotees do not express a clear consensus on what a Guadalupan vision means for their daily lives and for their participation in U.S. church and society.

Despite the limitations, inconsistencies, divergent views, and ambiguity that to some degree thwart Guadalupe's transformative influence, San Fernando leaders continue their plea for Guadalupan devotees to be ambassadors of the celestial mestiza and to promote their parish's penchant for dramatic public rituals. They also urge Guadalupe's faithful to provide a witness of faith, unity, and what Alejandro García-Rivera has called "subversive hospitality,"[71] a reversal of roles in which Mexican Americans are the Juan Diegos who welcome Anglo Americans and other San Antonians to their parish and its traditions and provide a model for a new future of respectful pluralism. As Father Elizondo puts it, public witness and ritual reversals of this sort help Mexican Americans to recognize their "self-worth, fundamental dignity, radical equality, and love" and constitute "the innermost and deepest beginning of liberation. It certainly does not stop there. But, on the other hand, there is no other authentic beginning."[72] San Fernando leaders are aware of the multiple challenges and obstacles that impede the advance of this liberating vision, especially the concern that Guadalupe's power to effect harmony can be undermined by a decline in devotional fervor if new generations are not formed in the Guadalupan and other religious traditions. As a new century dawns and the cathedral renovation and City Centre project provide the occasion for reimagining San Fernando's role as a cathedral faith community, the mestizaje of these new generations is at the heart of their future and the future of the congregation's Guadalupan devotion.

The Future of
Guadalupan Devotion

San Fernando leaders' views regarding the future of Guadalupan devotion—along with the views of various scholars and other observers—range from an optimistic confidence that devotional fervor will continue unabated to dire predictions that veneration of Guadalupe will fade through generational attrition, as did the distinctive faith expressions of numerous European Catholics who immigrated to the United States. Yet the San Fernando case illuminates several factors that influence the possible trajectories for Guadalupan devotion among cathedral congregants and other ethnic Mexicans. One important factor is the vision of pastoral leaders. Their influence at San Fernando has been evident in pastoral initiatives from lay town council members' labors during the Spanish colonial era to the efforts of Mexican American pastors, women religious, deacons, and lay congregational leaders in recent decades. But the capacity to implement a particular pastoral vision is never absolute, as many San Fernando leaders have discovered: Claretians who tried to link Guadalupe with proper reception of the sacraments, women who sought gender egalitarianism under Guadalupe's inspiration, justice advocates who pronounced a Guadalupan call to social activism, and proponents of exilic and mestizo understandings of Guada-

lupe have all found that congregants embraced and acted on their ideals to varying degrees.

Today at San Fernando, as the City Centre project expands parish facilities
and provides new opportunities to enrich the congregation's faith life and mission, lay leaders and clergy are once again articulating various priorities and concerns for the parish. Though the congregation has always maintained far more
links with Mexico than with dominant-culture U.S. Catholicism—the parish has
had only one Anglo American pastor in nearly three centuries—a growing connection to U.S. Catholicism is illuminated in changes like the recent cathedral
renovation, which mirrored a national trend for arranging worship space in a
manner that places the altar closer to the liturgical assembly. In the proximate
future the shortage of Catholic clergy could easily lead to a decrease in San Fernando's current contingent of two priests, amplifying the need to develop more
lay leaders and to foster an even greater spirit of collaboration between the clergy
and laity, especially the numerous women who are influential figures in the
parish and in their families and communities.

Parish leaders' recent efforts to consciously foster bilingualism, Mexican
Catholic devotions, and awareness of the mestizaje process reveal their recognition that the formation of young leaders and devotees is essential for the trans-
mission of traditions like Guadalupan devotion. Father David García is in the
midst of his second six-year term as rector, and some congregants already wonder aloud whether his replacement will be as dedicated, energetic, and committed to Guadalupan devotion and other ethnic Mexican faith expressions. Occasionally parish leaders dare to voice the fear that a new rector could inhibit or
end the prominence of ethnic Mexican traditions at San Fernando and decree a
worship style that rigidly conforms to official liturgical rubrics. But more often
lay leaders confidently assert that their parish community will continue to pros-
per even with changing and fewer clergy personnel, as it has for generations.
Nonetheless, the choice of archbishop, cathedral rector, and other pastoral leaders will play a crucial role in San Fernando's future, potentially altering current
trends like the vital interplay among liturgy, devotion, public ritual, and media
in parish traditions like the Guadalupe feast.

Contemporary efforts to engage Guadalupe as a guide and support for ethnic Mexicans adapting to life in the United States do not eliminate the importance of ongoing contact with Mexico—both through San Antonio's proximity
to the border and continuing Mexican immigration—which has arguably had
the most consistent and lasting historical influence on Guadalupan devotion at

San Fernando. This influence spans from Francisco de Florencia's book that inspired the Guadalupan dedication of the first Spanish expedition into the San Antonio area to today's ongoing participation of Mexican immigrants and the televised juxtaposition of the San Fernando serenata with the celebration at the Guadalupe basilica in Mexico City. Though in recent years parish leaders have acclaimed Guadalupe as a mestiza who calls her children to unite diverse peoples, her strong association with Mexican nationalism, identity, and human dignity have consistently intensified and sustained the fervor of Guadalupan devotion.

The arrival of Mexican nationals and the ongoing transnational migration across a porous border show no signs of abating. However, Mexico itself is ever evolving, and changes in socioeconomic and religious conditions there—such as increased urbanization, the impact of globalization, and the growth of Protestantism, especially Pentecostalism and evangelicalism—could alter the degree, expressions, and meanings of Guadalupan devotion among newcomers to the United States. For the foreseeable future continuing immigration and contact with Mexico will play a major and varied role in the shape of Guadalupan devotion at U.S. parishes like San Fernando: sustaining or increasing the passionate fervor for Guadalupe among Mexican Americans and other U.S. residents, prompting some parishioners to seek congregations where ethnic Mexican faith expressions are less conspicuous, and expanding Guadalupe's role as a mother who helps ethnic Mexicans adapt to U.S. society, among other possibilities. Moreover, the population of Latinos from Central and South America and the Caribbean, though still relatively small at San Fernando, will continue to grow and to diversify many U.S. communities and the feast days and religious traditions they celebrate, placing Guadalupe's within a wider constellation of patronal feasts and devotions. The increasingly pluralistic context in which Guadalupe is venerated will further mold the devotion's prominence, expressions, and significance in many locales.

If the San Fernando case is any indication, the striking parallels between the Guadalupe apparition narrative and the history of Guadalupan devotion reveals that the paradigmatic figures and story of Guadalupe, Juan Diego, and Juan de Zumárraga will extensively shape the future contours of Guadalupan devotion. For numerous San Fernando and other devotees the core experience of the devotion is the replication of Juan Diego's intimate, mystical encounter with their celestial mother. In innumerable conversations, prayers, and sustained gazes at her image, devotees relive this mystical encounter. Their experience of the consolation and acceptance Guadalupe offers Juan Diego is so potent that even those confessing their failures—such as men seeking forgiveness for violence against women—have presumed that they enjoy Guadalupe's continued love and support. Juan Diego's vindication before Bishop Zumárraga and his assistants also resonates with many devotees who have endured the sharp sting of hostility and rejection in their daily lives.

As sisters, daughters, and mothers, women devotees often identify not just with Juan Diego but with Guadalupe herself, a powerful but ambiguous figure of motherhood, womanhood, purity, activism, and strength. Given the difficulty for any human being to pursue personal change and conversion, it is not surprising that in faith communities like San Fernando neither women nor men tend to associate themselves with Bishop Zumárraga, the figure in the story who repents of his ethnocentrism and initial rejection of Guadalupe's poor Indigenous messenger. Guadalupe speaks most powerfully to women and the rejected precisely because the apparition story announces the possibility of personal and social transformation and the good news of their fundamental dignity and worth; her voice is more muted among those who dehumanize and demean others— the Zumárraga tendency that lurks inside all of us—because of the challenging demands self-examination entails. Like the apparition narrative, which only implicitly challenges the Spanish colonial order's systemic domination of the Indigenous peoples, San Fernando Guadalupan devotion has rarely included a direct critique of social structures and power dynamics.

The Guadalupe apparition narrative simultaneously presents devotees a reason for hope and a poignant reminder that, as a popular saying goes, "la vida es la lucha" (life is struggle). She is hope that the drama of Juan Diego and Juan de Zumárraga reveals a divine plan in which the humanity and dignity of the lowly are restored, injustice is set aright, strangers become friends, enemies are reconciled, and the love of a common mother prompts mutual respect and harmony. But she is also a reminder that, in ways her children often see only partially, the final resolution of this drama has yet to be realized in their personal lives, families, communities, and society. Guadalupan devotion is deeply rooted in the imaginative horizon of the apparition narrative, and its future trajectory is intrinsically linked with devotees' tendency to engage Guadalupe as a sacred but tragic heroine: tragic in the sense that her holy presence illuminates their failures and flaws and the ongoing need for a more humane and harmonious world, yet heroic because she engenders confident trust that the transformation of their lives and their world has already dawned with the help of her celestial aid. As with other foundational sacred narratives and icons, the dynamic interplay between varied Guadalupan visions of life as it is and life as it could be continues to shape the parameters and evolution of her followers' faith and devotion.

Guadalupan devotion is an embodied, flexible tradition that has enabled generations of diverse practitioners at San Fernando to learn, express, accept, change, and cope with essential elements of their lives: faith, illness, safety in battle, identity, changes in national government, daily struggles, exile, employment, economic status, male-female relations, social hierarchies, adaptation to life in the United States, the meaning of discipleship for mestizo believers, and many others. Devotees' fundamental conviction about their celestial mother is that she never abandons them. As contemporary parish leader Mary Esther Bernal put it, "She is love, but first and foremost she is hope in all that we face." The most certain statement about Guadalupe's future is that she will continue to abide amidst the evolving web of relationships, communal structures, needs, and desires that her devotees create and inhabit, serving as a mirror that simultaneously reinforces and transforms their attitudes, actions, and aspirations.

Notes

ABBREVIATIONS

ACM   Archives of Claretian Missionaries, Western Province, U.S.A., Claretian Center, Los Angeles
BA   Bexar Archives, Center for American History
CAH   Center for American History, University of Texas, Austin
CASA   Catholic Archives at San Antonio, Chancery Office, Archdiocese of San Antonio
CAT   Catholic Archives of Texas, Austin
NA   Nacogdoches Archives, Center for American History

INTRODUCTION: An Evolving Tradition

1. "Información por el sermón de 1556," 44 (first four quotations), 72 (last two quotations), 36–72. See also Poole, *Our Lady of Guadalupe*, 58–64; Brading, *Mexican Phoenix*, 268–275; Lundberg, *Unification and Conflict*, 204–216. With the single exception of a citation noted in chapter 2, all quotations from Spanish-language sources in this book are my translations.

2. Sahagún, "Sobre supersticiones"; Carrasco, *Religions of Mesoamerica*, 136–137; Broda, "Sacred Landscape of Aztec Calendar Festivals," 89–90.

3. "Información por el sermón de 1556," 36–141; Brading, *Mexican Phoenix*, 271–279.

4. De la Torre Villar and Navarro de Anda, *Testimonios históricos Guadalupanos*; J. B. Smith, *Image of Guadalupe*; Noguez, *Documentos guadalupanos*; Poole, *Our Lady of Guadalupe*; Escalada, *Enciclopedia guadalupana*; J. L. Guerrero, *Nican mopohua*; González Fernández, Chávez Sánchez, and Guerrero Rosado, *Encuentro de la Virgen de Guadalupe y Juan Diego*; Brading, *Mexican Phoenix*; Chávez Sánchez, *Virgen de Guadalupe y Juan Diego en las Informaciones Jurídicas*. The *Nican mopohua* was first published as part of Luis Laso de la Vega's *Huei tlamahuiçoltica* (1649), which is discussed later in the text. For a translation of this work, see Sousa, Poole, and Lockhart, *Story of Guadalupe*.

5. Sousa, Poole, and Lockhart, *Story of Guadalupe*, 89; Taylor, "Virgin of Guadalupe in New Spain"; Taylor, *Magistrates of the Sacred*, 277–300; Taylor, "Mexico's Virgin of Guadalupe."

6. "Información por el sermón de 1556," 52–53, 58–59, 62, 64, 67–71.

7. Taylor, "Virgin of Guadalupe in New Spain," 12; Taylor, *Magistrates of the Sacred*, 282–283; Lundberg, *Unification and Conflict*, 216–219; Lafaye, *Quetzalcóatl and Guadalupe*, 57, 242, 274; González Fernández, Chávez Sánchez, and Guerrero Rosado, *Encuentro de la Virgen de Guadalupe y Juan Diego*, 444–447; Gregory XIII, *Ut Deiparae semper virginis* (quotation); Poole, *Our Lady of Guadalupe*, 76–77.

8. Taylor, "Virgin of Guadalupe in New Spain," 12; Taylor, *Magistrates of the Sacred,* 283; Brading, *Mexican Phoenix,* 2 (quotation).

9. Brading, *Mexican Phoenix,* 2 (first quotation), 54; Enríquez de Almanza, "Carta al rey Felipe II" (second quotation); Poole, *Our Lady of Guadalupe,* 65, 73, 84–85, 87, 94.

10. Verdugo Quetzalmamalitzin, Testamento, 2 April 1563 (quotation); Cuadriello, Robledo Galván, and León Mariscal, *Reina de las Américas,* 14, 106–107. Historians debate the authorship and dating of the *Nican motecpana;* it was first published in Luis Laso de la Vega's *Huei tlamahuiçoltica* (1649). See Sousa, Poole, and Lockhart, *Story of Guadalupe,* 14, 92–115. For reprints or excerpts from other colonial-era wills that illuminate Guadalupan devotion, see González Fernández, Chávez Sánchez, and Guerrero Rosado, *Encuentro de la Virgen de Guadalupe y Juan Diego,* 351–352, 397–398, 404, 419–420, 422.

11. Poole, *Our Lady of Guadalupe,* 97–98; Brading, *Mexican Phoenix,* 47–55; Taylor, "Mexico's Virgin of Guadalupe," 282–288.

12. M. Sánchez, *Imagen de la Virgen María;* Brading, *Mexican Phoenix,* 55–70; Matovina, "Guadalupe at Calvary."

13. Sousa, Poole, and Lockhart, *Story of Guadalupe;* Brading, *Mexican Phoenix,* 81–88.

14. M. Sánchez, *Imagen de la Virgen María,* 218, 247–248, 257 (quotation); Sousa, Poole, and Lockhart, *Story of Guadalupe,* 97–99, 119; Lafaye, *Quetzalcóatl and Guadalupe,* esp. 248–253; Brading, *Mexican Phoenix,* 230. The story of Guadalupe curing Juan, the caretaker of Remedios, first appeared in Luis de Cisneros's 1621 work on Nuestra Señora de los Remedios. See Brading, *Mexican Phoenix,* 47–48.

15. De la Cruz, *Relación de la milagrosa aparición.*

16. Schulte, *Mexican Spirituality;* Brading, *Mexican Phoenix,* 165 (quotation), 96–101, 146–168; Carranza et al., *Siete sermones guadalupanos.*

17. To this day theologians typically analyze Guadalupe more as a part of salvation history than as a source for Mariology, or the theology of Mary. However, contemporary writers reverse the perspective of Sánchez and Laso de la Vega, claming not that Guadalupe abetted the Spanish conquerors but that she sided with the native peoples and defended them from the effects of Spanish victimization and subjugation. See, e.g., Elizondo, *Morenita;* Elizondo, *Guadalupe;* Siller Acuña, *Flor y canto del Tepeyac;* J. Rodriguez, *Our Lady of Guadalupe;* Nebel, *Santa María Tonantzin, Virgen de Guadalupe;* Guerrero, *Nican mopohua.*

18. Traslosheros H., "Construction of the First Shrine and Sanctuary of Our Lady of Guadalupe in San Luis Potosí," 10–11 (quotations); Poole, *Our Lady of Guadalupe,* 2, 180.

19. Chávez Sánchez, *Virgen de Guadalupe y Juan Diego en las Informaciones Jurídicas,* 177–178 (first two quotations); Poole, *Our Lady of Guadalupe,* 128–138; Becerro Tanco, *Felicidad de México;* De Florencia, *La Estrella del Norte de México;* Lafaye, *Quetzalcóatl and Guadalupe,* 274–278. The final two quotations are taken from the full title of Becerra Tanco's *Felicidad de México.*

20. Brading, *Mexican Phoenix,* 120–127.

21. Brading, *Mexican Phoenix,* 127–132; Cabrera y Quintero, *Escudo de armas de México;* Taylor, "Virgin of Guadalupe in New Spain," 14–15; Taylor, *Magistrates of the Sacred,* 285–286; Poole, *Our Lady of Guadalupe,* 176–178, 181–182, 187.

22. Harrington, "Mother of Death, Mother of Rebirth," 33 (first quotation); Kurtz, "Virgin of Guadalupe and the Politics of Becoming Human," 206 (second quotation); Poole, *Our Lady of Guadalupe,* 67, 70, 88; M. Smith, *Aztecs,* 60–64; Taylor, "Virgin of Guadalupe in New Spain," 19–21; Taylor, *Magistrates of the Sacred,* 291–294; Carrasco,

Religions of Mesoamerica, 135–138; Peterson, "Virgin of Guadalupe: Symbol of Conquest or Liberation?" I gratefully acknowledge Neto Valiente, whose questions, insights, and doctoral seminar essay helped shape my thinking on early Nahuatl devotion to Guadalupe.

23. Sousa, Poole, and Lockhart, *Story of Guadalupe,* 97 (quotations); Taylor, "Virgin of Guadalupe in New Spain," 21–24; Taylor, *Magistrates of the Sacred,* 294–296.

24. Sklar, *Dancing with the Virgin;* Giuriati and Kan et al., *No temas . . . yo soy tu madre;* O'Connor, "Virgin of Guadalupe and the Economics of Symbolic Behavior."

25. Elizondo, *Morenita;* Elizondo, *Guadalupe;* J. Rodriguez, *Our Lady of Guadalupe;* A. Guerrero, *Chicano Theology,* esp. 96–117, 139–148; Goizueta, *Caminemos con Jesús,* esp. 37–46, 70–76, 104–109; Espín, *Faith of the People,* 73–78; Goizueta, "Resurrection at Tepeyac"; García-Rivera, *Community of the Beautiful,* esp. 39–40, 56–59, 194; Alvarez Cuauhtemoc, "Lord Became Lady."

26. Since self-referential terminology provides important clues for understanding individual and collective identity, throughout this volume I attempt to reflect the language and meanings encountered in interviews and in written sources, including both the diverse expressions of individual informants and the general usages of specific historical eras. During the twentieth century the designation *Mexican American* emerged among people of Mexican heritage born or living in the United States, and they often used it as an expression of pride in their dual heritage. But since the 1960s some ethnic Mexicans have rejected the term as assimilationist and instead have called themselves *Chicanas* and *Chicanos,* usually as a means of expressing a strong ethnic consciousness and an orientation toward social struggle and justice. Others, like many of the parishioners I met at San Fernando, do not use the term *Chicano* in everyday speech and even react negatively to it as being too radical or militant. Additionally, both native-born persons of Mexican heritage and those who migrated from Mexico have at times been perceived as forming a single group or as being united in common activities like Guadalupan devotion, so the terms *Mexican-descent* and *ethnic Mexican* are used in this volume when referring to both groups jointly. Finally, ethnic Mexicans and Puerto Ricans, Cubans, Salvadorans, Guatemalans, and others from countries where Spanish is a primary language frequently employ the umbrella designations *Hispanic, Latino,* and *Latina* to reflect and promote the perception that they share a common language and heritage and a common struggle in adapting to life in the United States. No clear consensus on any one term is evident in Catholic parishes like San Fernando or in common parlance, though *Latino* and the gender inclusive *Latino/a* are gaining ascendancy among scholars. For a similar discussion of terminology and its significance for race relations, see S. Pitti, *Devil in Silicon Valley,* esp. 6–7.

27. Castillo, *Goddess of the Americas;* Gaspar de Alba, *Chicano Art Inside/Outside the Master's House,* esp. 47–48, 139–141, 221; Herrera-Sobek, *Santa Barraza: Artist of the Borderlands;* L. Pérez, "El Desorden."

28. Pulido, "Nuestra Señora de Guadalupe"; G. Sánchez, *Becoming Mexican American,* 166–170; Dolan and Hinojosa, *Mexican Americans and the Catholic Church;* Matovina, "Lay Initiatives in Worship on the Texas *Frontera*"; Engh, "Companion of the Immigrants"; G. Pitti, "Sociedades Guadalupanas in the San Francisco Archdiocese."

29. Matovina, *Tejano Religion and Ethnicity,* esp. 83–93; Matovina and Poyo, *¡Presente!;* Matovina and Riebe-Estrella, *Horizons of the Sacred,* esp. 2–7.

30. See, e.g., Orsi, *Madonna of 115th Street;* Orsi, *Thank You, St. Jude;* Taves, *House-*

hold of Faith; Taves, *Fits, Trances, and Visions;* Hall, *Lived Religion in America;* Tweed, *Our Lady of the Exile;* O'Toole, *Habits of Devotion.*

31. León, *Llorona's Children,* 5. For the significance of understanding the borderlands as a site of the formation of *mestiza/o* (mixed or hybrid) consciousness, identity, and religious expressions, see also Anzaldúa, *Borderlands / La Frontera.*

32. The generic term *Anglo American* is as equivocal as are other umbrella terms like Latino, Hispanic, and Native American. It refers generally to persons of European descent who have become "Americanized" as U.S. residents, but glosses over differences such as European country of origin, the historical era of arrival in the United States, and settlement patterns after arrival. In this volume I examine such distinctions only when they are pertinent to the social milieu of San Antonio and its inflection of Guadalupan devotion at San Fernando, particularly during the second half of the nineteenth century when Italians and especially Germans had a noteworthy linguistic and cultural presence in the city. Moreover, the use of the designation *Anglo American* in this volume reflects San Antonians' long-standing perceptions of an Anglo-Mexican dichotomy, which have significantly shaped their group identities, municipal politics, everyday interactions, and faith expressions like Guadalupan devotion.

33. Matovina, "Sacred Place and Collective Memory"; Matovina, "San Fernando Cathedral and the Alamo." The growing body of literature on these topics includes works such as McDannell, *Material Christianity;* Morgan, *Visual Piety;* Morgan, *Protestants and Pictures;* Wingerd, *Claiming the City.*

34. Robinson, "Houses of Worship in Nineteenth-Century Texas," 238.

35. The blurred line between Mary as intercessor and Mary as possessor of her own divine powers is not unique to Mexican-descent Catholics, of course. See, e.g., Johnson, "Mary and the Female Face of God"; Johnson, *Truly Our Sister,* 71–92.

36. Wright, "Local Church Emergence and Mission Decline"; Wright, "How Many Are 'A Few'?"; Wright, "Hispanic Church in Texas under Spain and Mexico." See also M. Sandoval, *On the Move,* esp. 18–22, 30–40.

37. Orsi, "Everyday Miracles," 20, n. 10; Bell, *Ritual Theory, Ritual Practice,* esp. 169–238; Bell, *Ritual: Perspectives and Dimensions,* 76–83.

38. Goizueta, "Symbolic World of Mexican American Religion," 121–122.

39. Díaz-Stevens, "Saving Grace"; Bell, *Ritual: Perspectives and Dimensions,* 38. See also Aquino, *Our Cry for Life,* 178–181; J. Rodriguez, *Our Lady of Guadalupe;* Castillo, *Goddess of the Americas;* Aquino, Machado, and Rodríguez, *Reader in Latina Feminist Theology,* esp. Lozano-Díaz, "Ignored Virgin or Unaware Women."

40. Tirres, "'Liberation' in the Latino(a) Context," 152. See also Espín, *Faith of the People,* esp. 6, 78–81, 96–104; Mejido, "Critique of the 'Aesthetic Turn' in U.S. Hispanic Theology"; Valentín, *Mapping Public Theology.*

41. As cited in Bell, *Ritual Theory, Ritual Practice,* 217–218, emphasis in original; see also Durkheim, *Elementary Forms of the Religious Life,* 145.

42. Espín, "Mexican Religious Practices, Popular Catholicism, and the Development of Doctrine," 141 (quotation); Espín, "Toward the Construction of an Intercultural Theology of Tradition"; Espín, *Faith of the People,* 63–90. See also Thiel, *Senses of Tradition;* Tilley, *Inventing Catholic Tradition.*

43. Gregory, *Salvation at Stake,* 11.

44. J. Rodriguez, *Our Lady of Guadalupe,* 128.

CHAPTER 1: "Nuestra Madre Querida"

1. Author's notes from observation and interviews at San Fernando, 11–12 December 2003. Unless otherwise indicated, all other information in this chapter is taken from these field notes.

2. Felipa Peña, interview by author, 4 December 1993.

3. *San Antonio Express* (hereafter *Express*), 11 February 2000 (quotations), 14 September 2001, 15 September 2001.

4. *Express*, 14 September 2001, 15 September 2001; Rivard, "San Fernando Still Stands" (quotations).

5. "San Fernando Restoration"; *Express*, 11 December 2003; D. García, "Roles for the Urban Cathedral in 21st-Century America," 603 (quotation).

6. This statement is also the proud claim of many San Fernando staff and parishioners. Although San Fernando was not declared a cathedral until 1874, the original sanctuary, which became a devotional area after the space reconfiguration of the renovation, dates from the time of the first parish church, on which construction began in 1738.

7. Quote taken from an interview of Richard Galindo in the video *Soul of the City / Alma del pueblo.*

8. The four canonical Gospels do not agree on the number and identity of the women at the empty tomb, and the name "Salome" is not accompanied by "Mary" in any of them, but "las tres Marías" is the way many ethnic Mexicans have traditionally referred to them. See Matthew 28:1, Mark 16:1, Luke 24:10, John 20:1.

9. Cathedrals for a New Century: Church Architecture at the Beginning of the Third Millennium conference, University of Notre Dame, South Bend, Indiana, 21–23 October 2001; "San Fernando Restoration" (first three quotations); "About the Defenders" (fourth quotation); "Defenders of the Magisterium Petition to Archbishop Flores" (last three quotations).

10. *Express*, 14 January 2004 (first three quotations), 1 February 2004; Dorsett, "Three Church Statues May Not Survive" (last quotation).

11. Gene Rodríguez, interview by author, 11 October 2003.

12. Prayer and song texts cited in this and the following two paragraphs are taken from a worship aid distributed to congregants for the mañanitas celebration.

13. For a fuller treatment of the attempt to integrate liturgy and popular devotion from the perspective of a San Fernando leader, see Empereur, "Popular Religion and the Liturgy."

14. Sally Gómez-Kelley, interview by author, 30 May 2002.

CHAPTER 2: Patroness of *la Frontera*, 1731–1836

1. Terán de los Ríos, Diary, 72; Massanet and companions, Diary, 358; De Florencia, *La Estrella del Norte de México.* For an English translation of the expedition diaries, see Hatcher, "Expedition of Don Domingo Terán de los Ríos," esp. 19, 54 (quotations).

2. Terán de los Ríos, Diary, 64; see also Hatcher, "Expedition of Don Domingo Terán de los Ríos," 13.

3. "Autos sobre diferentes noticias," Archivo General de México, Provincias Internas (typescript), vol. 181, CAH, as translated and cited in de la Teja, *San Antonio de Béxar,* 18

(quotation); Mörner, *Race Mixture in the History of Latin America*, esp. chapter 5, "Society of Castes: Rise and Decline"; Poyo, "Social Identity on the Hispanic Texas Frontier."

4. Castañeda, *Our Catholic Heritage in Texas*, 2:70–148, 211–267; Habig, *Alamo Chain of Missions*.

5. Poyo, "Canary Islands Immigrants of San Antonio," 41–46; de la Teja, *San Antonio de Béxar*, esp. 18, 76–79, 140, 144.

6. Recio de León, Statement of 16 October 1736; "Memorial of Father Benito Fernández Concerning the Canary Islanders, 1741," 274. I gratefully acknowledge Adán Benavides, who brought the Recio de León document and numerous other primary sources to my attention. The quotation cited from this document is his translation of the text.

7. Documents concerning the construction of the parish church at the Villa de San Fernando, 17 February–6 June 1738 (typescript), NA, 1:77 (quotation), 68–78; Castañeda, *Our Catholic Heritage in Texas*, 3:94–101; Cruz, *Let There Be Towns*, 134–138; Benavides, "Sacred Space, Profane Reality." For a translation of the 1738 documents from the Nacogdoches Archives, see De Zavala, *History and Legends of the Alamo and Other Missions in and around San Antonio*, 180–189.

8. Documents concerning the construction of the parish church at the Villa de San Fernando, 17 February–6 June 1738 (typescript), NA, 1:77.

9. De la Teja, "St. James at the Fair," 405.

10. Cruz, *Let There Be Towns*, 134–138; Benavides, "Sacred Space, Profane Reality," 14–17; San Fernando Combined Register, 1731–1760, CASA, 179 (new pagination in pencil); Hollon and Butler, *William Bollaert's Texas*, 224. Previous writers claim that parishioners completed the church construction several years earlier, but Benavides demonstrates with primary documentation that 1755 is the correct date.

11. Citizens of the villa of San Fernando to Baron de Ripperdá and others, 7 February 1771, NA, 5:30–31; *cabildo* (town council) of the villa of San Fernando and others, statements on feast days, 12 February 1772–9 January 1788, NA, 5:46b (quotation), 46a–46s; San Fernando Combined Register, 1731–1760, CASA, 151–153. For the Spanish custom of designating town or village patrons, see Christian, *Local Religion in Sixteenth-Century Spain*; Lafaye, *Quetzalcóatl and Guadalupe*, 86, 226, 254–255; Foster, *Culture and Conquest*, 160–166, 209–221.

12. De la Teja, *San Antonio de Béxar*, 148–150; report from the cabildo of the villa of San Fernando, 27 January 1747, BA; Domingo Cabello, statement on peace treaties with the Lipan Apaches, 30 September 1784, Archivo General de México, Provincias Internas (typescript), CAH, 64:111–112. The 1747 report from the San Fernando cabildo is summarized in Cruz, *Let There Be Towns*, 141–143. A synopsis of Cabello's 1784 report, which includes a description of the 1749 peace-treaty ritual, is in John, *Storms Brewed in Other Men's Worlds*, 284–286; Dunn, "Apache Relations in Texas," 260–262.

13. Tjarks, "Comparative Demographic Analysis of Texas," 309; Morfi, *History of Texas*, 92 (quotations).

14. Citizens of the villa of San Fernando to Baron de Ripperdá and others; cabildo of the villa de San Fernando and others, statements on feast days, NA, 5:46a–46s; de la Teja, *San Antonio de Béxar*, 21, 148–149; Morfi, *History of Texas*, 99; Tjarks, "Comparative Demographic Analysis of Texas"; Cabello to José Antonio Rengel, 24 December 1785, BA; John, *Storms Brewed in Other Men's Worlds*, 689–690.

15. Poyo and Hinojosa, *Tejano Origins in Eighteenth-Century San Antonio*, 140 (quota-

tion); Almaráz, "Harmony, Discord, and Compromise in Spanish Colonial Texas"; de la Teja, *San Antonio de Béxar;* R. Ramos, "From Norteño to Tejano," esp. 97–140.

16. De la Teja, *San Antonio de Béxar,* 149; Juan Gregorio de Campos, *Oración panegyrica a María Santísima en su portentosa imagen de Guadalupe,* as cited in Poole, *Our Lady of Guadalupe,* 181–182.

17. As cited in de la Teja, *San Antonio de Béxar;* 93 (quotation), 94.

18. Hinojosa and Fox, "Indians and Their Culture in San Fernando de Béxar," 113–120; Schuetz, "Indians of the San Antonio Missions," 94–99; Ruecking, "Ceremonies of the Coahuiltecan Indians of Southern Texas and Northeastern Mexico"; Mann, "Music and Popular Religiosity in Northern New Spain," 21–22; Solís, "Solís Diary of 1767," 123; Morfi, *History of Texas,* 97; *Guidelines for a Texas Mission,* 37–38.

19. Cabildo of the villa of San Fernando and others, statements on feast days, NA, 5:46n–46s; de la Teja, *San Antonio de Béxar,* 136, 148–149.

20. Tjarks, "Comparative Demographic Analysis of Texas," 338 (quotation); Poyo, "Immigrants and Integration in Late Eighteenth-Century Béxar," 90–99; de la Teja, *San Antonio de Béxar,* 24–29, 132.

21. Tjarks, "Comparative Demographic Analysis of Texas," 304–305; de la Teja and Wheat, "Béxar: Profile of a Tejano Community," 10–11; de la Teja, *San Antonio de Béxar,* 22, 35, 38, 40 (first quotation), 41, 44, 87, 104, 115, 123; Acosta and Winegarten, *Las Tejanas,* 35 (second quotation), 10–16, 25–36; Chipman and Joseph, *Notable Men and Women of Spanish Texas,* 269 (third quotation), 262–275; David Weber, *Spanish Frontier in North America,* 329–332; David Weber, *Mexican Frontier, 1821–1846,* 215–216.

22. Green, *Memoirs of Mary A. Maverick,* 53–54; Jean Marie Odin to Jean-Baptiste Étienne, 7 February 1842, CAT.

23. Taylor, "Virgin of Guadalupe in New Spain," 21–24; Brading, *Mexican Phoenix,* 228–236; Crimm, *De León,* 53–55; Manuel de Salcedo, regulations for celebrating the feasts of the Immaculate Conception and Our Lady of Guadalupe, 2 December 1810, NA, 12:78–81. For a published English translation of this document, see Webb, "Christmas and New Year in Texas," 358–359.

24. De la Teja, "Rebellion on the Frontier"; R. Ramos, "From Norteño to Tejano," 66–88; José Antonio Navarro, "Historical Fragments," *San Antonio Ledger,* 19 December 1857 (quotation), as cited in J. Navarro, *Defending Mexican Valor in Texas,* 68; Antonio Martínez to *ayuntamiento* (town council) of Béxar, 18 July 1821, BA; José Sandoval to ayuntamiento of Béxar, 21 July 1821, BA; Almaráz, *Governor Antonio Martínez and Mexican Independence in Texas,* 9–11.

25. [Martínez] to [José Angel Navarro], 30 October 1821, BA; [Martínez] to [Refugio de la Garza], 30 October 1821, BA; [ayuntamiento of Béxar] to José León Lobo Guerrero, 4 September 1822, BA; Father Francisco Maynes to *junta gubernativa* (governing council) of Texas, 5 June 1823, BA; [junta gubernativa] to ayuntamiento of Béxar, 6 June 1823, BA; Tomás Buentello to José Antonio Saucedo, 20 July 1827, BA; Tomás de Oquillas to Antonio Elozúa, 18 August 1827, BA; "Minutes of the City Council of the City of San Antonio, 1830 to 1835, Spanish Minute Book Two" (typescript), 11 December 1833, CAH; minutes of the junta for the Independence Day celebration, 12 September 1829, BA; de la Teja and Wheat, "Béxar: Profile of a Tejano Community," 22; R. Ramos, "From Norteño to Tejano," 211–216; Matovina, *Tejano Religion and Ethnicity,* 20–22.

26. National Congress decree on religious feasts and civic holidays, 27 November 1824, "Mission San Antonio de Valero Marriage Register, 1709–1788, 1797–1811,

1825," item #618 (second to last page), CASA; Berlandier, *Journey to Mexico during the Years 1826 to 1834*, 1:127 (quotations); Lafaye, *Quetzalcóatl and Guadalupe*.

27. David Weber, *Troubles in Texas, 1832*; Matovina, *Tejano Religion and Ethnicity*, 7–23; Tijerina, *Tejanos and Texas under the Mexican Flag*, esp. 93–136.

28. [Ayuntamiento of Béxar] to [Mariano Varela], 5 October 1815, BA; "Minutes of the City Council of the City of San Antonio, 1815 to 1820, Spanish Minute Book One" (typescript), 5 October 1815, 31 October 1816, CAH; ayuntamiento minutes of 21 November 1822, 22 November 1824, BA (see volume 66); "Minutes of the City Council of the City of San Antonio, 1830 to 1835, Spanish Minute Book Two" (typescript), 2–3 December 1830, 1 December 1831, 6 December 1832, 5 December 1833, CAH; ordinance issued by Ramón Músquiz, 7 December 1830, BA; Juan Seguín to Béxar *alcalde* (mayor), 2 December 1834, BA.

29. White, *1830 Citizens of Texas*, 79–112; de la Teja and Wheat, "Béxar: Profile of a Tejano Community," 9–12; Matovina, *Tejano Religion and Ethnicity*, 7–8.

30. Lundy, *Life, Travels, and Opinions of Benjamin Lundy*, 52–55.

31. Minutes of the junta for the Independence Day celebration, 12 September 1829, BA; de la Teja and Wheat, "Béxar: Profile of a Tejano Community," 22–23; [Ayuntamiento of Béxar] to [Mariano Varela], 5 October 1815, BA; "Minutes of the City Council of the City of San Antonio, 1815 to 1820, Spanish Minute Book One" (typescript), 5 October 1815, 31 October 1816, CAH; ayuntamiento minutes of 23 August 1821, 7 and 14 November 1822, 20 November 1823, BA (see volume 66); "Minutes of the City Council of the City of San Antonio, 1830 to 1835, Spanish Minute Book Two" (typescript), 2–3 December 1830, 1 December 1831, 6 December 1832, 5 December 1833, CAH; ordinance issued by Ramón Músquiz, 7 December 1830, BA; Juan Seguín to Béxar alcalde, 2 December 1834, BA.

32. Francisco Salazar and Antonio Hernández, list of foreigners at Béxar, 24 April 1828, BA; Brown, "Reminiscences of Jno. Duff Brown," 300; Matovina, *Tejano Religion and Ethnicity*, 8, 10–11, 14–16.

33. Wright, "Popular and Official Religiosity," esp. 535–557; Engh, "From *Frontera* Faith to Roman Rubrics," 90.

34. Christian, *Local Religion in Sixteenth-Century Spain*, 3.

35. Díaz-Stevens, *Oxcart Catholicism on Fifth Avenue*, 46.

CHAPTER 3 : Defender of *Dignidad*, 1836–1900

1. Foley, "Jean-Marie Odin, C.M."; Jean Marie Odin to Benoite (his sister), 3 May 1822, in Bony, *Vie de Mgr. Jean-Marie Odin*, 39 (quotations).

2. The term *Tejano* was extant in primary documentation as early as 1824, although most nineteenth-century references to people of Mexican heritage in Texas name them Mexicans or *mexicanos*. Contemporary historians have employed the word Tejano to designate the regional identity of Texas residents that began to evolve during the eighteenth century. In this study I employ the term and its feminine form, *Tejana*, to designate Texas-born and long-term ethnic Mexican residents whose sustained contact with the U.S. ethos distinguished them from new arrivals who migrated to San Antonio after its political separation from Mexico. The tensions, collaboration, and general interrelations between Mexican-descent San Antonio residents from the two sides of the U.S.-Mexican border

shaped their social life, civic involvement, collective identity, and Guadalupan devotion. See Benavides, "Tejano."

3. *Austin Texas Sentinel,* 29 August 1840 (quotation), and 5 and 26 September 1840; Odin to Anthony Blanc, 24 August 1840, CAT; Odin to Joseph Rosati, 27 August 1840, CAT; Odin to Jean-Baptiste Étienne, 28 August 1840, CAT; Odin, "Daily Journal" (photocopy), 6–8, CAT; Parisot and Smith, *History of the Catholic Church in the Diocese of San Antonio,* 62–71.

4. Wuthnow, Marty, Gleason, and Moore, "Sources of Personal Identity," 9. For a fuller treatment and more extensive bibliographic overview on the formation of ethnic identities in pluralistic societies, see Matovina, *Tejano Religion and Ethnicity,* 3–5, 49–93.

5. Jean Marie Odin to Jean-Baptiste Étienne, 7 February 1842, in *United States Catholic Magazine and Monthly Review* 3 (October 1844): 729. A copy of this letter is in CAT.

6. Broussard, "San Antonio during the Texas Republic"; Barr, *Texas in Revolt;* Matovina, *Alamo Remembered;* Lack, *Texas Revolutionary Experience;* Hardin, *Texian Iliad; Austin Texas Sentinel,* 23 and 25 March, 15 April 1840; *Houston Telegraph and Texas Register,* 8 April 1840; Nance, *Attack and Counter-Attack.*

7. Wooster, "Foreigners in the Principal Towns of Ante-Bellum Texas," 209; G. Jordan, "W. Steinert's View of Texas in 1849," 193–194; Carpenter, *State of Texas Federal Population Schedules, Seventh Census of the United States, 1850,* 1:111–189; *San Antonio Ledger,* 23 June 1853 (quotation). Unless otherwise noted, all other newspapers cited in this chapter were published in San Antonio.

8. Olmsted, *Journey through Texas,* 150 (quotation); Carpenter, *State of Texas Federal Population Schedules, Seventh Census of the United States, 1850,* 1:111–189; "Population Schedules of the Eighth Census of the United States, 1860"; Griswold del Castillo, *La Familia,* 61–64, 69–71, 142.

9. "Officers of the City Government" (typescript), San Antonio Public Library; Matovina, *Tejano Religion and Ethnicity,* 51–52, 74–75; R. W. Brahan, Jr., to John D. Coffee, 20 January [1855], in Boom, "Texas in the 1850s," 283 (first quotation); Reid, *Reid's Tramp,* 69 (second and third quotations); Olmsted, *Journey through Texas,* 163 (fourth quotation); Lundy, *Life, Travels, and Opinions of Benjamin Lundy,* 48 (fifth quotation).

10. Seguín, *Personal Memoirs of John N. Seguín,* iv, 18; de la Teja, *Revolution Remembered,* 1–70.

11. Smith and Judah, *Chronicles of the Gringos,* 93; Odin to Propagation of the Faith, 9 April 1847, CAT; Freeman, "W. G. Freeman's Report on the Eighth Military Department," 168; Mansfield, "Colonel J. K. F. Mansfield's Report of the Inspection of the Department of Texas in 1856," 135–141.

12. Foley, "From Linares to Galveston"; Odin to John Timon, 14 July 1840, CAT; Odin to Blanc, 24 August 1840; Odin to Rosati, 27 August 1840; Odin to Étienne, 28 August 1840, CAT; Odin to James Fransoni, 15 December 1840, CAT; Odin to Étienne, 11 April 1841, CAT; Odin, "Daily Journal" (photocopy), 6–8, CAT; Vanderholt, "San Fernando Cathedral in San Antonio," 53–81. For further treatment of the native priests' removal, see Matovina, *Tejano Religion and Ethnicity,* 42–43.

13. Domenech, *Missionary Adventures in Texas and Mexico,* 11; Matovina, *Tejano Religion and Ethnicity,* 64–67; Claude Marie Dubuis to Odin, 22 March 1853, Incarnate Word Archives, Incarnate Word Generalate, San Antonio.

14. Matovina, *Tejano Religion and Ethnicity*, 52–55, 59–65; *San Antonio Ledger,* 10 July 1851.

15. *San Antonio Ledger,* 6 March 1851; Lawrence, *Texas in 1840,* xviii-xix; McCalla, *Adventures in Texas,* 81–83; *Texas Baptist,* 2 February 1860; Matovina, *Tejano Religion and Ethnicity,* 39–41, 59–64.

16. *San Antonio Herald,* 14 August 1855, 3 February 1858; *San Antonio Ledger,* 6 November 1858. See also De León, *They Called Them Greasers.*

17. Olmsted, *Journey through Texas,* 126, 164; "Recollections of Texas," 114; *Texas Presbyterian,* 15 January 1848; R. Ramos, "From Norteño to Tejano," 360–368.

18. *Bejareño,* 7 and 21 July 1855; *San Antonio Ledger,* 14 and 21 July 1855; Matovina, "Religion and Ethnicity at San Antonio," 44–47; Matovina, *Tejano Religion and Ethnicity,* 70–74. Translations from the *Bejareño* are mine. The translation in the *San Antonio Ledger* has several inaccuracies.

19. *Correo,* 26 May 1858; Weeks, *Debates of the Texas Convention,* 235, 473–474; J. Navarro, *Defending Mexican Valor in Texas,* 19–21.

20. Muir, *Texas in 1837,* 103 (quotation); McDowell, *Letters from the Ursuline,* 261, 277.

21. Odin to Étienne, 11 April 1841, CAT (first quotation); Engelmann, "Second Illinois in the Mexican War," 383; Esparza, "Esparza, the Boy of the Alamo, Remembers," 220 (second quotation); McDowell, *Letters from the Ursuline,* 260–261, 271–273, 283, 312–313; *San Antonio Daily Herald,* 25 December 1858; S. King, "Early Days in San Antonio"; Newcomb, "Christmas in San Antonio Half a Century Ago"; French, "Mrs. French's Reminiscences," 98; Barnes, *Combats and Conquests of Immortal Heroes,* 121; *Correo,* 8 July 1858; Steinert, *North America, Particularly Texas,* 85; Crimmins, "Robert E. Lee in Texas," 19–20. Sarah L. French's reminiscences incorrectly identify the 24 June feast of San Juan with Cinco de Mayo (5 May).

22. Esparza, "Esparza, the Boy of the Alamo, Remembers," 219; French, "Mrs. French's Reminiscences," 98.

23. Green, *Memoirs of Mary A. Maverick,* 53 (first quotation); Odin to Étienne, 7 February 1842 (second, third, and fourth quotations), CAT; *San Antonio Ledger,* 16 December 1852, 12 December 1857, 18 December 1858 (fifth quotation); *Alamo Star,* 11 and 16 December 1854; McDowell, *Letters from the Ursuline,* 170, 272, 276; French, "Mrs. French's Reminiscences," 98.

24. See esp. Odin to Étienne, 7 February 1842, CAT.

25. McDowell, *Letters from the Ursuline,* 272–273; *Alamo Star,* 6 May 1854; S. King, "Early Days in San Antonio."

26. McDowell, *Letters from the Ursuline,* 273; *Alamo Star,* 2 September 1854.

27. McClintock, "Journal of a Trip Through Texas," 146; Hollon and Butler, *William Bollaert's Texas,* 229–230.

28. McDowell, *Letters from the Ursuline,* 272, 276; *San Antonio Ledger,* 12 May 1853; Newcomb, "Christmas in San Antonio Half a Century Ago"; Morrell, *Flowers and Fruits from the Wilderness,* 118.

29. S. King, "Early Days in San Antonio" (first quotation); *San Antonio Daily Ledger,* 19 August 1858 (second quotation); *Alamo Star,* 22 January 1855; Matovina, *Tejano Religion and Ethnicity,* 55- 56.

30. *San Antonio Ledger,* 12 December 1857; *Alamo Star,* 11 December 1854.

31. Green, *Memoirs of Mary A. Maverick*, 53–56, 97–118; G. Smith, *Life and Times of George Foster Pierce*, 375.

32. Engelmann, "Second Illinois in the Mexican War," 384 (first quotation); "T. E. G. to Editors, December 1846"; Olmsted, *Journey through Texas*, 150 (second quotation); *San Antonio Ledger*, 8 September 1853 (third quotation).

33. Green, *Memoirs of Mary A. Maverick*, 53–54 (quotation); Odin to Étienne, 7 February 1842, CAT.

34. Chipman, *Spanish Texas*, 253; David Weber, *Mexican Frontier, 1821–1846*, 215–216; Carroll, *Homesteads Ungovernable*, 99–101; Griswold del Castillo, *La Familia*, 43 (second quotation), 75 (third quotation), 81 (first quotation), 82.

35. "Officers of the City Government"; De León, "*In Re* Ricardo Rodríguez," 57 (quotations), 58–63; *San Antonio Express* (hereafter *Express*), 31 January 1896, p. 8.

36. J. Davis, *San Antonio*, 27–35; Sobré, *San Antonio on Parade*, 20–34; De León and Stewart, "Tale of Three Cities"; Stewart and De León, *Not Room Enough*, esp. 21–38; Barr, "Occupational and Geographic Mobility in San Antonio, 1870–1900"; E. King, *Texas, 1874*, 108, 111 (quotations).

37. J. Davis, *San Antonio*, 29; *San Antonio Herald*, 28 March 1866, p. 2 (first quotation); Morrison, *San Antonio, Texas*, 3 (second and third quotations); Stewart and De León, *Not Room Enough*, 16–17, 25.

38. J. Davis, *San Antonio*, 30; Sobré, *San Antonio on Parade*, 206 (quotation); Maguire, *Century of Fiesta in San Antonio*.

39. Pycior, "*La Raza* Organizes"; Arnold, *Folklore, Manners, and Customs*, 7–10; Ríos and Castillo, "Toward a True Chicano Bibliography," 23–24; Ríos, "Toward a True Chicano Bibliography—Part II," 47; J. Davis, *San Antonio*, 31; *Express*, 22 September 1883, p. 1; 24 February 1884, p. 4.

40. *San Antonio Herald*, 16 September 1869; *Express*, 17 September 1878, p. 4 (quotations); 16 September 1880, p. 4; 16 September 1884, p. 4; 16 September 1886, p. 8; 8 September 1887, p. 5; 15 September 1893, p. 8; 16 September 1895, p. 5; Sobré, *San Antonio on Parade*, 79–100. Numerous other reports of Mexican Independence Day celebrations appeared in the San Antonio press during the last decades of the nineteenth century. Many of these are cited in De León, *Apuntes Tejanos*.

41. Vanderholt, "San Fernando Cathedral in San Antonio," 53–81; Robinson, *Reflections of Faith*, 115, 116 (quotation); Gould, *Alamo City Guide*, 34.

42. Parisot and Smith, *History of the Catholic Church in the Diocese of San Antonio*, 76–91; *Express*, 24 December 1882, p. 2 (first quotation); 25 June 1869, p. 3 (second quotation); Sweet and Knox, *On a Mexican Mustang, through Texas*, 368 (third and fourth quotations), 369.

43. Esparza, "Esparza, the Boy of the Alamo, Remembers," 219–220; French, "Mrs. French's Reminiscences," 100; *Express*, 25 December 1881, p. 4; 24 December 1882, p. 2; 10 January 1888, p. 3; 25 December 1890, p. 3; 29 December 1893, p. 6; 7 January 1894, p. 9; 8 April 1894, p. 6; 11 April 1894, p. 4; 13 April 1894, p. 5; 17 April 1894, p. 6; 22 April 1894, p. 11; 27 April 1894, p. 6; and 28 April 1907, p. 9 (quotation); Gamio, *Mexican Immigration*, 122–124.

44. "San Fernando Cathedral Census Book thru ca. 1901," CASA; Parisot, *Reminiscences of a Texas Missionary*, 175 (first quotation); *San Antonio Herald*, 3 November 1871, 25 October 1875, p. 3; 9 June 1876, p. 3; *Express*, 16 October 1889, p. 3; 8 June 1894, p. 8;

(second quotation); Corner, *San Antonio de Béxar,* 12, 31–32; Lanier, *Sidney Lanier's Historical Sketch,* 31 (third quotation); Morrison, *San Antonio, Texas,* 13. Lanier wrote his historical sketch of San Antonio in the early 1870s. The sketch is also in Corner, *San Antonio de Béxar,* 68–94.

45. *Express,* 25 December 1890, p. 3 (first quotation); 24 December 1882, p. 2; 26 December 1882, p. 2 (second quotation); McDanield and Taylor, *Coming Empire,* 126; *La Fe Católica,* 15, 22, and 29 May 1897; 5 June 1897.

46. *San Antonio Herald,* 13 December 1868, p. 3 (first two quotations); 15 December 1868, p. 3; 9 April 1871, p. 2 (fourth and fifth quotations); *Express,* 13 December 1878, p. 4; 13 December 1883, p. 4; 13 December 1892, p. 2 (third quotation); *El Regidor,* 9 December 1893, p. 2; *San Antonio Light,* 9 December 1897, p. 5; 11 December 1899, p. 5 (sixth quotation).

47. De León, *They Called Them Greasers,* 56–57; R. Ramos, "From Norteño to Tejano," 370–372; *San Antonio Herald,* 23 August 1868, p. 2; 17 September 1868, p. 3; 11 November 1868, p. 3; 15 December 1868, p. 3 (quotation); 27 January 1869, p. 3; and 20 April 1869, p. 3.

48. *Express,* 13 December 1883, p. 4 (first quotation); Brading, *Mexican Phoenix,* 288–310; *El Regidor,* 12 October 1895, p. 3 (last three quotations); 19 October 1895, p. 3.

49. *Express,* 13 December 1892, p. 2.

50. De León, *Tejano Community,* 203 (first quotation); Camarillo, *Chicanos in a Changing Society,* 65 (second quotation); Matovina, "Lay Initiatives in Worship on the Texas Frontera," 108–111; Matovina and Poyo, *¡Presente!,* 44–89; Engh, *Frontier Faiths,* 107–120, 165–186. Eyewitness accounts of Guadalupe celebrations in the nineteenth-century Southwest are in Matovina and Poyo, *¡Presente!,* 65–67, 72–73; Domenech, *Missionary Adventures in Texas and Mexico,* 357–359; and Colton, *Three Years in California,* 224–225.

51. Granjon, *Along the Rio Grande,* 39.

52. Ramírez, "Liturgy from the Mexican American Perspective," 296.

CHAPTER 4: Companion in *el Exilio,* 1900–1940

1. *La Prensa,* 15 December 1931, pp. 1–2; Brading, *Mexican Phoenix,* 312. All newspapers cited in this chapter were published in San Antonio.

2. *San Antonio Express* (hereafter *Express*) 13 December 1921, 6 December 1931 (first quotation); G. Hinojosa, "Mexican-American Faith Communities," 78 (second quotation); *Southern Messenger,* 15 December 1921, p. 4; *Magazín de La Prensa,* 13 December 1931; *La Prensa,* 11–15 December 1931; Arthur J. Drossaerts, American Board of Catholic Missions report, 1928, CASA (third quotation).

3. *Hoja parroquial de San Fernando* (hereafter *Hoja parroquial*), 15 and 22 November 1931, 29 November 1931 (first quotation), 6 December 1931, 13 December 1931 (fourth quotation), CASA; "San Fernando Cathedral Chronicles," 2:18 (second quotation), ACM; "Actos de la Sociedad de Vasallos," 1925–1934, 108 (third quotation); *Southern Messenger,* 3 December 1931, p. 5; 10 December 1931, p. 4; *Express,* 6 and 10 December 1931; *San Antonio Light,* 10 December 1931; *La Prensa,* 12 December 1931, pp. 1, 6; 13 December 1931, p. 5; 14 December 1931, p. 2.

4. For the purposes of this study, exiles are those who have fled political and social forces in their homeland; they usually arrive with a firm resolve to return home at the earliest possible opportunity, whether they eventually act on their desire or not. Immigrants

or émigrés, on the other hand, come to a new land seeking reunification with family members, economic or educational opportunity, or the fulfillment of some other personal goal. To be sure, not everyone fits neatly into one of these categories or the other, as the number of self-proclaimed exiles who settled permanently in San Antonio attests. Nonetheless, many exiles differ from immigrants in their experience of resettlement, their approach to self-identity, and their expressions of religious devotion.

5. Griswold del Castillo, *La Familia*, 59 (quotations), 103; T. Jordan, "Century and a Half of Ethnic Change in Texas," 392–397; Gonzales, *Mexican Revolution*; Meyer, *Cristero Rebellion*; Gamio, *Mexican Immigration*, 13–23, 55, 116, 172.

6. Balderrama and Rodríguez, *Decade of Betrayal*; San Antonio Public Service Company, *Economic and Industrial Survey* (San Antonio, 1940), as cited in R. García, *Rise of the Mexican American Middle Class*, 29; American Public Welfare Association, *Public Welfare Survey of San Antonio*, 20–21.

7. "Growth of the San Antonio Archdiocese: In Town Parishes by Chronology" (typescript), 1989, CASA; R. García, *Rise of the Mexican American Middle Class*, 157–158; San Antonio Baptist Association, *Baptist Century around the Alamo*, 56–58, 159–160, 170–171; Brackenridge and García-Treto, *Iglesia Presbiteriana*, 132–135; Nañez, *History of the Rio Grande Conference of the United Methodist Church*, 71; Ziehe, *Centennial Story of the Lutheran Church in Texas*, 2:184; Machado, *Of Borders and Margins*, 88–92, 97–101; Arthur J. Drossaerts, Speech to the National Catholic Charities Conference, New Orleans, 12 November 1929, CASA.

8. "San Fernando Cathedral Annual Parish Reports," 1911–1940, CASA; *Express*, 10 December 1930; Stecker, "History of San Fernando Cathedral," 46.

9. G. Hinojosa, "Mexican-American Faith Communities," 36; J. Davis, *San Antonio*, 41; Arnold, *Folklore, Manners, and Customs*, 43; *La Prensa*, 4 June 1923, p. 3 (first quotation); Badillo, "Between Alienation and Ethnicity," 69–71; Zamora, *World of the Mexican Worker in Texas*, esp. 167–170, 190–193; Menefee and Cassmore, *Pecan Shellers of San Antonio*, 16–19; Vargas, "Tejana Radical"; Blackwelder, "Emma Tenayuca"; "San Fernando Cathedral Chronicles," 1:129 (second quotation), 1:144.

10. J. Davis, *San Antonio*, 36–41; R. García, *Rise of the Mexican American Middle Class*, esp. 74–75 (quotation); Knox, *Economic Status of the Mexican American Immigrant*; American Public Welfare Association, *Public Welfare Survey of San Antonio*, 22–23.

11. Gutiérrez, *Walls and Mirrors*, 27, 181; "Officers of the City Government" (typescript), San Antonio Public Library.

12. *La Prensa*, 28 February 1930, p. 6.

13. Victor S. Clark, *Mexican Labor in the United States*, Bureau of Labor Bulletin, no. 78 (Washington, DC: Department of Commerce, 1908), reprinted in Servín, *Awakened Minority*, 58; Sáenz, *Mexico-Americanos en la gran guerra*, 289, 292.

14. Orozco, "Origins of the League of United Latin American Citizens"; Márquez, *LULAC*; R. García, *Rise of the Mexican American Middle Class*, 3 and 11 (quotations), 253–299.

15. Ríos and Castillo, "Toward a True Chicano Bibliography," 23–24; Ríos, "Toward a True Chicano Bibliography—Part II," 47; *La Prensa*, 26 November 1916, p. 3; 16 February 1930, p. 3; Ríos-McMillan, "Biography of a Man and His Newspaper," 139; *El Imparcial de Texas*, 23 December 1920, p. 1; Pycior, "*La Raza* Organizes," 96–104; Arnold, *Folklore, Manners, and Customs*, 7–10; Gonzalas, *Mexican Family in San Antonio*, 1–2.

16. Gamio, *Mexican Immigration,* 54–56, 129–130 (quotations); Gamio, *Mexican Immigrant;* G. Sánchez, *Becoming Mexican American,* 120–123; Gutiérrez, *Walls and Mirrors,* esp. 56–68.

17. Pycior, "*La Raza* Organizes," esp. 85–89, 223; Arnold, *Folklore, Manners, and Customs,* 19–21; Gamio, *Mexican Immigrant,* 46 (first quotation); Gamio, *Mexican Immigration,* 94 (second quotation).

18. *La Prensa,* 13 February 1933, p. 3 (quotation); Di Stefano, "'Venimos a Luchar': A Brief History of *La Prensa*'s Founding"; Ríos-McMillan, "Biography of a Man and His Newspaper"; F. Hinojosa, *El México de Afuera;* Treviño, "*Prensa y Patria*"; Ríos and Castillo, "Toward a True Chicano Bibliography," 23–24; Ríos, "Toward a True Chicano Bibliography—Part II," 47. I am grateful to Juanita Luna Lawhn, whose extensive research and insightful analysis helped me understand the function and significance of *La Prensa.* The Ríos-McMillan article was one of several papers on *La Prensa* published in *Americas Review* 17 (fall/winter 1989). A copy of the Hinojosa book is available at the Nettie Lee Benson Latin American Collection, University of Texas, Austin.

19. Luna Lawhn, "Victorian Attitudes Affecting the Mexican Woman Writing in *La Prensa*"; Luna Lawhn, "*El Regidor* and *La Prensa*"; Gonzalas, *Mexican Family in San Antonio,* 9 (first quotation); Gamio, *Mexican Immigration,* 129 (second quotation); Acosta and Winegarten, *Las Tejanas,* 84–93, 118–126, 191–192; Ruiz, *From Out of the Shadows,* 72–98; Orozco, "Origins of the League of United Latin American Citizens."

20. Gamio, *Mexican Immigration,* 94 (first quotation); Ruiz, *From Out of the Shadows,* 51–52 (second and third quotations), 51–71; Ruiz, "'Star Struck'"; Barker, "Los Tejanos de San Antonio"; Gonzalas, *Mexican Family in San Antonio,* 37–39; Gamio, *Mexican Immigrant,* 235 (fourth quotation); Arthur J. Drossaerts, pastoral letter, 31 January 1926, CASA (last three quotations).

21. Ruiz, *From Out of the Shadows,* 70–71 (first quotation), 51–71; Gamio, *Mexican Immigrant,* 102 (second and third quotations).

22. G. Hinojosa, "Mexican-American Faith Communities," 58; "San Fernando Cathedral Chronicles," 1:12 (quotations); *Anales de la Congregación de Misioneros Hijos del Inmaculado Corazón de María* (1917–1918): 185, ACM (hereafter *Anales*). Exiled women religious also served at San Antonio during these decades, but they were not prominent in the San Fernando congregation.

23. Fernández, *Compendio histórico,* 2:587–615; "Historia de la Catedral de San Fernando," unpublished manuscript, c. 1945, ACM. This unsigned manuscript was written by a Claretian.

24. *Anales* (1905–1906): 601–2, (1909–1910): 249 (first quotation); Serrano, "Missionary Work among the Mexicans" (second and third quotations); "San Fernando Cathedral Annual Parish Reports," 1911–1940, CASA; "San Fernando Cathedral Chronicles," 1:14, 1:54, 1:113, 1:291, 2:6–41, 2:81; Stecker, "History of San Fernando Cathedral," 57–58; *Southern Messenger,* 7 December 1911, p. 8; 14 December 1911, p. 8; *Hoja parroquial,* 8 June 1930; 25 January, 22 February, 8, 15, and 22 March, 5 and 12 April, 8 and 29 November, and 6 December 1931; "Historia de la Catedral de San Fernando," unpublished manuscript, c. 1945, ACM, 52–53. Various reports of Claretian preaching, leadership in devotional services, and collaboration with parochial school and catechetical efforts are in the *Anales* and the "San Fernando Cathedral Chronicles."

25. *Hoja parroquial,* 8 June 1930 and 4, 11, and 18 October and 8 November 1931;

"Actos de la Sociedad de Vasallos," 1925–1934, 103–109; "San Fernando Cathedral Chronicles," 1:291, 2:17, 2:20.

26. *Hoja parroquial*, 12 April–24 May 1931, 15 November–13 December 1931; "San Fernando Cathedral Chronicles," 2:18, 2:41; *Southern Messenger*, 3 December 1931, p. 5; *Express*, 6 December 1931. The quotation is from the *Hoja parroquial* of 19 April 1931.

27. *La Fe Católica*, 27 March 1897–4 August 1900; *Hoja parroquial*, 5 January–28 December 1930; E. Rodríguez, "Hispanic Community and Church Movements," 209 (quotation), 210.

28. *Anales* (1913–1914): 562 (quotation); "Actos de la Sociedad de Vasallos," 1925–1934, 24; "Actos de la Sociedad de Vasallas," 9. Numerous entries in the "San Fernando Cathedral Chronicles" for 1914–1954 (vols. 1 and 2), the *Hoja parroquial*, and the minutes of the Vasallos and Vasallas reflect Claretian efforts to support parish associations. I am grateful to Josefina Rodríguez, a member of the Vasallas for over five decades, for lending me various annual reports and the 1926–1933 minutes of the women's section. At her request, these documents will be housed in the special collections of Our Lady of the Lake University, San Antonio.

29. "Actos de la Sociedad de Vasallos," 1925–1934, 1 (quotation), 2–4. For an English translation of an excerpt from the minutes of the San Fernando Vasallos organizational meeting, see Matovina and Poyo, *¡Presente!*, 157–158.

30. "Actos de la Sociedad de Vasallos, 1925–1934, esp. 1 (first quotation), 2–7, 20, 33 (second quotation), 51; "Actos de la Sociedad de Vasallos," 1940–1945, 1–21; "Actos de la Sociedad de Vasallas"; "San Fernando Cathedral Chronicles," 1:165–300, 2:1–118; *Hoja parroquial*, 1930–1931. See also *Reglamento de la Asociación Nacional de los Vasallos de Cristo Rey*, 7, CASA; its cover has a photograph of the Vasallos member medallion.

31. *Hoja parroquial*, 11 May 1930 (first quotation), 23 November 1930 (second quotation), 15 November 1931 (third and fourth quotations).

32. *La Prensa*, 11 December 1923, p. 9 (quotation); "San Fernando Cathedral Annual Parish Reports," 1911–1940, CASA. For the various religious and social activities of the Hijas, see "San Fernando Cathedral Chronicles," vol. 1, 2:1–118; *Hoja parroquial*, 1930–1931; and various newspaper reports, such as those in *Southern Messenger*, 6 December 1917, p. 8; 15 December 1921, p. 8; 5 December 1929, p. 12; 4 December 1930, p. 12; 5 December 1940, p. 8; and *La Prensa*, 9 December 1923, p. 8.

33. "San Fernando Cathedral Chronicles," vol. 1, esp. pp. 150, 165, and vol. 2; *Hoja parroquial*, 1930–1931, esp. 18 May 1930 and 23 August 1931.

34. "Actos de la Sociedad de Vasallos," 1925–1934, 47, 49, 53–55.

35. Tarango, "Hispanic Woman and Her Role in the Church," 58 (first two quotations); G. Hinojosa, "Mexican-American Faith Communities," 62; "San Fernando Cathedral Chronicles," 2:12 (third quotation); *Hoja parroquial*, 15 March, 12 April, 10 May, and 21 June–5 July 1931. Other reports on developments in the young men's pious society at the parish are in "San Fernando Cathedral Chronicles," vol. 2, and *Hoja parroquial*, April–December 1931, but the frequency of these reports and the level of participation pale in comparison to those of the Hijas.

36. *Hoja parroquial*, January–December 1930; "San Fernando Cathedral Chronicles," 1:282–300, 2:3–6; "Actos de la Sociedad de Vasallos," 1925–1934, 80–95; "Actos de la Sociedad de Vasallas," 81–104 (from loose pages preserved in an envelope). For outdoor processions to celebrate el Santo Entierro, first communion rites, and Christ the King,

see, e.g., "San Fernando Cathedral Chronicles," 2:52; *Hoja parroquial*, 18 May and 19 and 26 October 1930.

37. For sources on the Guadalupe celebrations presented in this and the following paragraph, see annual December listings in "San Fernando Cathedral Chronicles," vols. 1 and 2; *Hoja parroquial*, 1930–1931; "Actos de la Sociedad de Vasallos," 1925–1934; "Actos de la Sociedad de Vasallos," 1940–1945; "Actos de la Sociedad de Vasallas." See also *Anales* (1917–1918): 182–83, 185, 190; Poster announcing "Solemne Triduo a Nuestra Madre Santísima de Guadalupe en la Catedral de San Fernando," 1933, CAT; and other sources listed in note 3 above. San Antonio newspapers contain numerous other reports of San Fernando Guadalupe celebrations; e.g., *San Antonio Light*, 11 December 1905, 12 December 1914, 12 December 1933; *La Prensa*, 13 December 1914, pp. 1, 3; 12 December 1926, p. 18; 12 December 1928, p. 6; 12 December 1929, p. 7; 13 December 1933, pp. 1–2; 12 December 1934, pp. 1–2; *Express*, 13 December 1914, 11 December 1928, 10 December 1930, 10 December 1932, 10 December 1933; *Southern Messenger*, 17 December 1914, p. 12; 21 December 1933, p. 10; *El Regidor*, 15 December 1915, p. 1.

38. *La Prensa*, 10 October 1920, p. 12; 12 December 1924, p. 3; 12 December 1925, p. 1; 12 December 1929, p. 7; 12 December 1931, p. 6; 12 December 1933, p. 1; *Magazín de La Prensa*, 13 December 1931, 5; Altamirano, "La Fiesta de Guadalupe," 1210.

39. *La Prensa*, 12 December 1916, p. 7 (first and second quotations), 14 December 1919, p. 13; 11 December 1921, p. 3; 12 December 1925, p. 3; 13 December 1926, p. 8; 12 December 1928, p. 6; 13 December 1930, p. 3; 11 December 1932, p. 4; 12 December 1934, p. 8 (fourth quotation); 13 December 1934, p. 8; 12 December 1937, pp. 3, 9; *San Antonio Light*, 12 December 1914 (third quotation); *Express*, 10 December 1930; *Hoja parroquial*, 13 December 1931 (fifth quotation). For earlier Guadalupe sermons and writings that developed insights similar to those of exiled Mexican clergy, see Brading, *Mexican Phoenix*, esp. 244–252, 298–304.

40. *La Prensa*, 13 December 1916, p. 5 (fifth quotation); 17 October 1920, p. 9 (first two quotations); 13 December 1934, pp. 1, 8 (third and fourth quotations).

41. Bruce-Novoa, "*La Prensa* and the Chicano Community," 154; F. Hinojosa, *El México de Afuera*, 9–10. See also *La Prensa*, 13 December 1914, p. 1.

42. Gamio, *Mexican Immigrant*, 211 (first quotation), 242 (second and third quotations); Arnold, *Folklore, Manners, and Customs*, 21 (fourth quotation), 22–24; *El Imparcial de Texas*, 19 December 1918, p. 11 (last three quotations).

43. *La Prensa*, 17 October 1920, p. 9 (fifth and sixth quotations); 12 December 1929, p. 7 (second, third, and fourth quotations); 12 December 1930, p. 7 (seventh and eighth quotations); 13 December 1933, p. 1; 12 December 1934, p. 8 (first quotation); Altamirano, "La Fiesta de Guadalupe," 1209; Brading, *Mexican Phoenix*, 290–291.

44. *La Prensa*, 12 December 1924, p. 3; 12 December 1925, 3.

45. *Hoja parroquial*, 29 November and 13 December 1931.

46. *San Antonio Light*, 13 December 1916 (quotation); Gonzalas, *Mexican Family in San Antonio*, 16–17; *La Prensa*, 12 December 1925, p. 9; 12 December 1935, p. 2.

47. Johnson, "Marian Tradition and the Reality of Women"; Johnson, *Truly Our Sister*, 47–70; *La Prensa*, 11 December 1932, p. 4; Luna Lawhn, "Victorian Attitudes Affecting the Mexican Woman Writing in *La Prensa*"; Luna Lawhn, "*El Regidor* and *La Prensa*." Jovita González also published a Guadalupe article in *La Prensa* (12 December 1933, p. 4), but it is a short summary of the traditional Guadalupe apparition narrative and does not relate any of her own reflections.

48. "San Fernando Cathedral Chronicles," 1:186–187.

49. Dolan and Hinojosa, *Mexican Americans and the Catholic Church*, 65, 74, 163, 248, 266, 281–282; Engh, "Companion of the Immigrants," 42.

50. Dolan and Hinojosa, *Mexican Americans and the Catholic Church*, 61 (first quotation), 186 (fourth quotation), 185–187; Balderrama, *In Defense of La Raza*, 77 (second quotation), 78 (third quotation), 73–90; G. Sánchez, *Becoming Mexican American*, 13 (last quotation), 167–170; Engh, "Companion of the Immigrants," 43.

51. Tweed, *Our Lady of the Exile*, 95–96.

52. Douglas, *Natural Symbols*, 91. See also Douglas's subsequent and related short work, *Cultural Bias*, and Bell, *Ritual: Perspectives and Dimensions*, 33–46.

53. Devra Weber, *Dark Sweat, White Gold*, 60 (quotations), 57–62. See also Groody, *Border of Death*, *Valley of Life*.

CHAPTER 5: Celestial *Mestiza*, 1940–2003

1. See Elizondo's *Mestizaje, La Morenita, Galilean Journey, Future Is Mestizo*, and *Guadalupe*; and Matovina, *Beyond Borders*. See also Lockhart, *Nahuas after the Conquest*; Espín, *Faith of the People*, 133–142; Gracia, *Hispanic/Latino Identity*.

2. U.S. Bureau of the Census, *Census of Population: 1970;* U.S. Census Bureau, Census 2000 Summary File; Grebler, Moore, and Guzmán, *Mexican-American People*, 42, 112–117; Landolt, *Mexican-American Workers of San Antonio*, 44; Gaquin and DeBrandt, *2000 County and City Extra*, 1059. Figures for foreign-born residents in the 2000 census are for Bexar County, where San Antonio is located. U.S. Bureau of the Census, State and County QuickFacts.

3. *San Antonio Express* (hereafter, *Express*), 14 June 1957; Ríos-McMillan, "Biography of a Man and His Newspaper," 147 (quotation), 146–148; Bruce-Novoa, "*La Prensa* and the Chicano Community," 155–156. Unless otherwise noted, the *Express* and all other newspapers cited in this chapter were published in San Antonio.

4. Pycior, "*La Raza* Organizes," 223–232; R. Rosales, *Illusion of Inclusion*, 168–170; Márquez, *LULAC*; Gutiérrez, *Walls and Mirrors*, 135–136, 143–144, 164–167, 193–194, 201–202.

5. Sloss-Vento, *Alonso S. Perales;* R. García, *Rise of the Mexican American Middle Class*, 282–289; M. García, "Catholic Social Doctrine and Mexican American Political Thought"; Perales, *Are We Good Neighbors?*, 150 (quotation); M. García, *Mexican Americans*, 49–51; Allsup, *American G.I. Forum*; H. Ramos, *American GI Forum*.

6. F. Rosales, *Chicano!*, esp. 215–222, 264–266; A. Navarro, *Mexican American Youth Organization*; Acosta and Winegarten, *Las Tejanas*, 195 (quotation).

7. Rogers, *Cold Anger*, 105–126; Warren, *Dry Bones Rattling*, esp. 47–57, 233–234; Matovina, "Latino Catholics and American Public Life," 59–64; Miller, *On the Border*, 12–13; "Power, Action, Justice: 1974–1999" (COPS twenty-fifth anniversary program), 21 (quotation), copy in possession of author. The observant reader will note that Edmundo Rodríguez is one of four persons with the same last name mentioned in this chapter; the others are Josefina, Gene, and Esther Rodríguez. None of them are related to each another.

8. "Officers of the City Government" (typescript), San Antonio Public Library; R. Rosales, *Illusion of Inclusion*, esp. 50, 62–81, 90–96; Rogers, *Cold Anger*, 75–76.

9. "Officers of the City Government" (typescript); R. Rosales, *Illusion of Inclusion*, esp. 110–116, 120–121, 143–144, 159–177; Acosta and Winegarten, *Las Tejanas*, 266, 272–273.

10. Ríos-McMillan, "Biography of a Man and His Newspaper," 136–137, 142; Buitron, "Who Are We?," 134–146, 166–170; *Express*, 3 July 2001 (quotation).

11. J. Davis, *San Antonio*, 40–43; Fisher, *San Antonio: Outpost of Empires*, 81–99.

12. Bronder, *Social Justice and Church Authority*, esp. 69, 100–101; Vanderholt, "San Fernando Cathedral in San Antonio," 101 (first quotation); Robert E. Lucey to J. L. Manning, 4 January 1944, as cited in Privett, *U.S. Catholic Church and Its Hispanic Members*, 153 (second quotation).

13. Romero, "Charism and Power"; Matovina, "Representation and Reconstruction of Power"; R. Martínez, *PADRES; Archdiocese of San Antonio*, 46; Tarango and Matovina, "Las Hermanas"; Medina, *Las Hermanas*.

14. Flores, "People Filled with Hope," 61; McMurtrey, *Mariachi Bishop*.

15. Mary Navarro Farr, interview by author, 1 July 2001.

16. Bean and Bradshaw, "Intermarriage between Persons of Spanish and Non-Spanish Surname," 393–394; Griswold del Castillo, *La Familia*, 116–120; Williams, *Mexican American Family*, 23–27, 44–51, 65–70.

17. Ruiz, *From Out of the Shadows*, 147; Pesquera, "'In the Beginning He Wouldn't Lift Even a Spoon,'" 181, 187 (quotations).

18. Skerry, *Mexican Americans*, 38–41; R. Rosales, *Illusion of Inclusion*, esp. 9–12; Landolt, *Mexican-American Workers of San Antonio*, 69, 71; U.S. Bureau of the Census, 2000 Census of Population and Housing, 10.

19. [Werlenbaker], *San Antonio*, 146; R. Rosales, *Illusion of Inclusion*; Renaud González, "Remember the Alamo," 28.

20. Recuerdo de la Solemne Novena a Cristo Rey en la Catedral de San Fernando, 1944; Pamphlet for Vasallos Holy Hour during World War II; "Actos de la Sociedad de Vasallos," 1940–1945, 83; "Actos de la Sociedad de Vasallos," 1945–1948; "Actos de la Sociedad de Vasallos," 1948–1952, 83–84. I gratefully acknowledge Josefina Rodríguez, who gave me the first two sources cited in this note from her private collection of San Fernando memorabilia.

21. Boletín, San Fernando Cathedral, 9 March 1958, copy from personal files of Josefina Rodríguez; "San Fernando Cathedral Chronicles," 4:4, ACM; Hijas de María information sheet, n.d., copy from personal files of Carmen Cedillo; Carmen Cedillo, interview by author, 1 August 1995.

22. "San Fernando Cathedral Chronicles," 3:65–66, 2:230; Josefina Rodríguez, interview by author, 1 August 1995. Various passages in the "San Fernando Cathedral Chronicles" cite other Cursillo retreats. For further explication of the Cursillo, see K. Davis, "Cursillo de Cristiandad."

23. The statue the Guadalupanas secured is visible in the illustrations on pages 25 and 160.

24. "San Fernando Cathedral Chronicles," 3:36, 3:112 (quotation); *Alamo Messenger*, 12 December 1957, p. 1. Various passages in the "San Fernando Cathedral Chronicles" record the activities of the Guadalupanas from the organization's 1949 foundation until the termination of the Chronicles when the Claretians left the parish in 1978. For a parallel study of the Guadalupanas in Kansas City and northern California, see Torres, "Our Lady of Guadalupe in the Society of the Guadalupanas"; G. Pitti, "Sociedades Guadalupanas in the San Francisco Archdiocese."

25. "San Fernando Cathedral Chronicles," vol. 4, esp. pp. 25, 81, 111, 128; author's notes from parish focus group, 4 October 1994 (quotation).

26. *Alamo Register*, 28 May 1943, sec. 2, p. 4; de Luna, "*Evangelizadoras del barrio.*"

27. *Today's Catholic*, 14 April 1978, p. 2 (first quotation); 11 November 1977, p. 1 (second quotation); Felipa Peña, interview by author, 24 May 1997; Jacobson, "San Antonio Gem Regains Its Sparkle," 38.

28. Elizondo, *Future Is Mestizo*, 38 (first quotation); Mexican American Cultural Center brochure, 1977, Archives of the Mexican American Cultural Center, San Antonio (second, third, and fourth quotations); Elizondo, "Mexican American Cultural Center Story"; E. Rodríguez, "Hispanic Community and Church Movements," 224–234. The texts cited from the Mexican American Cultural Center brochure of 1977 are also in Matovina and Poyo, *¡Presente!*, 224–225.

29. Elizondo and Matovina, *San Fernando Cathedral*, 11 (first quotation); Warner, "Elizondo's Pastoral Theology in Action," 51–52 (last three quotations).

30. "San Fernando Cathedral Chronicles," 3:189, 3:192.

31. Elizondo and Matovina, *San Fernando Cathedral*, 86–111; D. García, "Roles for the Urban Cathedral in 21st-Century America"; *La Gran Posada* (video); *Soul of the City / Alma del pueblo* (video); *Express*, 3 September 1985; D. Martínez, "Spanish TV Mass."

32. Frank Paredes, Jr., interview by author, 28 February 1994; Patti Elizondo, "Serenata Guadalupana Experience" (typescript presented to author), December 1994; Landa, "Cultures Thrive by Living Tradition."

33. Guadalupe Alvarado de Mandujano, interview by author, 8 December 1993; D. García, "Processions"; D. García, "Roles for the Urban Cathedral in 21st-Century America," 607–608; *La Gran Posada* (video).

34. Gene Rodríguez, interview by author, 1 December 1993; *Express*, 29 May 1995; Bill Thornton, interview by author, 18 February 1994.

35. Jarboe, "Celestial Center of San Antonio."

36. Author's notes from parish focus group, 9 March 1994; Guadalupe Alvarado de Mandujano, interview by author, 8 December 1993; author's notes from focus group of parishioners and scholars visiting San Fernando, 29 August 1994.

37. Author's notes from focus groups of parishioners and scholars visiting San Fernando, 2 April and 29 August 1994 and 15 April 1995.

38. *Alamo Register*, 18 December 1942, p. 5 (first two quotations); pamphlet for Vasallos Holy Hour during World War II, copy from personal files of Josefina Rodríguez; *Ecos de la Catedral*, 16 June 1918, p. 4; "San Fernando Cathedral Annual Parish Report," 1940, CASA; "Actos de la Sociedad de Vasallos," 1940–1945, 59 (third quotation). For further reports of San Fernando's Guadalupe celebrations each December during World War II, see pertinent entries in "Actos de la Sociedad de Vasallos," 1940–1945; "San Fernando Cathedral Chronicles," vol. 2; and *La Prensa*, 11 December 1941, p. 4. *Ecos de la Catedral* was a San Fernando parish publication in the early twentieth century and is available at CAT.

39. Information in this paragraph and further elaboration on the archdiocesan celebrations in the three paragraphs that follow are taken from numerous newspaper reports, including *Southern Messenger*, 9 December 1954, p. 1; 16 December 1954, p. 1; 6 December 1956, p. 1; 20 December 1956, p. 7; *Alamo Register*, 17 December 1954, p. 1; 23 November 1956, p. 1; 7 December 1956, p. 1; 21 December 1956, pp. 1–3; *Alamo Messenger*, 28 November 1957, p. 1 (quotation); 5 December 1957, pp. 1–2; 4 December 1958, pp. 1, 6; 3 December 1959, pp. 1, 10; 10 December 1959, p. 1; 1 December 1960, p. 1; 8 December 1960, pp. 1, 11; 1 December 1961, p. 1; 8 December 1961, p. 1; 7 December

1962, p. 1; 29 November 1963, p. 12; 6 December 1963, pp. 1, 8; 13 December 1963, p. 7; 27 November 1964, p. 12; 4 December 1964, pp. 1, 11; 11 December 1964, pp. 1–2; *Express*, 11, 12, and 13 December 1954; 13 December 1956; 12 December 1957; 12 and 13 December 1959; 12 December 1960; 9 December 1962; *San Antonio Light*, 13 December 1954; 9, 12 and 13 December 1956; 12 December 1957 (quotation); 11 December 1958; 13 December 1959; 12 December 1963; *La Prensa*, 14 December 1954, p. 2; 12 December 1957, pp. 1, 23; 20 December 1959, p. 15. See also pertinent entries in "San Fernando Cathedral Chronicles," vol. 3. Archbishop Lucey oversaw the founding of the *Alamo Register* as the San Antonio archdiocesan newspaper in 1942, and the *Southern Messenger*, a Catholic newspaper that the Menger family had published in San Antonio since 1893, continued publication until the two papers merged and formed the *Alamo Messenger* in 1956. The name of the newspaper was changed to *Today's Catholic* in 1972.

40. *Alamo Messenger*, 4 December 1958, p. 1.

41. *Alamo Register*, 13 December 1946, p. 3; *La Prensa*, 11 December 1949, p. 4; 12 December 1949, p. 1; 12 December 1950, p. 2; 12 December 1951, p. 1; 13 December 1953, p. 1; 11 December 1955, p. 4; and 12 December 1955, pp. 1–2; various entries in the "San Fernando Cathedral Chronicles."

42. Alfredo Ramírez, interview by author, 14 March 1994; author's notes from observation and interviews at San Fernando, 10–12 October 2003 (last three quotations). See also sources cited in note 41.

43. Josefina Rodríguez, interview by author, 1 August 1995.

44. Elizondo and Matovina, *San Fernando Cathedral*, 59 (first quotation); author's notes from observation and interviews at San Fernando, 10–12 October 2003 (last two quotations).

45. *San Antonio Light*, 10 and 11 December 1989; *Express*, 10, 11, 12, and 16 December 1989.

46. Warner, "Elizondo's Pastoral Theology in Action," 52–53; author's notes from focus group of parishioners and scholars visiting San Fernando, 12 December 1996; Janie García, interview by author, 3 December 1993.

47. Gene Rodríguez, interviews by author, 1 December 1993, 11 October 2003; author's notes from observation and interviews at San Fernando, 10–12 October 2003 (last two quotations); Chávez, "Virgin of Guadalupe Tattoos."

48. Carter, *Culture of Disbelief*; Gene Rodríguez, interview by author, 11 October 2003.

49. Brading, *Mexican Phoenix*, 298–299, 302–303, 324; *La Prensa*, 12 December 1945, p. 3 (quotations); 12 December 1950, pp. 3–4; 12 December 1951, p. 2; 12 December 1954, p. 7; 11 December 1955, p. 1; 11 December 1958, pp. 3, 23.

50. Elizondo, *La Morenita*, 112 (first quotation); Elizondo, *Future Is Mestizo*, 65 (second quotation); *San Antonio Light*, 11 December 1991 (third quotation). See also Elizondo, *Mestizaje, Galilean Journey*, and *Guadalupe*; and Matovina, *Beyond Borders*.

51. *La Prensa*, 13 December 1953, p. 1; 11 December 1955, p. 1; Elizondo, *Guadalupe*, 114; Elizondo, *Galilean Journey*, 44. See also *La Prensa*, 12 December 1950, p. 4; 13 December 1953, p. 1.

52. Josefina Rodríguez, interview by author, 1 August 1995; author's notes from parish focus group, 8 December 1993; R. Rosales, *Illusion of Inclusion*, 109 (quotation).

53. Robert E. Lucey, "Conditions in the Southwest Necessitating the Organization of the Confraternity of Christian Doctrine," address to the First Regional Inter-American

Congress of the Confraternity of Christian Doctrine, 23 October 1947, CASA; Hirsley and Casuso, "Hispanic Catholics Feel Pull of Protestant Fervor"; *Alamo Messenger*, 27 November 1964, p. 12; *Today's Catholic*, 12 September 1986, p. 9.

54. *La Prensa*, 13 December 1954, p. 2 (first two quotations); author's notes from parish leaders' manuscript evaluation session, 28 May 2002 (third quotation).

55. Mary Esther Bernal, interviews by author, 6 February 1994, 11 October 2003.

56. Author's notes from observation and interviews at San Fernando, 10–12 October 2003.

57. Tina Cantú Navarro, interview by author, 12 October 2003; *La Gran Posada* (video).

58. Cisneros, "Tejano Soul of San Antonio," 25; Cisneros, "Guadalupe the Sex Goddess," 50–51 (last three quotations); Cisneros, "Tepeyac."

59. Peter Paul Ruiz, interview by author, 12 December 2003.

60. References for the archdiocesan Guadalupe celebrations at San Fernando during the 1950s and 1960s are in note 39 above.

61. Information in this paragraph derives from my participation and observation at San Fernando for over a decade.

62. Author's notes from observation and interviews at San Fernando, 11–12 December 2003.

63. Stevens-Arroyo, "Correction, *Sí*; Defection, *No*."

64. Zulema Escamilla Galindo, interview by author, 18 March 1994.

65. M. Navarro, "In Many Churches, Icons Compete for Space"; García-Rivera, "Let's Capture the Hispanic Imagination"; Engh, "With Her People"; Dahm, *Parish Ministry in a Hispanic Community*, 161–167; Figueroa Deck, "Hispanic Ministry Comes of Age"; A. Pérez, "History of Hispanic Liturgy since 1965."

66. Gracia, *Hispanic/Latino Identity*, 108.

67. John Paul II, *Ecclesia in America*, #11.

68. Bañuelas, "U.S. Hispanic Theology," 279.

69. Ibid., 280.

70. M. Sánchez, *Imagen de la Virgen María*, 179, 191. For Sánchez's claim of Mexican divine election and its subsequent development in other Guadalupan writings, see Lafaye, *Quetzalcóatl and Guadalupe*, esp. 248–252; Schulte, *Mexican Spirituality*, esp. 133–168.

71. Theologian Alejandro García-Rivera has visited San Fernando Cathedral on various occasions, and we have had ongoing conversations about the San Fernando congregation and its religious traditions.

72. Elizondo, "Child in a Manger," 69.

Bibliography

Acosta, Teresa Palomo, and Ruth Winegarten. *Las Tejanas: 300 Years of History*. Austin: University of Texas Press, 2003.

"Actos de la Sociedad de Vasallas de Cristo Rey de la Catedral de San Fernando." 1926–1933. Special Collections, Our Lady of the Lake University, San Antonio.

"Actos de la Sociedad de Vasallos de Cristo Rey de la Catedral de San Fernando." 1925–1934, 1940–1945, 1945–1948, and 1948–1952. Catholic Archives at San Antonio, Chancery Office, Archdiocese of San Antonio.

Alamo Messenger (San Antonio). 1956–1972. Name changed to *Today's Catholic* in 1972. Catholic Archives at San Antonio, Chancery Office, Archdiocese of San Antonio.

Alamo Register (San Antonio). 1942–1956. Merged with the *Southern Messenger* and became the *Alamo Messenger* in 1956. Catholic Archives at San Antonio, Chancery Office, Archdiocese of San Antonio.

Alamo Star (San Antonio). 1854–1855. Center for American History, University of Texas, Austin; San Antonio Public Library.

Allsup, Carl. *The American G.I. Forum: Origins and Evolution*. Austin: Center for Mexican American Studies of the University of Texas at Austin, 1982.

Almaráz, Félix D., Jr. *Governor Antonio Martínez and Mexican Independence in Texas: An Orderly Transition*. 1975. Reprint, San Antonio: Bexar County Historical Commission, 1979.

———. "Harmony, Discord, and Compromise in Spanish Colonial Texas: The Río San Antonio Experience, 1691–1741." *New Mexico Historical Review* 67 (October 1992): 329–356.

Altamirano, Ignacio Manuel. "La Fiesta de Guadalupe." In *Paisajes y leyendas, tradiciones y costumbres de México*. 1884. Reprinted in Ernesto de la Torre Villar and Ramiro Navarro de Anda, eds. *Testimonios históricos Guadalupanos*. Mexico City: Fondo de Cultura Económica, 1982, 1128–1210.

Alvarez Cuauhtemoc, Juan. "The Lord Became Lady: A Chicano Theological Interpretation of Our Lady of Guadalupe." *Swedish Missiological Themes* 92, no. 2 (2004): 195–226.

American Public Welfare Association. *Public Welfare Survey of San Antonio, Texas*. Chicago: American Public Welfare Association, 1940.

Anzaldúa, Gloria. *Borderlands / La Frontera: The New Mestiza*, 2nd ed. San Francisco: Aunt Lute Books, 1999.

Aquino, María Pilar. *Our Cry for Life: Feminist Theology from Latin America*. Maryknoll, NY: Orbis, 1993.

Aquino, María Pilar, Daisy L. Machado, and Jeanette Rodríguez, eds. *A Reader in Latina Feminist Theology: Religion and Justice*. Austin: University of Texas Press, 2002.

Archdiocese of San Antonio: 1874–1974. San Antonio: n.p., 1974.

Archives of Claretian Missionaries, Western Province, USA, Claretian Center, Los Angeles. Records of Claretian order's work at San Fernando, 1902–1978, esp. "San Fernando Cathedral Chronicles, 1914–1978."

Arnold, Charles A. *Folklore, Manners, and Customs of the Mexicans in San Antonio, Texas.* 1928. Reprint, San Francisco: R and R Research Associates, 1971.

Austin Texas Sentinel. 1840–1841. Center for American History, University of Texas, Austin.

Badillo, David A. "Between Alienation and Ethnicity: The Evolution of Mexican American Catholicism in San Antonio, 1910–1940." *Journal of American Ethnic History* 16 (summer 1997): 62–83.

Balderrama, Francisco E. *In Defense of La Raza: The Los Angeles Mexican Consulate and the Mexican Community, 1929–1936.* Tucson: University of Arizona Press, 1982.

Balderrama, Francisco E., and Raymond Rodríguez. *Decade of Betrayal: Mexican Repatriation in the 1930s.* Albuquerque: University of New Mexico Press, 1995.

Bañuelas, Arturo. "U.S. Hispanic Theology." *Missiology: An International Review* 20 (April 1992): 275–300.

Barker, E. Shannon. "Los Tejanos de San Antonio: Mexican Immigrant Family Acculturation, 1880–1929." Ph.D. diss., George Washington University, 1996.

Barnes, Charles Merritt. *Combats and Conquests of Immortal Heroes: Sung in Song and Told in Story.* San Antonio: Guessaz & Ferlet, 1910.

Barr, Alwyn. "Occupational and Geographic Mobility in San Antonio, 1870–1900." *Social Science Quarterly* 51 (September 1970): 396–403.

———. *Texas in Revolt: The Battle for San Antonio, 1835.* Austin: University of Texas Press, 1990.

Bean, Frank D., and Benjamin S. Bradshaw. "Intermarriage between Persons of Spanish and Non-Spanish Surname: Changes from the Mid-Nineteenth to the Mid-Twentieth Century." *Social Science Quarterly* 51 (September 1970): 389–395.

Becerra Tanco, Luis. *Felicidad de Mexico.* 1675. Reprinted in Ernesto de la Torre Villar and Ramiro Navarro de Anda, eds. *Testimonios históricos Guadalupanos.* Mexico City: Fondo de Cultura Económica, 1982, 309–333.

Bejareño (San Antonio). 1855–1856. Center for American History, University of Texas, Austin.

Bell, Catherine. *Ritual: Perspectives and Dimensions.* New York: Oxford University Press, 1997.

———. *Ritual Theory, Ritual Practice.* New York: Oxford University Press, 1992.

Benavides, Adán. "Sacred Space, Profane Reality: The Politics of Building a Church in Eighteenth-Century Texas." *Southwestern Historical Quarterly* 107 (July 2003): 1–33.

———. "Tejano." In *The New Handbook of Texas,* 6:238–239. Austin: The Texas State Historical Association, 1996.

Berlandier, Jean Louis. *Journey to Mexico during the Years 1826 to 1834.* 2 vols, trans. Sheila M. Ohlendorf, Josette M. Bigelow, and Mary M. Standifer. Austin: Texas State Historical Association, 1980.

Bexar Archives, Center for American History, University of Texas, Austin. Official correspondence, decrees, and records from the Spanish colonial and Mexican periods.

Blackwelder, Julia Kirk. "Emma Tenayuca: Vision and Courage." In *The Human Tradition in Texas,* ed. Ty Cashion and Jesús F. de la Teja, 191–208. Wilmington, DE: Scholarly Resources, 2001.

Bony, Abbe. *Vie de Mgr. Jean-Marie Odin: Missionaire lazarist, archeveque de la Nouvelle Orleans.* Paris: Imprimerie de D. Dumoulin, 1896.

Boom, Aaron M. "Texas in the 1850s, as Viewed by a Recent Arrival." *Southwestern Historical Quarterly* 70 (October 1966): 281–288.

Brackenridge, R. Douglas, and Francisco O. García-Treto. *Iglesia Presbiteriana: A History of Presbyterians and Mexican Americans in the Southwest,* 2nd ed. San Antonio: Trinity University Press, 1987.

Brading, D. A. *Mexican Phoenix: Our Lady of Guadalupe, Image and Tradition across Five Centuries.* Cambridge: Cambridge University Press, 2001.

Broda, Johanna. "The Sacred Landscape of Aztec Calendar Festivals: Myth, Nature, and Society." In *To Change Place: Aztec Ceremonial Landscapes,* ed. Davíd Carrasco, 74–120. Niwot: University Press of Colorado, 1991.

Bronder, Saul E. *Social Justice and Church Authority: The Public Life of Archbishop Robert E. Lucey.* Philadelphia: Temple University Press, 1982.

Broussard, Ray F. "San Antonio during the Texas Republic: A City in Transition." *Southwestern Studies* 5 (1967): 3–40.

Brown, John Duff. "Reminiscences of Jno. Duff Brown." *Quarterly of the Texas State Historical Association* 12 (April 1909): 296–311.

Bruce-Novoa, Juan. "*La Prensa* and the Chicano Community." *Americas Review* 17 (fall/ winter 1989): 150–162.

Buitron, Richard A., Jr. "Who Are We? The Quest for Tejano Identity in San Antonio, Texas, 1913–the Present." Ph.D. diss., Florida State University, Tallahassee, 2002.

Cabrera y Quintero, Cayetano de. *Escudo de armas de México.* Mexico City: Viuda de D. Joseph Bernardo de Hogal, 1746. Facsimile edition, Mexico City: Seguro Social, 1981.

Camarillo, Albert. *Chicanos in a Changing Society: From Mexican Pueblos to American Barrios in Santa Barbara and Southern California, 1848–1930.* Cambridge, MA: Harvard University Press, 1979.

Carpenter, V. K., comp. *The State of Texas Federal Population Schedules, Seventh Census of the United States, 1850.* Huntsville, AR: Century Enterprises, 1969.

Carranza, Francisco Javier, et al. *Siete sermones guadalupanos (1709–1765).* México: Centro de Estudios de Historia de México Condumex, 1994.

Carrasco, Davíd. *Religions of Mesoamerica: Cosmovision and Ceremonial Centers.* San Francisco: Harper & Row, 1990.

Carroll, Mark M. *Homesteads Ungovernable: Families, Sex, Race, and the Law in Frontier Texas, 1823–1860.* Austin: University of Texas Press, 2001.

Carter, Stephen L. *The Culture of Disbelief: How American Law and Politics Trivialize Religious Devotion.* New York: Basic Books, 1993.

Castañeda, Carlos. *Our Catholic Heritage in Texas, 1519–1936.* 7 vols. Austin: Von Boeckmann-Jones, 1936–1958.

Castillo, Ana, ed. *Goddess of the Americas / La Diosa de las Américas: Writings on the Virgin of Guadalupe.* New York: Riverhead Books, 1996.

Catholic Archives at San Antonio, Chancery Office, Archdiocese of San Antonio. Archdiocesan and San Fernando parish records; papers of Archbishops Arthur J. Drossaerts and Robert E. Lucey; "Mission San Antonio de Valero Marriage Register."

Catholic Archives of Texas, Austin. Correspondence and daily journal of Bishop Jean Marie Odin, 1840–1861; San Fernando parish records.

Center for American History, University of Texas, Austin. Archivo General de México, Provincias Internas; "Minutes of the City Council of the City of San Antonio, 1815 to 1820, 1830 to 1835"; Bexar Archives; Nacogdoches Archives.

Chávez, Arturo. "Virgin of Guadalupe Tattoos: Embodied Symbols and the Construction of Race and Gender among Mexican American Men." Ph.D. diss., Iliff School of Theology, Denver, forthcoming.

Chávez Sánchez, Eduardo. *La Virgen de Guadalupe y Juan Diego en las Informaciones Jurídicas de 1666*, 2nd ed. Mexico City: Ángel Servin, 2002.

Chipman, Donald E. *Spanish Texas, 1519–1821*. Austin: University of Texas Press, 1992.

Chipman, Donald E., and Harriett Denise Joseph. *Notable Men and Women of Spanish Texas*. Austin: University of Texas Press, 1999.

Christian, William A., Jr. *Local Religion in Sixteenth-Century Spain*. Princeton, NJ: Princeton University Press, 1981.

Cisneros, Sandra. "Guadalupe the Sex Goddess." In *Goddess of the Americas / La Diosa de las Américas: Writings on the Virgin of Guadalupe*, ed. Ana Castillo, 46–51. New York: Riverhead Books, 1996.

———. "The Tejano Soul of San Antonio." *New York Times Magazine.* 17 May 1992, 24–25, 36–41.

———. "Tepeyac." In *Woman Hollering Creek and Other Stories*, 21–23. New York: Random House, 1991.

Colton, Walter. *Three Years in California*. Stanford, CA: Stanford University Press, 1949.

Corner, William, ed. and comp. *San Antonio de Béxar: A Guide and History*. 1890. Reprint, San Antonio: Graphic Arts, 1977.

Correo (San Antonio). 1858. Center for American History, University of Texas, Austin.

Crimm, Ana Carolina Castillo. *De León: A Tejano Family History*. Austin: University of Texas Press, 2003.

Crimmins, M. L. "Robert E. Lee in Texas: Letters and Diary." *West Texas Historical Association Year Book* 8 (June 1932): 3–24.

Cruz, Gilbert R. *Let There Be Towns: Spanish Municipal Origins in the American Southwest, 1610–1810*. College Station: Texas A&M University Press, 1988.

Cuadriello, Jaime, Carmen de Monserrat Robledo Galván, and Beatriz Berndt León Mariscal. *La Reina de las Américas: Works of Art from the Museum of the Basílica de Guadalupe*. Chicago: Mexican Fine Arts Center Museum, 1996.

Dahm, Charles W. *Parish Ministry in a Hispanic Community*. Mahwah, NJ: Paulist, 2004.

Davis, John L. *San Antonio: A Historical Portrait*. Austin: Encino, 1978.

Davis, Kenneth G. "Cursillo de Cristiandad: Gift of the Hispanic Church." *Chicago Studies* 38 (fall/winter 1999): 318–328.

De Florencia, Francisco. *La Estrella del Norte de México*. 1688. Reprinted in Ernesto de la Torre Villar and Ramiro Navarro de Anda, eds. *Testimonios históricos Guadalupanos*. Mexico City: Fondo de Cultura Económica, 1982, 359–399.

De la Cruz, Mateo. *Relación de la milagrosa aparición de la santa imagen de la Virgen de Guadalupe de México*. Puebla: Viuda de Borja, 1660. Reprinted in Ernesto de la Torre Villar and Ramiro Navarro de Anda, eds. *Testimonios históricos Guadalupanos*. Mexico City: Fondo de Cultura Económica, 1982, 267–281.

De la Teja, Jesús F. "Rebellion on the Frontier." In *Tejano Journey, 1770–1850*, ed. Gerald E. Poyo, 15–30. Austin: University of Texas Press, 1996.

————, ed. *A Revolution Remembered: The Memoirs and Selected Correspondence of Juan N. Seguín.* Austin: State House Press, 1991.

————. "St. James at the Fair: Religious Ceremony, Civic Boosterism, and Commercial Development on the Colonial Mexican Frontier." *Americas* 57 (January 2001): 395–416.

————. *San Antonio de Béxar: A Community on New Spain's Northern Frontier.* Albuquerque: University of New Mexico Press, 1995.

De la Teja, Jesús F., and John Wheat. "Béxar: Profile of a Tejano Community, 1820–1832." *Southwestern Historical Quarterly* 89 (July 1985): 7–34.

De la Torre Villar, Ernesto, and Ramiro Navarro de Anda, eds. *Testimonios históricos Guadalupanos.* Mexico City: Fondo de Cultura Económica, 1982.

De León, Arnoldo. *Apuntes Tejanos.* Vol. 1. Austin: Texas State Historical Association, 1978.

————. "*In Re* Ricardo Rodríguez: An Attempt at Chicano Disfranchisement in San Antonio, 1896–1897." In *En aquel entonces: Readings in Mexican-American History,* ed. Manuel G. Gonzales and Cynthia M. Gonzales, 57–63. Bloomington: Indiana University Press, 2000.

————. *The Tejano Community, 1836–1900.* 1982. Reprint, Albuquerque: University of New Mexico Press, 1997.

————. *They Called Them Greasers: Anglo Attitudes toward Mexicans in Texas, 1821–1900.* Austin: University of Texas Press, 1983.

De León, Arnoldo, and Kenneth L. Stewart. "A Tale of Three Cities: A Comparative Analysis of the Socioeconomic Conditions of Mexican-Americans in Los Angeles, Tucson, and San Antonio, 1850–1900." *Journal of the West* 24 (April 1985): 64–74.

De Luna, Anita. "*Evangelizadoras del barrio:* The Rise of the Missionary Catechists of Divine Providence." *U.S. Catholic Historian* 21 (winter 2003): 53–71.

De Zavala, Adina. *History and Legends of the Alamo and Other Missions in and around San Antonio,* ed. Richard Flores. Houston: Arte Público, 1996.

Defenders of the Magisterium. "About the Defenders," n.d. Available at www.dotm.org.

————. Petition to Archbishop Flores, n.d. Available at www.dotm.org.

Di Stefano, Onofre. "'Venimos a Luchar': A Brief History of *La Prensa's* Founding." *Aztlán* 16, nos. 1–2 (1987): 95–118.

Díaz-Stevens, Ana María. *Oxcart Catholicism on Fifth Avenue: The Impact of Puerto Rican Migration upon the Archdiocese of New York.* Notre Dame, IN: University of Notre Dame Press, 1993.

————. "The Saving Grace: The Matriarchal Core of Latino Catholicism." *Latino Studies Journal* 4 (September 1993): 60–78.

Dolan, Jay P., and Allan Figueroa Deck, eds. *Hispanic Catholic Culture in the U.S.: Issues and Concerns.* Notre Dame, IN: University of Notre Dame Press, 1994.

Dolan, Jay P., and Gilberto M. Hinojosa, eds. *Mexican Americans and the Catholic Church, 1900–1965.* Notre Dame, IN: University of Notre Dame Press, 1994.

Domenech, Abbe [Emanuel]. *Missionary Adventures in Texas and Mexico: A Personal Narrative of Six Years' Sojourn in Those Regions.* Translated from French. London: Longman, Brown, Green, Longmans, and Roberts, 1858.

Dorsett, Amy. "Three Church Statues May Not Survive." *San Antonio Express,* 15 January 2004.

Douglas, Mary. *Cultural Bias*. London: Royal Anthropological Institute, 1978.

————. *Natural Symbols: Explorations in Cosmology*. New York: Pantheon, 1970.

Dubuis, Claude Marie, to Jean Marie Odin, 22 March 1853. Incarnate Word Archives, Incarnate Word Generalate, San Antonio.

Dunn, William Edward. "Apache Relations in Texas, 1718–1750." *Quarterly of the Texas State Historical Association* 14 (January 1911): 198–274.

Durkheim, Émile. *The Elementary Forms of the Religious Life* (1912). In *Durkheim on Religion*, ed. W. S. F. Pickering, 102–166. Atlanta: Scholars Press, 1994.

Ecos de la Catedral (San Antonio). 1918. Catholic Archives of Texas, Austin.

Elizondo, Virgilio. "A Child in a Manger: The Beginning of a New Order of Existence." In *Proclaiming the Acceptable Year*, ed. Justo L. González, 64–70. Valley Forge: Judson, 1982.

————. *The Future Is Mestizo: Life Where Cultures Meet*, 2nd ed. Boulder: University Press of Colorado, 2000.

————. *Galilean Journey: The Mexican-American Promise*, rev. ed. Maryknoll, NY: Orbis, 2000.

————. *Guadalupe: Mother of the New Creation*. Maryknoll, NY: Orbis, 1997.

————. *Mestizaje: The Dialectic of Cultural Birth and the Gospel*. 3 vols. San Antonio: Mexican American Cultural Center Press, 1978.

————. "The Mexican American Cultural Center Story." *Listening: Journal of Religion and Culture* 32 (fall 1997): 152–160.

————. *La Morenita: Evangelizer of the Americas*. San Antonio: Mexican American Cultural Center Press, 1980.

Elizondo, Virgilio, and Timothy Matovina. *San Fernando Cathedral: Soul of the City*. Maryknoll, NY: Orbis, 1998.

Empereur, James L. "Popular Religion and the Liturgy: The State of the Question." *Liturgical Ministry* 7 (summer 1998): 105–120.

Engelmann, Otto B., trans. and ed. "The Second Illinois in the Mexican War: Mexican War Letters of Adolph Engelmann, 1846–1847." *Journal of the Illinois State Historical Society* 26 (January 1934): 357–452.

Engh, Michael E. "Companion of the Immigrants: Devotion to Our Lady of Guadalupe among Mexicans in the Los Angeles Area, 1900–1940." *Journal of Hispanic/Latino Theology* 5 (August 1997): 37–47.

————. "From *Frontera* Faith to Roman Rubrics: Altering Hispanic Religious Customs in Los Angeles, 1855–1880." *U.S. Catholic Historian* 12 (fall 1994): 85–105.

————. *Frontier Faiths: Church, Temple, and Synagogue in Los Angeles, 1846–1888*. Albuquerque: University of New Mexico Press, 1992.

————. "With Her People: The Barrio and 'La Virgen.'" *America*, 6–13 January 2003, 15–16.

Enríquez de Almanza, Martín. "Carta al rey Felipe II" (1575). Reprinted in Ernesto de la Torre Villar and Ramiro Navarro de Anda, eds. *Testimonios históricos Guadalupanos*. Mexico City: Fondo de Cultura Económica, 1982, 148–149.

Escalada, Xavier. *Enciclopedia guadalupana: Apéndice códice 1548: Estudio científico de su autenticidad*. México: n.p., 1997.

Esparza, Enrique. "Esparza, the Boy of the Alamo, Remembers." In *Rise of the Lone Star: A Story of Texas Told by Its Pioneers*, ed. Howard R. Driggs and Sarah S. King, 213–231. New York: Frederick A. Stokes, 1936.

Espín, Orlando O. *The Faith of the People: Theological Reflections on Popular Catholicism.* Maryknoll, NY: Orbis, 1997.

———. "Mexican Religious Practices, Popular Catholicism, and the Development of Doctrine." In *Horizons of the Sacred: Mexican Traditions in U.S. Catholicism,* ed. Timothy Matovina and Gary Riebe-Estrella, 139–152. Ithaca, NY: Cornell University Press, 2002.

———. "Toward the Construction of an Intercultural Theology of Tradition." *Journal of Hispanic/Latino Theology* 9 (February 2002): 22–59.

La Fe Católica (San Antonio), 1897–1900. Center for American History, University of Texas, Austin.

Fernández, Cristóbal. *Compendio histórico de la Congregación de los Hijos del Inmaculado Corazón de María.* Vol. 2. Madrid: Editorial Coculsa, 1967.

Figueroa Deck, Allan. "Hispanic Ministry Comes of Age." *America,* 17 May 1986, 400–402.

Fisher, Lewis F. *San Antonio: Outpost of Empires.* San Antonio: Maverick, 1997.

Flores, Patricio F. "A People Filled with Hope." In *Proceedings of the II Encuentro Nacional Hispano de Pastoral,* 60–61. Washington, DC: United States Catholic Conference, 1978.

Foley, Patrick. "From Linares to Galveston: Texas in the Diocesan Scheme of the Roman Catholic Church to the Mid-Nineteenth Century." *Catholic Southwest: A Journal of History and Culture* 8 (1997): 25–44.

———. "Jean-Marie Odin, C.M., Missionary Bishop Extraordinaire of Texas." *The Journal of Texas Catholic History and Culture* 1 (1990): 42–60.

Foster, George M. *Culture and Conquest: America's Spanish Heritage.* Chicago: Quadrangle Books, 1960.

Freeman, W. G. "W. G. Freeman's Report on the Eighth Military Department," ed. M. L. Crimmins. *Southwestern Historical Quarterly* 51 (October 1947): 167–174.

French, Sarah L. "Mrs. French's Reminiscences of Early Days in Béxar." In S. J. Wright, *San Antonio de Béxar: Historical, Traditional, Legendary,* 96–101. Austin: Morgan, 1916.

Gamio, Manuel. *The Mexican Immigrant: His Life-Story.* Chicago: University of Chicago Press. 1931. Reprint, New York: Arno, 1969.

———. *Mexican Immigration to the United States: A Study of Human Migration and Adjustment.* Chicago: University of Chicago Press, 1930. Reprint, New York: Arno, 1969.

Gaquin, Deirdre A., and Katherine A. DeBrandt, eds. *2000 County and City Extra: Annual Metro, City, and County Data Book,* 9th ed. Lanham, MD: Bernan, 2000.

García, David. "Processions: The Soul of the City." *Modern Liturgy* 25 (November 1998): 16–18.

———. "Roles for the Urban Cathedral in 21st-Century America." *Origins* 31 (21 February 2002): 603–609.

García, Mario T. "Catholic Social Doctrine and Mexican American Political Thought." In *El Cuerpo de Cristo: The Hispanic Presence in the U.S. Catholic Church,* ed. Peter Casarella and Raúl Gómez, 292–311. New York: Crossroad, 1998.

———. *Mexican Americans: Leadership, Ideology, and Identity, 1930–1960.* New Haven: Yale University Press, 1989.

García, Richard A. *Rise of the Mexican American Middle Class: San Antonio, 1929–1941.* College Station: Texas A&M University Press, 1991.

García-Rivera, Alejandro. *The Community of the Beautiful: A Theological Aesthetics*. Collegeville, MN: Liturgical Press, 1999.
————. "Let's Capture the Hispanic Imagination." *U.S. Catholic* 57 (July 1994): 34–35.
Gaspar de Alba, Alicia. *Chicano Art Inside/Outside the Master's House: Cultural Politics and the CARA Exhibition*. Austin: University of Texas Press, 1998.
Giuriati, Paolo, and Elio Masferrer Kan et al. *No temas . . . yo soy tu madre: Un estudio socioantropológico de los peregrinos a la Basílica de Guadalupe*. Mexico City: Plaza y Valdés Editores, 1998.
Goizueta, Roberto S. *Caminemos con Jesús: Toward a Hispanic/Latino Theology of Accompaniment*. Maryknoll, NY: Orbis, 1995.
————. "Resurrection at Tepeyac: The Guadalupan Encounter." *Theology Today* 56 (October 1999): 336–345.
————. "The Symbolic World of Mexican American Religion." In *Horizons of the Sacred: Mexican Traditions in U.S. Catholicism*, ed. Timothy Matovina and Gary Riebe-Estrella, 119–138. Ithaca, NY: Cornell University Press, 2002.
Gonzalas, Kathleen May. *The Mexican Family in San Antonio, Texas*. 1928. Reprint, San Francisco: R and R Research Associates, 1971.
Gonzales, Michael J. *The Mexican Revolution, 1910–1940*. Albuquerque: University of New Mexico Press, 2002.
González Fernández, Fidel, Eduardo Chávez Sánchez, and José Luis Guerrero Rosado. *El encuentro de la Virgen de Guadalupe y Juan Diego*, 4th ed. Mexico City: Editorial Porrúa, 2001.
Gould, Stephen. *The Alamo City Guide, San Antonio, Texas*. New York: Macgowan & Slipper, 1882.
Gracia, Jorge J. E. *Hispanic/Latino Identity: A Philosophical Perspective*. Malden, MA: Blackwell, 2000.
La Gran Posada. San Antonio: HTN Productions, 1998. Videocassette.
Granjon, Henry. *Along the Rio Grande: A Pastoral Visit to Southwest New Mexico in 1902*, ed. Michael Romero Taylor, trans. Mary W. de López. Albuquerque: University of New Mexico Press, 1986.
Grebler, Leo, Joan W. Moore, and Ralph C. Guzmán. *The Mexican-American People: The Nation's Second Largest Minority*. New York: Free Press, 1970.
Green, Rena Maverick, ed. *Memoirs of Mary A. Maverick*. San Antonio: Alamo, 1921.
Gregory, Brad S. *Salvation at Stake: Christian Martyrdom in Early Modern Europe*. Cambridge: Harvard University Press, 1999.
Gregory XIII. *Ut Deiparae semper virginis*, 2 March 1576. Reprinted in Fidel González Fernández, Eduardo Chávez Sánchez, and José Luis Guerrero Rosado. *El encuentro de la Virgen de Guadalupe y Juan Diego*, 4th ed. Mexico City: Editorial Porrúa, 2001, 557–560.
Griswold del Castillo, Richard. *La Familia: Chicano Families in the Urban Southwest, 1848 to the Present*. Notre Dame, IN: University of Notre Dame Press, 1984.
Groody, Daniel G. *Border of Death, Valley of Life: An Immigrant Journey of Heart and Spirit*. Lanham, MD: Rowman and Littlefield, 2002.
Guerrero, Andrés G. *A Chicano Theology*. Maryknoll, NY: Orbis, 1987.
Guerrero, José Luis. *El Nican mopohua: Un intento de exégesis*. 2 vols. Mexico City: Realidad, Teoría y Práctica, 1998.
Guidelines for a Texas Mission: Instructions for the Missionary of Mission Concepción in San Antonio, Texas, trans. Benedict Leutenegger. San Antonio: Old Spanish Missions Historical Research Library, 1976.

Gutiérrez, David G. *Walls and Mirrors: Mexican Americans, Mexican Immigrants, and the Politics of Ethnicity*. Berkeley: University of California Press, 1995.

Habig, Marion A. *The Alamo Chain of Missions: A History of San Antonio's Five Old Missions*. Chicago: Franciscan Herald Press, 1976.

Hall, David D., ed. *Lived Religion in America: Toward a History of Practice*. Princeton, NJ: Princeton University Press, 1997.

Hardin, Stephen L. *Texian Iliad: A Military History of the Texas Revolution*. Austin: University of Texas Press, 1994.

Harrington, Patricia. "Mother of Death, Mother of Rebirth: The Mexican Virgin of Guadalupe." *Journal of the American Academy of Religion* 56 (winter 1988): 25–50.

Hatcher, Mattie Austin. "The Expedition of Don Domingo Terán de los Rios into Texas." In *Wilderness Mission: Preliminary Studies of the Texas Catholic Historical Society*, vol. 2, ed. Jesús F. de la Teja, 1–66. Austin: Texas Catholic Historical Society, 1999.

Herrera-Sobek, María, ed. *Santa Barraza: Artist of the Borderlands*. College Station: Texas A&M University Press, 2001.

Hinojosa, Federico Allen. *El México de Afuera y su reintegracíon a la patria*. San Antonio: Artes Gráficas, 1940.

Hinojosa, Gilberto M. "Mexican-American Faith Communities in Texas and the Southwest." In *Mexican Americans and the Catholic Church, 1900–1965*, ed. Jay P. Dolan and Gilberto M. Hinojosa, 9–125. Notre Dame, IN: University of Notre Dame Press, 1994.

Hinojosa, Gilberto M., and Anne A. Fox. "Indians and Their Culture in San Fernando de Béxar." In *Tejano Origins in Eighteenth-Century San Antonio*, ed. Gerald E. Poyo and Gilberto M. Hinojosa, 105–120. Austin: University of Texas Press, 1991.

Hirsley, Michael, and Jorge Casuso. "Hispanic Catholics Feel Pull of Protestant Fervor." *Chicago Tribune*, 7 January 1990.

Hollon, W. Eugene, and Ruth Lapham Butler, eds. *William Bollaert's Texas*. Norman: University of Oklahoma Press, 1956.

Houston Telegraph and Texas Register. 1835–1848. Center for American History, University of Texas, Austin; Houston Public Library.

El Imparcial de Texas (San Antonio). 1917–1921. Ethnic and Gender Studies Library, University of California, Santa Barbara.

"Información por el sermón de 1556." Reprinted in Ernesto de la Torre Villar and Ramiro Navarro de Anda, eds. *Testimonios históricos Guadalupanos*. Mexico City: Fondo de Cultura Económica, 1982, 36–141.

Jacobson, Susan. "A San Antonio Gem Regains Its Sparkle." *San Antonio* 9 (March 1975): 32–38.

Jarboe, Jan. "Celestial Center of San Antonio." *San Antonio Express*, 21 December 1986.

John, Elizabeth A. H. *Storms Brewed in Other Men's Worlds: The Confrontation of Indians, Spanish, and French in the Southwest, 1540–1795*. 1975. Reprint, Lincoln: University of Nebraska Press, 1981.

John Paul II. *Ecclesia in America*. In *Origins* 28 (4 February 1999): 565–592.

Johnson, Elizabeth A. "The Marian Tradition and the Reality of Women." *Horizons* 12 (spring 1985): 116–135.

———. "Mary and the Female Face of God." *Theological Studies* 50 (September 1989): 500–526.

———. *Truly Our Sister: A Theology of Mary in the Communion of Saints*. New York: Continuum, 2003.

Jordan, Gilbert J., ed. and trans. "W. Steinert's View of Texas in 1849." *Southwestern Historical Quarterly* 80 (October 1976): 177–200.

Jordan, Terry G. "A Century and a Half of Ethnic Change in Texas, 1836–1986." *Southwestern Historical Quarterly* 89 (April 1986): 385–422.

King, Edward. *Texas, 1874: An Eyewitness Account of Conditions in Post-Reconstruction Texas*, ed. Robert S. Gray. Houston: Cordovan, 1974.

King, Sarah Brackett. "Early Days in San Antonio Recalled by a Pioneer Resident of the City." *San Antonio Light*, 4 February 1917, 14.

Knox, William J. *The Economic Status of the Mexican American Immigrant in San Antonio, Texas*. 1927. Reprint, San Francisco: R and R Research Associates, 1971.

Kurtz, Donald V. "The Virgin of Guadalupe and the Politics of Becoming Human." *Journal of Anthropological Research* 38 (summer 1982): 194–210.

Lack, Paul D. *The Texas Revolutionary Experience: A Political and Social History, 1835–1836*. College Station: Texas A&M University Press, 1992.

Lafaye, Jacques. *Quetzalcóatl and Guadalupe: The Formation of Mexican National Consciousness, 1531–1813*. Chicago: University of Chicago Press, 1976.

Landa, Victor. "Cultures Thrive by Living Tradition." *San Antonio Express*, 2 April 1994.

Landolt, Robert Garland. *The Mexican-American Workers of San Antonio, Texas*. New York: Arno, 1976.

Lanier, Sidney. *Sidney Lanier's Historical Sketch*. San Antonio: Accurate Litho, 1980.

Lawrence, A. B. *Texas in 1840; or, the Emigrant's Guide to the New Republic; Being the Result of Observation, Enquiry and Travel in that Beautiful Country. By an Emigrant, Late of the United States*. New York: William W. Allen, 1840.

León, Luis D. *La Llorona's Children: Religion, Life, and Death in the U.S.-Mexican Borderlands*. Berkeley: University of California Press, 2004.

Lockhart, James. *The Nahuas after the Conquest: A Social and Cultural History of the Indians of Central Mexico, Sixteenth through Eighteenth Centuries*. Stanford: Stanford University Press, 1992.

Lozano-Díaz, Nora O. "Ignored Virgin or Unaware Women: A Mexican-American Protestant Reflection on the Virgin of Guadalupe." In *A Reader in Latina Feminist Theology: Religion and Justice*, ed. María Pilar Aquino, Daisy L. Machado, and Jeanette Rodríguez, 204–216. Austin: University of Texas Press, 2002.

Luna Lawhn, Juanita. "*El Regidor* and *La Prensa*: Impediments to Women's Self-Definition." In *Third Woman: The Sexuality of Latinas*, ed. Norma Alarcón, Ana Castillo, and Cherríe Moraga, 134–142. Berkeley: Third Woman Press, 1989.

———. "Victorian Attitudes Affecting the Mexican Woman Writing in *La Prensa* during the Early 1900s and the Chicana of the 1980s." In *Missions in Conflict: Essays on U.S.-Mexican Relations and Chicano Culture*, ed. Renate von Bardeleben, Dietrich Briesemeister, and Juan Bruce-Novoa, 65–71. Tübingen: Narr, 1986.

Lundberg, Magnus. *Unification and Conflict: The Church Politics of Alonso de Montúfar OP, Archbishop of Mexico, 1554–1572*. Uppsala, Sweden: Swedish Institute of Missionary Research, 2002.

Lundy, Benjamin. *The Life, Travels, and Opinions of Benjamin Lundy*. 1847. Reprint, New York: Negro Universities Press, 1969.

Machado, Daisy L. *Of Borders and Margins: Hispanic Disciples in Texas, 1888–1945*. Oxford: Oxford University Press, 2003.

Maguire, Jack. *A Century of Fiesta in San Antonio*. Austin: Eakin, 1990.

Mann, Kristin Dutcher. "Music and Popular Religiosity in Northern New Spain." *Catholic Southwest: A Journal of History and Culture* 12 (2001): 7–27.

Mansfield, J. K. F. "Colonel J. K. F. Mansfield's Report of the Inspection of the Department of Texas in 1856." *Southwestern Historical Quarterly* 42 (October 1938): 133–143.

Márquez, Benjamin. *LULAC: The Evolution of a Mexican American Political Organization*. Austin: University of Texas Press, 1993.

Martínez, Demetria. "Spanish TV Mass: Evangelism at Its Finest." *National Catholic Reporter*, 17 March 1989, 27.

Martínez, Richard Edward. *PADRES: The National Chicano Priest Movement*. Austin: University of Texas Press, 2005.

Massanet, Fray Damián, and companions. "Diary of the missionary friars, 16 May–2 August 1691." In *Boletín del Archivo General de la Nación* 28, no. 2 (1957): 349–375.

Matovina, Timothy. *The Alamo Remembered: Tejano Accounts and Perspectives*. Austin: University of Texas Press, 1995.

———, ed. *Beyond Borders: Writings of Virgilio Elizondo and Friends*. Maryknoll, NY: Orbis, 2000.

———. "Guadalupe at Calvary: Patristic Theology in Miguel Sánchez's *Imagen de la Virgen María* (1648)." *Theological Studies* 64 (December 2003): 795–811.

———. "Latino Catholics and American Public Life." In *Can Charitable Choice Work? Covering Religion's Impact on Urban Affairs and Social Services*, ed. Andrew Walsh, 56–77. Hartford, CT: The Leonard E. Greenberg Center for the Study of Religion in Public Life, 2001.

———. "Lay Initiatives in Worship on the Texas *Frontera*, 1830–1860." *U.S. Catholic Historian* 12 (fall 1994): 107–120.

———. "Religion and Ethnicity at San Antonio: Germans and Tejanos in the Wake of U.S. Annexation." *Catholic Southwest: A Journal of History and Culture* 10 (1999): 29–49.

———. "Representation and Reconstruction of Power: The Rise of PADRES and Las Hermanas." In *What's Left? Liberal American Catholics*, ed. Mary Jo Weaver, 220–237. Bloomington: Indiana University Press, 1999.

———. "Sacred Place and Collective Memory: San Fernando Cathedral, San Antonio, Texas." *U.S. Catholic Historian* 15 (winter 1997): 33–50.

———. "San Fernando Cathedral and the Alamo: Sacred Place, Public Ritual, and Construction of Meaning." *Journal of Ritual Studies* 12 (winter 1998): 1–13.

———. *Tejano Religion and Ethnicity: San Antonio, 1821–1860*. Austin: University of Texas Press, 1995.

Matovina, Timothy, and Gary Riebe-Estrella, eds. *Horizons of the Sacred: Mexican Traditions in U.S. Catholicism*. Ithaca, NY: Cornell University Press, 2002.

Matovina, Timothy, and Gerald E. Poyo, eds. *¡Presente! U.S. Latino Catholics from Colonial Origins to the Present*. Maryknoll, NY: Orbis, 2000.

McCalla, W[illiam] L. *Adventures in Texas, Chiefly in the Spring and Summer of 1840*. Philadelphia: Privately printed, 1841.

McClintock, William A. "Journal of a Trip Through Texas and Northern Mexico in 1846–1847." *Southwestern Historical Quarterly* 34 (October 1930): 141–158.

McDanield, H. F., and N.A. Taylor. *The Coming Empire; or, Two Thousand Miles in Texas on Horseback*. New York: A. S. Barnes, 1877.

McDannell, Colleen. *Material Christianity: Religion and Popular Culture in America*. New Haven: Yale University Press, 1995.

212   *Bibliography*

McDowell, Catherine, ed. *Letters from the Ursuline, 1852–1853.* San Antonio: Trinity University Press, 1977.

McMurtrey, Martin. *Mariachi Bishop: The Life Story of Patrick Flores.* San Antonio: Corona, 1987.

Medina, Lara. *Las Hermanas: Chicana/Latina Religious-Political Activism in the U.S. Catholic Church.* Philadelphia: Temple University Press, 2004.

Mejido, Manuel J. "A Critique of the 'Aesthetic Turn' in U.S. Hispanic Theology: A Dialogue with Roberto Goizueta and the Positing of a New Paradigm." *Journal of Hispanic/Latino Theology* 8 (February 2001): 18–48.

"Memorial of Father Benito Fernández Concerning the Canary Islanders, 1741," trans. Benedict Leutenegger. *Southwestern Historical Quarterly* 82 (January 1979): 265–296.

Menefee, Selden C., and Orin C. Cassmore. *The Pecan Shellers of San Antonio: The Problem of Underpaid and Unemployed Mexican Labor.* Washington, DC: United States Government Printing Office, 1940. Reprinted in *Mexican Labor in the United States.* New York: Arno, 1974.

Mexican American Cultural Center brochure, 1977. Archives of the Mexican American Cultural Center, San Antonio.

Meyer, Jean A. *The Cristero Rebellion: The Mexican People between Church and State, 1926–1929,* trans. Richard Southern. Cambridge: Cambridge University Press, 1976.

Miller, Char, ed. *On the Border: An Environmental History of San Antonio.* Pittsburgh: University of Pittsburgh Press, 2001.

Morfi, Juan Agustín. *History of Texas, 1673–1779,* trans. Carlos Eduardo Castañeda. Albuquerque: Quivira Society, 1935.

Morgan, David. *Protestants and Pictures: Religion, Visual Culture, and the Age of American Mass Production.* Oxford: Oxford University Press, 1999.

———. *Visual Piety: A History and Theory of Popular Religious Images.* Berkeley: University of California Press, 1998.

Mörner, Magnus. *Race Mixture in the History of Latin America.* Boston: Little, Brown, 1967.

Morrell, Z. N. *Flowers and Fruits from the Wilderness; or, Thirty-Six Years in Texas and Two Winters in Honduras.* Boston: Gould and Lincoln, 1872.

Morrison, Andrew, comp. *San Antonio, Texas.* 1891. Reprint, San Antonio: Privately printed, 1977.

Muir, Andrew Forest, ed. *Texas in 1837: An Anonymous, Contemporary Narrative.* Austin: University of Texas Press, 1988.

Nacogdoches Archives, Center for American History, University of Texas, Austin. Official records of the Spanish colonial period.

Nance, Joseph Milton. *Attack and Counter-Attack: The Texas-Mexican Frontier, 1842.* Austin: University of Texas Press, 1964.

Nañez, Alfredo. *History of the Rio Grande Conference of the United Methodist Church.* Dallas: Bridwell Library, Southern Methodist University, 1980.

Navarro, Armando. *Mexican American Youth Organization: Avant-Garde of the Chicano Movement in Texas.* Austin: University of Texas Press, 1995.

Navarro, José Antonio. *Defending Mexican Valor in Texas: José Antonio Navarro's Historical Writings, 1853–1857,* ed. David R. McDonald and Timothy M. Matovina. Austin: State House Press, 1995.

Navarro, Mireya. "In Many Churches, Icons Compete for Space; Multiple Shrines to Patron Saints Testify to a Rivalry of the Devout." *New York Times,* 29 May 2002.

Nebel, Richard. *Santa María Tonantzin, Virgen de Guadalupe: Continuidad y transformación religiosa en México.* Mexico City: Fondo de Cultura Económica, 1995.

Newcomb, James P. "Christmas in San Antonio Half a Century Ago." *San Antonio Express,* 18 December 1904, 26.

Noguez, Xavier. *Documentos guadalupanos: Un estudio sobre las fuentes de información tempranas en torno a las mariofanías en el Tepeyac.* Mexico City: Fondo de Cultura Económica, 1993.

O'Connor, Mary. "The Virgin of Guadalupe and the Economics of Symbolic Behavior." *Journal for the Scientific Study of Religion* 28, no. 2 (1989): 105–119.

Odin, Jean Marie. Personal correspondence 1840–1861. Catholic Archives of Texas, Austin; University of Notre Dame Archives, Notre Dame, Indiana.

"Officers of the City Government" (typescript). San Antonio Public Library, San Antonio, Texas.

Olmsted, Frederick Law. *A Journey through Texas; or, A Saddle-Trip on the Southwestern Frontier: With a Statistical Index.* New York: Dix, Edwards & Co., 1857.

Orozco, Cynthia E. "The Origins of the League of United Latin American Citizens (LULAC) and the Mexican American Civil Rights Movement in Texas with an Analysis of Women's Political Participation in a Gendered Context, 1910–1929." Ph.D. diss., University of California at Los Angeles, 1992.

Orsi, Robert A. "Everyday Miracles: The Study of Lived Religion." In *Lived Religion in America: Toward a History of Practice,* ed. David D. Hall, 3–21. Princeton, NJ: Princeton University Press, 1997.

———. *The Madonna of 115th Street: Faith and Community in Italian Harlem, 1880–1950,* 2nd ed. New Haven: Yale University Press, 2002.

———. *Thank You, St. Jude: Women's Devotion to the Patron Saint of Hopeless Causes.* New Haven: Yale University Press, 1996.

O'Toole, James M. ed. *Habits of Devotion: Catholic Religious Practice in Twentieth-Century America.* Ithaca, NY: Cornell University Press, 2004.

Parisot, P. F. *The Reminiscences of a Texas Missionary.* San Antonio: Johnson Bros., 1899.

Parisot, P. F., and C. J. Smith. *History of the Catholic Church in the Diocese of San Antonio, Texas.* San Antonio: Carrico & Bowen, 1897.

Perales, Alonso S. *Are We Good Neighbors?* 1948. Reprint, New York: Arno, 1974.

Pérez, Arturo J. "The History of Hispanic Liturgy since 1965." In *Hispanic Catholic Culture in the U.S.: Issues and Concerns,* ed. Jay P. Dolan and Allan Figueroa Deck, 360–408. Notre Dame, IN: University of Notre Dame Press, 1994.

Pérez, Laura Elisa. "El Desorden, Nationalism, and Chicana/o Aesthetics." In *Between Woman and Nation: Nationalisms, Transnational Feminisms, and the State,* ed. Caren Kaplan, Norma Alarcón, and Minoo Moallem, 19–46. Durham, NC: Duke University Press, 1999.

Pesquera, Beatríz M. "'In the Beginning He Wouldn't Lift Even a Spoon': The Division of Household Labor." In *Building with Our Own Hands: New Directions in Chicana Studies,* ed. Adela de la Torre and Beatríz M. Pesquera, 181–195. Berkeley: University of California Press, 1993.

Peterson, Jeanette Favrot. "The Virgin of Guadalupe: Symbol of Conquest or Liberation?" *Art Journal* 51 (winter 1992): 39–47.

214   *Bibliography*

Pitti, Gina Marie. "The Sociedades Guadalupanas in the San Francisco Archdiocese, 1942–1962." *U.S. Catholic Historian* 21 (winter 2003): 83–98.

Pitti, Stephen J. *The Devil in Silicon Valley: Northern California, Race, and Mexican Americans.* Princeton, NJ: Princeton University Press, 2003.

Poole, Stafford. *Our Lady of Guadalupe: The Origins and Sources of a Mexican National Symbol, 1531–1797.* Tucson: University of Arizona Press, 1995.

"Population Schedules of the Eighth Census of the United States, 1860." Washington, DC: The National Archives, 1967. Text-fiche, roll 1288: 1–192a.

Poyo, Gerald E. "The Canary Islands Immigrants of San Antonio: From Ethnic Exclusivity to Community in Eighteenth-Century Béxar." In *Tejano Origins in Eighteenth-Century San Antonio,* ed. Gerald E. Poyo and Gilberto M. Hinojosa, 41–58. Austin: University of Texas Press, 1991.

———. "Immigrants and Integration in Late Eighteenth-Century Béxar." In *Tejano Origins in Eighteenth-Century San Antonio,* ed. Gerald E. Poyo and Gilberto M. Hinojosa, 85–103. Austin: University of Texas Press, 1991.

———. "Social Identity on the Hispanic Texas Frontier." In *Recovering the U.S. Hispanic Literary Heritage,* ed. Virgina Sánchez-Korrol and María Herrera-Sobek, 3:384–401. Houston: Arte Público, 1999.

Poyo, Gerald E., and Gilberto M. Hinojosa, eds. *Tejano Origins in Eighteenth-Century San Antonio.* Austin: University of Texas Press, 1991.

La Prensa (San Antonio). 1913–1962. San Antonio Public Library; San Antonio College library; Ethnic and Gender Studies Library, University of California, Santa Barbara.

Privett, Stephen A. *The U.S. Catholic Church and Its Hispanic Members: The Pastoral Vision of Archbishop Robert E. Lucey.* San Antonio: Trinity University Press, 1988.

Pulido, Alberto L. "Nuestra Señora de Guadalupe: The Mexican Catholic Experience in San Diego." *Journal of San Diego History* 37 (fall 1991): 236–254.

Pycior, Julie Leininger. "*La Raza* Organizes: Mexican American Life in San Antonio, 1915–1930, as reflected in *Mutualista* Activities." Ph.D. diss., University of Notre Dame, 1979.

Ramírez, Ricardo. "Liturgy from the Mexican American Perspective." *Worship* 51 (July 1977): 293–298.

Ramos, Henry A. J. *The American GI Forum: In Pursuit of the Dream, 1948–1983.* Houston: Arte Público, 1998.

Ramos, Raúl Alberto. "From Norteño to Tejano: The Roots of Borderlands Ethnicity, Nationalism, and Political Identity in Bexar, 1811–1861." Ph.D. diss., Yale University, 1999.

Recio de León, Juan. Statement of 16 October 1736. In *Ramo de la Historia,* 524:139. *Archivo General de México* (microfilm). Nettie Lee Benson Latin American Collection, University of Texas, Austin.

"Recollections of Texas. By a Returned Emigrant." *North American Miscellany* 2 (17 May 1851): 113–120.

El Regidor (San Antonio). 1890–1915. San Antonio College library; San Antonio Public Library.

Reid, John C. *Reid's Tramp; or, a Journal of the Incidents of Ten Months Travel through Texas, New Mexico, Arizona, Sonora, and California Including Topography, Climate, Soil, Minerals, Metals, and Inhabitants; with a Notice of the Great Inter-Oceanic Rail Road.* 1858. Reprint, Austin: Steck, 1935.

Renaud González, Bárbara. "Remember the Alamo, Part II." *The Nation*, 15 March 1999, 25–29.

Ríos, Hermino. "Toward a True Chicano Bibliography—Part II." *El Grito: A Journal of Contemporary Mexican-American Thought* 5 (summer 1972): 40–47.

Ríos, Hermino, and Guadalupe Castillo. "Toward a True Chicano Bibliography: Mexican American Newspapers, 1848–1942." *El Grito: A Journal of Contemporary Mexican-American Thought* 3 (summer 1970): 17–24.

Ríos-McMillan, Nora. "A Biography of a Man and His Newspaper." *Americas Review* 17 (fall/winter 1989): 136–149.

Rivard, Robert. "San Fernando Still Stands, A Refuge for San Antonio." *San Antonio Express-press*, 16 September 2001.

Robinson, Willard B. "Houses of Worship in Nineteenth-Century Texas." *Southwestern Historical Quarterly* 85 (January 1982): 235–298.

———. *Reflections of Faith: Houses of Worship in the Lone Star State*. Waco, TX: Baylor University Press, 1994.

Rodríguez, Edmundo. "The Hispanic Community and Church Movements: Schools of Leadership." In *Hispanic Catholic Culture in the U.S.: Issues and Concerns*, ed. Jay P. Dolan and Allan Figueroa Deck, 206–239. Notre Dame, IN: University of Notre Dame Press, 1994.

Rodriguez, Jeanette. *Our Lady of Guadalupe: Faith and Empowerment among Mexican-American Women*. Austin: University of Texas Press, 1994.

Rogers, Mary Beth. *Cold Anger: A Story of Faith and Power Politics*. Denton: University of North Texas Press, 1990.

Romero, Juan. "Charism and Power: An Essay on the History of PADRES." *U.S. Catholic Historian* 9 (winter/spring 1990): 147–163.

Rosales, F. Arturo. *Chicano! The History of the Mexican American Civil Rights Movement*, 2nd rev. ed. Houston: Arte Público, 1997.

Rosales, Rodolfo. *The Illusion of Inclusion: The Untold Political Story of San Antonio*. Austin: University of Texas Press, 2000.

Ruecking, Frederick., Jr. "Ceremonies of the Coahuiltecan Indians of Southern Texas and Northeastern Mexico." *Texas Journal of Science* 6 (September 1954): 330–339.

Ruiz, Vicki L. *From Out of the Shadows: Mexican Women in Twentieth-Century America*. Oxford: Oxford University Press, 1998.

———. "'Star Struck': Acculturation, Adolescence, and Mexican American Women, 1920–1950." In *Small Worlds: Children and Adolescents in America, 1850–1950*, ed. Elliott West and Paula Petrik, 61–80. Lawrence: University Press of Kansas, 1992.

Sáenz, J. Luz. *Los Mexico-Americanos en la gran guerra y su contingente en pró de la democracia, la humanidad y la justicia*. San Antonio: Artes Gráficas, 1933.

Sahagún, Bernardino de. "Sobre supersticiones," appendix to *Historia general de las cosas de Nueva España*, Book XI (1576). Reprinted in Ernesto de la Torre Villar and Ramiro Navarro de Anda, eds. *Testimonios históricos Guadalupanos*. Mexico City: Fondo de Cultura Económica, 1982, 142–144.

San Antonio Baptist Association. *A Baptist Century around the Alamo, 1858–1958*. San Antonio: Perry, 1958.

San Antonio Daily Herald. 1857–1860. San Antonio Public Library.

San Antonio Daily Ledger. 1858–1859. Center for American History, University of Texas, Austin; San Antonio Public Library.

San Antonio Express. 1869–2004. San Antonio Public Library.

San Antonio Herald. 1855–1878. Center for American History, University of Texas, Austin; San Antonio Public Library.

San Antonio Ledger. 1851–1860. Center for American History, University of Texas, Austin; Library of Congress; San Antonio Public Library.

San Antonio Light. 1888–1993. San Antonio Public Library.

Sánchez, George J. *Becoming Mexican American: Ethnicity, Culture, and Identity in Chicano Los Angeles, 1900–1945.* Oxford: Oxford University Press, 1993.

Sánchez, Miguel. *Imagen de la Virgen María.* Mexico City: Viuda de Bernardo Calderón, 1648. Reprinted in Ernesto de la Torre Villar and Ramiro Navarro de Anda, eds. *Testimonios históricos Guadalupanos.* Mexico City: Fondo de Cultura Económica, 1982, 152–267.

Sandoval, Moises. *On the Move: A History of the Hispanic Church in the United States.* Maryknoll, NY: Orbis, 1990.

"San Fernando Cathedral Chronicles, 1914–1978." 4 vols. Archives of Claretian Missionaries, Western Province, USA, Claretian Center, Los Angeles.

"The San Fernando Restoration." *San Antonio Express,* 28 March 2003 (special insert).

Schuetz, Mardith Keithly. "The Indians of the San Antonio Missions." Ph.D. diss., University of Texas, Austin, 1980.

Schulte, Francisco Raymond. *Mexican Spirituality: Its Sources and Mission in the Earliest Guadalupan Sermons.* Lanham, MD: Rowman and Littlefield, 2002.

Seguín, Juan N. *Personal Memoirs of John N. Seguín from the Year 1834 to the Retreat of General Woll from the City of San Antonio in 1842.* San Antonio: Ledger Book and Job Office, 1858. Reprinted in *A Revolution Remembered: The Memoirs and Selected Correspondence of Juan N. Seguín,* ed. Jesús F. de la Teja. Austin: State House Press, 1991.

Serrano, R[afael]. "Missionary Work among the Mexicans." *Southern Messenger,* 30 June 1910, 6.

Servín, Manuel P. *An Awakened Minority: The Mexican Americans.* New York: Macmillan, 1974.

Siller Acuña, Clodomiro L. *Flor y canto del Tepeyac: Historia de las apariciones de Santa María de Guadalupe; Texto y comentario.* Xalapa, Veracruz: Servir, 1981.

Skerry, Peter. *Mexican Americans: The Ambivalent Minority.* New York: Free Press, 1993.

Sklar, Deidre. *Dancing with the Virgin: Body and Faith in the Fiesta of Tortugas, New Mexico.* Berkeley: University of California Press, 2001.

Sloss-Vento, Adela. *Alonso S. Perales: His Struggle for the Rights of Mexican-Americans.* San Antonio: Artes Gráficas, 1977.

Smith, George G. *The Life and Times of George Foster Pierce.* Sparta, GA: Hancock, 1888.

Smith, Jody Brant. *The Image of Guadalupe,* 2nd ed. Macon, GA: Mercer University Press, 1994.

Smith, Michael E. *The Aztecs.* Cambridge, MA: Blackwell, 1996.

Smith, Winston, and Charles Judah, eds. *Chronicles of the Gringos: The U.S. Army in the Mexican War, 1846–1848, Accounts of Eyewitnesses and Combatants.* Albuquerque: University of New Mexico Press, 1968.

Sobré, Judith Berg. *San Antonio on Parade: Six Historic Festivals.* College Station: Texas A&M University Press, 2003.

Solís, Gaspar José. "The Solís Diary of 1767." Translated by Peter P. Forrestal. In *Prepar-*

ing the Way: Preliminary Studies of the Texas Catholic Historical Society, vol. 1, ed. Jesús F. de la Teja, 101–148. Austin: Texas Catholic Historical Society, 1997.

Soul of the City / Alma del pueblo. Houston: JM Communications, 1996. Videocassette.

Sousa, Lisa, Stafford Poole, and James Lockhart, eds. and trans. *The Story of Guadalupe: Luis Laso de la Vega's Huei tlamahuiçoltica of 1649.* Stanford: Stanford University Press, 1998.

Southern Messenger (San Antonio). 1893–1956. Merged with the *Alamo Register* and became the *Alamo Messenger* in 1956. Catholic Archives of Texas, Austin; Catholic Archives at San Antonio, Chancery Office, Archdiocese of San Antonio.

Stecker, Mary of Providence. "The History of San Fernando Cathedral." M.A. thesis, Catholic University of America, Washington, DC, 1940.

Steinert, Wilhelm. *North America, Particularly Texas, in the Year 1849: A Travel Account*, ed. Terry G. Jordan-Bychkov, trans. Gilbert J. Jordan. 1850. Reprint, Dallas: William P. Clements Center for Southwest Studies, Southern Methodist University, 1999.

Stevens-Arroyo, Anthony M. "Correction, *Si*; Defection, *No*: Hispanics and U.S. Catholicism." *America*, 7–14 July 2003, 16–18.

Stewart, Kenneth L., and Arnoldo De León. *Not Room Enough: Mexicans, Anglos, and Socioeconomic Change in Texas, 1850–1900.* Albuquerque: University of New Mexico Press, 1993.

Sweet, Alex E., and J. Armoy Knox. *On a Mexican Mustang, through Texas, from the Gulf to the Rio Grande.* Hartford, CT: S. S. Scranton, 1883.

Tarango, Yolanda. "The Hispanic Woman and Her Role in the Church." *New Theology Review* 3 (November 1990): 56–61.

Tarango, Yolanda, and Timothy Matovina. "Las Hermanas." In *Hispanics in the Church: Up from the Cellar*, ed. Philip E. Lampe, 95–120. San Francisco: Catholic Scholars Press, 1994.

Taves, Ann. *Fits, Trances, and Visions: Experiencing Religion and Explaining Experience from Wesley to James.* Princeton, NJ: Princeton University Press, 1999.

———. *The Household of Faith: Roman Catholic Devotions in Mid-Nineteenth Century America.* Notre Dame, IN: University of Notre Dame Press, 1986.

Taylor, William B. *Magistrates of the Sacred: Priests and Parishioners in Eighteenth-Century Mexico.* Stanford: Stanford University Press, 1996.

———. "Mexico's Virgin of Guadalupe in the Seventeenth Century: Hagiography and Beyond." In *Colonial Saints: Discovering the Holy in the Americas*, ed. Allan Greer and Jodi Bilinkoff, 277–298. New York: Routledge, 2003.

———. "The Virgin of Guadalupe in New Spain: An Inquiry into the Social History of Marian Devotion." *American Ethnologist* 14 (February 1987): 9–33.

"T. E. G. to Editors, December 1846." *The United States Catholic Magazine and Monthly Review* 6 (April 1847): 219–220.

Terán de los Ríos, Domingo. Diary. In *Boletín del Archivo General de la Nación* 28, no. 1 (1957): 59–112.

Texas Baptist. 1860–1861. Center for American History, University of Texas, Austin.

Texas Presbyterian. 1847–1848. Center for American History, University of Texas, Austin.

Thiel, John E. *Senses of Tradition: Continuity and Development in Catholic Faith.* New York: Oxford University Press, 2000.

Tijerina, Andrés. *Tejanos & Texas under the Mexican Flag, 1821–1836.* College Station: Texas A&M University Press, 1994.

Tilley, Terrence W. *Inventing Catholic Tradition.* Maryknoll, NY: Orbis, 2000.

Tirres, Christopher D. "'Liberation' in the Latino(a) Context: Retrospect and Prospect." In *New Horizons in Hispanic/Latino(a) Theology,* ed. Benjamín Valentín, 138–162. Cleveland: Pilgrim Press, 2003.

Tjarks, Alicia V. "Comparative Demographic Analysis of Texas, 1777–1793." *Southwestern Historical Quarterly* 77 (January 1974): 291–338.

Today's Catholic (San Antonio). 1972–2004. Previously called the *Alamo Messenger.* Catholic Archives at San Antonio, Chancery Office, Archdiocese of San Antonio.

Torres, Theresa. "Our Lady of Guadalupe in the Society of the Guadalupanas in Kansas City, Missouri: An Empirical and Theological Analysis." Ph.D. diss., Catholic University of America, Washington, DC, 2002.

Traslosheros H., Jorge E. "The Construction of the First Shrine and Sanctuary of Our Lady of Guadalupe in San Luis Potosí, 1654–1664." *Journal of Hispanic/Latino Theology* 5 (August 1997): 7–19.

Treviño, Roberto R. *"Prensa y Patria:* The Spanish-Language Press and the Biculturation of the Tejano Middle Class, 1920–1940." *Western Historical Quarterly* 22 (November 1991): 451–472.

Tweed, Thomas A. *Our Lady of the Exile: Diasporic Religion at a Cuban Catholic Shrine in Miami.* Oxford: Oxford University Press, 1997.

U.S. Bureau of the Census. *Census of Population: 1970.* Vol. 1, part 45, tables 6 and 96. Washington, DC: Government Printing Office, 1973.

———. Census 2000 Summary File 1 (SF1) 100-Percent Data, Detailed Tables for Place.

———. State and County QuickFacts. Available at http://quickfacts.census.gov/qfd/states/48/48029.html.

———. 2000 Census of Population and Housing, figures for Bexar County. Available at http://txsdc.utsa.edu/data/census/2000/sf3/profiles/htm/county/Bexar/htm.

Valentín, Benjamín. *Mapping Public Theology: Beyond Culture, Identity, and Difference.* Harrisburg, PA: Trinity Press International, 2002.

———, ed. *New Horizons in Hispanic/Latino(a) Theology.* Cleveland: Pilgrim Press, 2003.

Vanderholt, James F. "San Fernando Cathedral in San Antonio, Texas: A Presentation of Priestly Ministry through a Study of Its History." D.Min. diss., San Francisco Theological Seminary, 1987.

Vargas, Zaragosa. "Tejana Radical: Emma Tenayuca and the San Antonio Labor Movement during the Great Depression." *Pacific Historical Review* 66 (November 1997): 553–580.

Verdugo Quetzalmamalitzin, Francisco. Testamento (Will), 2 April 1563. Reprinted in Fidel González Fernández, Eduardo Chávez Sánchez, and José Luis Guerrero Rosado. *El encuentro de la Virgen de Guadalupe y Juan Diego,* 4th ed. Mexico City: Editorial Porrúa, 2001, 363–364.

Warner, R. Stephen. "Elizondo's Pastoral Theology in Action: An Inductive Appreciation." In *Beyond Borders: Writings of Virgilio Elizondo and Friends,* ed. Timothy Matovina, 47–57. Maryknoll, NY: Orbis, 2000.

Warren, Mark R. *Dry Bones Rattling: Community Building to Revitalize American Democracy.* Princeton, NJ: Princeton University Press, 2001.

Webb, Walter Prescott. "Christmas and New Year in Texas." *Southwestern Historical Quarterly* 44 (January 1941): 357–379.

Weber, David J. *The Mexican Frontier, 1821–1846: The American Southwest under Mexico.* Albuquerque: University of New Mexico Press, 1982.

———. *The Spanish Frontier in North America.* New Haven: Yale University Press, 1992.

———, ed. *Troubles in Texas, 1832: A Tejano Viewpoint from San Antonio with a Translation and Facsimile,* trans. Conchita Hassell Winn and David J. Weber. Dallas: Wind River, 1983.

Weber, Devra. *Dark Sweat, White Gold: California Farm Workers, Cotton, and the New Deal.* Berkeley: University of California Press, 1994.

Weeks, William F., comp. *Debates of the Texas Convention.* Houston: J. W. Cruger, 1846.

[Werlenbaker, G.P.]. *San Antonio: City in the Sun.* New York: McGraw-Hill, 1946.

White, Gifford. *1830 Citizens of Texas.* Austin: Eakin, 1983.

Williams, Norma. *The Mexican American Family: Tradition and Change.* Dix Hills, NY: General Hall, 1990.

Wingerd, Mary Lethert. *Claiming the City: Politics, Faith, and the Power of Place in St. Paul.* Ithaca, NY: Cornell University Press, 2001.

Wooster, Ralph A. "Foreigners in the Principal Towns of Ante-Bellum Texas." *Southwestern Historical Quarterly* 66 (October 1962): 208–220.

Wright, Robert E. "The Hispanic Church in Texas under Spain and Mexico." *U.S. Catholic Historian* 20 (fall 2002): 15–33.

———. "How Many Are 'A Few'? Catholic Clergy in Central and Northern New Mexico, 1780–1851." In *Seeds of Struggle / Harvest of Faith: The Papers of the Archdiocese of Santa Fe Catholic Cuarto Centennial Conference on the History of the Catholic Church in New Mexico,* ed. Thomas J. Steele, Paul Rhetts, and Barbe Awalt, 219–261. Albuquerque: LPD, 1998.

———. "Local Church Emergence and Mission Decline: The Historiography of the Catholic Church in the Southwest during the Spanish and Mexican Periods." *U.S. Catholic Historian* 9 (winter/spring 1990): 27–48.

———. "Popular and Official Religiosity: A Theoretical Analysis and a Case Study of Laredo–Nuevo Laredo, 1755–1857." Ph.D. diss., Graduate Theological Union, Berkeley, CA, 1992.

Wuthnow, Robert, Martin E. Marty, Philip Gleason, and Deborah Dash Moore. "Sources of Personal Identity: Religion, Ethnicity, and the American Cultural Situation." *Religion and American Culture: A Journal of Interpretation* 2 (winter 1992): 1–22.

Zamora, Emilio. *The World of the Mexican Worker in Texas.* College Station: Texas A&M University Press, 1993.

Ziehe, H. C. *A Centennial Story of the Lutheran Church in Texas.* 2 vols. Seguin, TX: South Texas Printing, 1954.

Index